PROGRESSIVE CITIES

Progressive Cities

THE COMMISSION GOVERNMENT

MOVEMENT IN AMERICA, 1901–1920

BY BRADLEY ROBERT RICE

University of Texas Press, Austin and London

The publication of this book was
assisted by a grant from the
Andrew W. Mellon Foundation

Library of Congress Cataloging in Publication Data

Rice, Bradley Robert, 1948–
    Progressive cities.

    Bibliography: p.
    Includes index.
    1. Municipal government by commission—History.
I. Title.
JS342.R55   352'.0085'0973   77-8458
ISBN 0-292-76441-3

Copyright © 1977 by University of Texas Press

Printed in the United States of America

CONTENTS

TABLES

ACKNOWLEDGMENTS

THIS BOOK had its inception in the urban government seminars of Robert L. Lineberry and the Progressive Era politics seminars of Lewis L. Gould. Professor Gould's guidance has been continuous and invaluable. He helped in numerous ways, but I am especially grateful for the sources he discovered for me in the course of his own research.

Many colleagues and friends have given me support and advice in the course of this project, but I owe special thanks to three. Lyle W. Dorsett and John C. Livingston of the University of Denver read the entire manuscript at an earlier stage and offered helpful suggestions for revision. The switch of a few control cards enabled the data which Richard M. Bernard and I gathered for a co-authored article in the *Journal of Urban History* to be used for the present work. Of course, the implications and conclusions I draw from that data and the other evidence are my own responsibility.

Richard S. Childs and the staff of the Murray Seasongood Library of the National Municipal League went out of their way to help. Mr. Childs, the acknowledged "father of the city manager plan," spent portions of three days with me and allowed me full access to his personal papers. He truly believed that the full story of the commission government movement needed to be told.

To my father, whose twenty-five years as a city attorney whetted my interest in municipal government, and to my mother, whose encouragement is never ending, I will always be indebted. My wife, Vivian, is glad to see the work completed, and it might not have been without her unwavering support.

INTRODUCTION

Fiddlesticks, you may say. Good men can accomplish these things under any system. But they can't. Good men have tried here and elsewhere. Something has always been wrong with the system.
—in defense of the Des Moines Plan
July 1908[1]

THE PROPONENTS of the commission plan of city government believed that structure mattered. They had a progressive hope that good government would necessarily flow from efficient machinery. Opponents argued that "the mere matter of the form of municipal government has little to do with good government";[2] but such proclamations did not cause the reformers to waver. Modern political scientists have pointed out that many socioeconomic, cultural, and demographic variables influence public policy. But they have also confirmed the reformist assumption that structure does have a noticeable, if sometimes undesirable, impact on policy and participation.[3] The commission government movement developed from a growing feeling in the late nineteenth century that the conspicuous failures of American municipal government could be remedied by modifying the administrative structure of city charters.

Except for a few places in New England that clung to the town meeting concept, by 1850 virtually all cities in the United States operated under some variation of the mayor-council plan. This arrangement provided for a mayor elected by the entire city and a council selected from individual districts or wards. Municipalities existed under the umbrella of state jurisdiction and control since American municipal corporations legally were creatures of the rural-dominated state legislatures. Often the states added to city charters so many boards, commissions, and agencies that the mayors and councils retained little actual power. Such semi-autonomous bodies sometimes controlled public works, parks, public health, and other essential functions of the municipality. Charters seldom concentrated power administratively; thus, when cities were able to achieve unity of action, it was often only by informal means.[4]

Sometimes such informal concentration of power came through the so-called boss system. Historians have often told the tales of the urban political machines that William Marcy Tweed of New York, James McManes of Philadelphia, and other "bosses" of the Gilded Age built. But if the bosses brought efficiency and centralized administration, it was sometimes at the expense of honesty. Corruption was often the price of a unified municipal corporation. Some citizens who were not willing to pay the price sought ways to improve city government through charter reform. Such efforts were not confined to the boss-ridden cities but were common all over the country wherever urban government failed to satisfy influential groups of active citizens. Improved administration, these reformers argued would allow the city to cope better with the problems of rapidly growing populations.

One historian has dubbed such crusaders "structural reformers" and contrasted them with "social reformers" who aimed at substantive improvement in the quality of urban life. The latter worked at improving housing, sanitation, transportation, and general social conditions.[5] The distinction between the social and structural traditions of urban reform is a useful one, but it must be used with care. "Structural" refers only to the machinery of municipal government and does not imply that adjustments in the form of administration would effect major changes in a community's social structure. Those in the structural tradition might better be called administrative reformers. Furthermore, the two approaches were not mutually exclusive. Some social change advocates realized that governmental efficiency could expedite social services, and on occasion the efforts of administrative reformers had humanitarian effects.

Administrative municipal reforms popular in the late nineteenth century included a wide range of specific measures for city charters. A few cities initiated civil service procedures designed to rob machine politicians of their spoils. Some towns chose to elect at least some of their aldermen from the city at large rather than from individual wards where the alleged machines flourished. Structural reformers argued that municipal elections should be nonpartisan and should not occur at the same time as state and national balloting because traditional party politics had no place in local matters. In addition, there was also a fairly widespread effort to make the mayor a stronger administrator so that he could streamline city government. A handful of states even made progress toward home rule for cities in order to free municipalities from excessive legislative interference.

Many of the advocates of such structural changes came together in 1894 to form the National Municipal League (NML). The league publicized ideas for municipal reform and generally stimulated interest in city government. Their annual Conference for Good Government was the central meeting place for administrative reformers. Social reformers sometimes received a hearing, but their reception was not enthusiastic. In 1900 the league consolidated many of the suggestions for changes in municipal administration into a unified model program. The league called for limited home rule as an important first step toward allowing cities to reform themselves. The model charter proposed that a strong mayor with the authority to appoint most subordinates without council confirmation be in charge of general administration. The aldermen would retain only the power of appropriation and the responsibility of making ordinances. The plan provided for a council-appointed auditor or comptroller to keep careful tabs on municipal expenditures. Because excessive debt burdened many cities, the program suggested that each charter limit indebtedness to a specified percentage of assessed valuation except for revenue bonds. Realizing that public service corporations were often a source of corruption in urban politics, the league outlined restrictions on the granting of long-term franchises. It also called for the separation of local from state and national elections. In short, the NML program gathered in one place most of the city charter experiments of the previous three decades. But all of the league's proposals presupposed that the mayor-council system would continue to be the universal governmental arrangement of the American city.[6]

Many city reformers, on the other hand, had more faith in the electoral process than they had in NML-type charter tinkering. Some of the colorful reform mayors of the late nineteenth and early twentieth centuries, many of whom were in the social reform tradition, are as well known as the notorious bosses. Good government sponsors in numerous cities regarded such mayors as Seth Low of Brooklyn, Samuel M. Jones of Toledo, and Tom Johnson of Cleveland as examples of how strong leadership could redeem a municipality. Although Hazen S. Pingree of Detroit and others proved that reformers could use machine tactics as well as the unsavory bosses could, the impact of elected leaders was often more transitory than that of institutionalized reform structures. For example, George Washington Plunkitt, the famous Tammany lieutenant who told his story to William Riordon, explained that bosses and machines did not generally fear elected crusaders, because they were merely "morning glories" that bloomed in reform enthusiasm and faded in electoral apathy.[7]

Prior to 1901, efforts to cleanse city government usually fit one of these approaches. Reformers either tried to improve their charters with a whole arsenal of specific devices or they concentrated on voting out the scoundrels in favor of reformist candidates. Both of these categories continued past 1901 and, for that matter, are still very much a part of city politics today. But in 1900–1901, events in Galveston, Texas, gave birth to a new alternative for structural reformers. This fresh concept in civic administration was the commission form of city government.

During its evolution as a progressive solution to municipal problems, the commission format was variously known as the Galveston plan, the Texas idea, and the Des Moines plan. Since Galveston invented the basic organization and Des Moines popularized the addition of related reform techniques, the new type of government is probably best described as the Galveston–Des Moines plan. So popular did the new idea become that towns could reap advertising benefits for being in the forefront of municipal innovation if they used the commission plan. Consequently, some cities boasted that they had the system, knowning full well that their charters had little resemblance to Galveston's. But there were certain essentials necessary before a city could claim commission status. Benjamin DeWitt, an early historian of the progressive movement, explained:

> In every case, however, no matter how much charters may differ as to minor details, they have certain fundamental features in common. These fundamental features of commission charters are four:
> 1. Authority and responsibility are centralized.
> 2. The number of men in whom this authority and this responsibility are vested is small.

3. These few men are elected from the city at large and not by wards or districts.
4. Each man is at the head of a single department.[8]

The most radical departure the new scheme made was the combination of legislative and executive functions in one body. The plan disregarded the federal model of separation of powers. Sitting together, the commission was a typical policy- and ordinance-making council; but, separately, each commissioner administered a specific department on a day-to-day basis. The original Galveston charter provided for a mayor-president plus commissioners of finance and revenue, waterworks and sewerage, streets and public property, and fire and police. Later commission cities followed a similar division of responsibility.

Many governmental procedures not essential to the commission plan became widely identified with it. These nonessential features included initiative, referendum, recall, nonpartisan elections, civil service examinations, and most of the NML model charter except the strong mayor. Local debates over the adoption of the Galveston–Des Moines plan often became enmeshed in arguments over such incidental devices.

Armed with the commission plan, good-government forces could promise to do more than tinker with charters or elect short-lived reform administrations. They could offer a whole new system of government. In the years between 1901 and 1920 the drive for the plan became nationwide, and observers consistently identified it with the progressive spirit of the era. By 1911, when over 100 cities boasted commission charters, Woodrow Wilson could declare, "No single movement of reform in our governmental methods has been more significant than the rapid adoption of the so-called commission form of government in the cities of the country." When the United States entered the First World War, nearly 500 cities had adopted the system. The commission plan had reached its peak. By 1976 only 215 cities, including 163 or 4 percent of those with populations over 5,000, retained the plan.[9]

Historians have long treated the movement as part of the reform surge of the Progressive Era. Long-time urban government scholar Ernest S. Griffith described the Galveston–Des Moines plan and its attendant reforms as "one of the finest expressions of progressive thought and motivation."[10] Numerous other historians have also placed the system alongside various progressive measures. Textbooks and general works treating either urban history or the Progressive Era routinely acknowledge the city commission plan as an important component of municipal progressivism. Yet there has been no full-scale historical account of commission government since a rather encyclopedic 1918 effort.[11]

Of course, it makes no sense to ascertain if commission government was a progressive measure unless the term *progressive* itself is a useful one. Some teachers and writers have misused the concept to oversimplify the period of prevalent reform ranging from the 1890s until the First World War or some time shortly thereafter. Efforts popular in the 1950s to profile the typical progressive unfortunately accentuated the tendency to see a unity in the period.

A scholarly counterattack demonstrated that such profiles of leading progressives were of dubious value because the measurable characteristics of the typical progressive leader did not substantially differ from those of his conservative counterpart. Political leaders on both sides of the fence tended to be middle-class business and professional people. But futher study revealed that upper-class elements comprised the leadership for some so-called progressive measures. Still more research determined that lower-class voters, especially in Massachusetts, Wisconsin, and California, supplied much of the electoral support for progressive reforms.[12] Surely, some historians argued, such a diverse collection including upper classes, middle classes, and lower classes could not constitute a definable "movement."

Moreover, there was no agreement by either contemporaries or historians on just what issues constituted progressivism. There were varied approaches, such as the activist New Nationalism of Theodore Roosevelt or the negative New Freedom of Woodrow Wilson. Lawmakers who agreed on one issue, such as business regulation, might differ on tariff revision. Progressivism encompassed issues from railroad regulation to language simplification, from tenement-house design to ballot design, from seamen's protection to women's rights, and from rural problems to urban woes.

Since modern scholarship has established that there was no one group of people or any particular set of issues that could unanimously be defined as "progressive," Peter Filene suggested that the so-called progressive movement was no more than a collection of "shifting coalitions around different issues with the specific nature of those coalitions varying." To one historian, progressivism was a useful term only with a lower-case *p* and only when referring broadly to "the reformist surge of the era irrespective of the group or issue involved." Another has suggested that the period might better be called "an age of modernization."[13] But most scholars are not ready completely to abandon the term *progressive*. Although it may no longer reliably identify specific people or particular issues, it does serve to designate a period in which the nation was struggling for solutions to new problems of an urban-industrial society. Change was in vogue. Reform, however defined, was the battle cry.

Although *progressive* was a value-laden term to the contemporaries who applied it to their own pet issues, it need not be so to historians. Unfortunately, some scholars have used their own modern standards of liberalism to specify which measures deserve to be called progressive and which do not. Since charter tinkering and commission government changed only the machinery and not necessarily the social conscience of city hall, some historians have doubted the "progressiveness" of such measures. The ideology of the scholar and the motives of the reformers, while important, should be kept separate from the question of a measure's "progressiveness." If a significant number of contemporaries regarded a particular issue as part of the reform surge—or modernization impulse—of the era, historians should treat it as such. Clearly, structural municipal reform in general and the commission system in particular were, for better or worse as historians may decide, part and parcel of the progressive impulse. DeWitt's 1915 work, *The Progressive Movement*, is at once both a history and a primary document. That he gave so much space to charter reform is indicative that informed opinion considered it a major component of progressivism. Theodore Roosevelt and Woodrow Wilson might have differed on many counts, but neither doubted the progressive credentials of the commission movement.[14]

Once a particular issue, such as municipal reform, is defined as a facet of progressivism, it is still necessary to go beyond that essentially rhetorical classification to investigate a second question concerning who favored and opposed such governmental or social change and why they did so. This study establishes that the major long-term importance of the commission movement was as a transition to the council-manager plan. But commission proponents obviously could not have had that stalking-horse role as their original purpose. Thus, it is necessary to demonstrate what their initial motives were.

The two most important studies of the commission movement are suggestive articles published in the early 1960s by James Weinstein and Samuel P. Hays. Their findings are so similar that they have often been linked together and widely referred to as the Hays-Weinstein thesis. As stated by Hays, the argument runs: "The movement for reform in municipal government, therefore, constituted an attempt by upper-class, advanced professional and large business groups to take formal political power from the previously dominant lower- and middle-class elements so that they might advance their own conceptions of desirable public policy."[15] Neither article purported to be a comprehensive history of the commission and city manager movements; quite to the contrary, both ended with calls for further research on the questions they posed.

Weinstein set out to show how organized business's advocacy of the commission and manager plans "illuminates the goals and political ideology of businessmen in the period when America emerged as the world's leading industrial power." Hays, on the other hand, was looking beyond the business community "in order to achieve a more complete understanding of social change in the Progressive Era." Both authors, but especially Hays, stressed that reform ideology must be carefully distinguished from reform practice if historians are to be able to identify the motivations of the reformers. They found that lower-class spokesmen and voters made such a distinction. These groups were more concerned with the practical application of urban government than with the ideology of democracy, efficiency, and business principles. Consequently, they generally opposed Chamber of Commerce–sponsored good-government campaigns.[16]

One weakness common to both Hays' and Weinstein's treatments, as well as to others, was a tendency to blur the commission and manager plans together. In fact, the manager concept was clearly a successor to the commission idea. It was a response to the weaknesses of the commission format. Although the manager plan amplified and refined the arguments upon which the Galveston–Des Moines form was based, commission government was much more a product of the Progressive Era than was its successor. The present work separates the commission movement from the manager plan and is a case study of the former as a Progressive Era reform.

This study will describe and analyze the origin, diffusion, and decline of the commission plan movement and in that process will test the Hays-Weinstein thesis. This is not a study of municipal administration but of municipal innovation, governmental ideas, and the motives for change. Nor is it a study of individual cities, although it naturally begins with case studies of the movement's pioneer municipalities.

How a substantially different system of municipal administration could spread to hundreds of cities in forty-two states in less than twenty years has posed an intriguing question for historians. Thomas M. Scott's typology of the four stages of diffusion of municipal innovation can provide a partial explanation. He applies his theory to the expansion of the city manager scheme, but the model could also apply to the commission plan movement. The study identifies the four stages as prechoice, innovation, emulation, and institutionalization.[17]

In the prechoice stage "all communities have similar structures of government because no alternatives are available."[18] This, of course, was the situation prevailing before Galveston stumbled onto the commission government idea in 1901. For all practical purposes, the only course open to the cities of Texas and the nation outside New England at this time was the mayor-council structure with its various alterations concerning mayoral power, independent boards, and method of election of aldermen. Despite such Gilded Age precedents as the commissionlike arrangements in Sacramento, Memphis, New Orleans, and Washington, D.C., administration by a small board vested with both executive and legislative functions was not really an available alternative to cities seeking charter reform. Actually, the commission system did not completely emerge from prechoice status until after 1903 when Galveston's ruling body became fully elective and thereby attractive to other cities. The process of social learning that eventually led to the widespread imitation of the island city's innovation could then begin.

The second stage in the spread of municipal change is the innovative step. At this point "new alternatives . . . become available and state law permits their adoption." Cities that opt for a new invention early in its evolution are the movement's "pioneers." Scott argued that "these pioneer communities have special characteristics which provide optimal conditions for innovative political change."[19] As Chapter 1 will show, Galveston was commission government's initial pioneer, but others followed within their own state or region. The great hurricane of 1900 provided the optimal conditions necessary for the island city to initiate radical change in its form of government. Chapter 3 demonstrates how the determined leadership of the press and business elite of Des Moines made their city the new plan's nothern pioneer. In some states political, social, and physical conditions made certain cities ripe for innovation while others resisted. Situations conducive to structural reform did not need to be catastrophic as in Galveston or even drawn out and hard fought as in Des Moines. After studying the various charter forms available during the Progressive Era, some cities adopted commission government with virtually no controversy. Conditions for change could be both ideological and practical and often involved such seemingly incidental matters as the timing of legislative sessions and the personalities of politicians and others in leadership positions.

Third in the steps of innovation diffusion is emulation. By this time so many cities in a state or region have followed the pioneers' examples that social conditions and extra effort become less and less important in the assumption of a innovative program. For example, in 1905 Houston's adoption of the Galveston plan was a pioneering move, but by 1907, when Dallas, Fort Worth, El Paso, and two smaller Texas municipalities took up the system, there was more emulation than pathbreaking. Of course, compared to the dozens of Lone Star communities that later obtained commission charters, the 1907 towns were relative pioneers. Even as the Texas idea was entering the emulation stage in its own state, the system was still innovative in Iowa. Similarly, as Iowa and much of the Midwest reached the emulative point, other sections were having their own pioneer commission agitations. Short-ballot advocate Richard S. Childs explained how the simple process of emulation helped diffuse the commission system. "Unquestionably," he wrote in 1914, "the plan is popular wherever tried and spreads with most rapidity among the nearby cities which have the best opportunity for intimate observation of its operation."[20]

Fourth among the stages of municipal innovation is institutionalization. This comes "when the formal and informal institutions in the state encourage and expect (perhaps require) the acceptance of or conformity to what was formerly the innovative idea."[21] In 1910 an enthusiastic partisan of the Des Moines plan praised his city's charter and noted "there are those who believe that the present generation will see the general abandonment of the mayor-and-council type of municipal government with which the country has long been familiar." A short time later, Henry Bruere's mildly critical study of commision government for the New York Bureau of Municipal Research found some support for the belief that the new form might become the "characteristic American plan of city organization."[22]

Despite such predictions, the commission movement never quite reached the institutional stage on a nationwide basis. A few states did require that certain classes of cities use the plan; and in others, especially Texas and Oklahoma, the scheme threatened to become the municipal norm but fell short of the mark. Satisfaction with existing plans, shortcomings of the commission structure, and competition from a new innovation—the council-manager plan—combined to keep the Galveston–Des Moines arrangement from becoming fully institutionalized across the country.

The commission government movement not only reveals much about the Progressive Era in which the plan was nurtured; it also has relevance for present-day urban politics. Well over five million people reside in cities that still retain the plan. Moreover, its direct successor, the council-manager system, prevails in 2,441 cities, including 70 in the over-100,000 population class.[23] Furthermore, such charter features as nonpartisan elections, at-large representation, direct democracy, and others received important impetus from the commission movement. These provisions are permanent fixtures of urban government in thousands of cities. In short, the story of the commission movement and its legacies is an important chapter in the nation's urban history.

PROGRESSIVE CITIES

CHAPTER ONE

THE GALVESTON PLAN

*T*HE invention of the commission plan of municipal government was a response to "the greatest hurricane disaster in our nation's history."[1] On September 8, 1900, wind whipped and water inundated the island city of Galveston, Texas, taking over 6,000 lives and destroying at least $17 million worth of property. Private relief from throughout the state and nation poured into Galveston and the surrounding area, but the responsibility for long-term rehabilitation lay with the citizens of the stricken city. Before the storm, Galveston had been a prosperous Gulf port of nearly 40,000, but death and a steady exodus of victims cut the population by almost a fourth within a few days after the disaster. About 4,000 homes lay in ruins although the better residential sections and the downtown area suffered less damage.[2]

An ad hoc group called the Central Relief Committee took charge of the situation and coordinated the grim business of disposing of bodies and maintaining order—initially under martial law. The committee confined itself to consideration of the immediate problems of recovery, but some citizens soon began to ponder the city's long-term prospects. Only two weeks after the storm, the city council minutes revealingly indicate that "the members indulged in a discussion as to the future of the city government." One alderman wanted the entire body to resign in favor of a commission appointed by the governor. His suggestion may well have originated in a group of businessmen that met a week to ten days after the disaster to formulate plans for Galveston's rebuilding. The editor of the *Galveston Tribune* was privy to the discussions of the stricken city's most influential leaders, and twenty days after the hurricane he wrote of the urgent need to devise a new municipal government.[3]

Some businessmen wanted a new city government because they had lost confidence in the existing one. Later partisans of the commission system often characterized Galveston's administration as corrupt and incompetent both before and immediately after the September 1900 storm. One Harvard professor wrote in 1912, "Prior to 1901 Galveston was one of the worst-governed urban communities in the whole country."[4] A journalist charged that "the city was bankrupt by a board of ward-aldermen who had out-Tweeded Tweed."[5] After the great hurricane, according to the daughter of Galveston's first commission play mayor, "an impotent city council sat upon the ruins of

Note: This chapter previously appeared in the *Southwestern Historical Quarterly*, vol. 78 (April 1975), and is published here by permission of the Texas State Historical Association.

their former council-chamber quarreling listlessly among themselves."[6] Charles A. Beard perpetuated the myth, writing that "the local government was paralyzed, because the problems connected with the reparation of the ruin were too much for the old political machine which had control." Even some modern scholarly works make it appear that the old council simply collapsed under pressure, but in fact charter reform had been on Galveston's agenda for some time.[7]

The 1890s marked the beginning of efforts by organized businessmen in Galveston to minimize the effects of ward politics in their city. Prior to that time the city had operated under a typical mayor-council charter with twelve aldermen elected by wards. New charter amendments effective for the 1891 and 1893 elections provided that an additional four councilmen be elected at large. But this system did not go far enough for the businessmen. In 1895 the Chamber of Commerce proposed a charter amendment that would establish a council of twelve members elected at large. Some compromise resulted in a system by which candidates would reside in and represent specific wards but would be elected by the city as a whole. Consequently, the wards retained the appearance of direct representation but not the substance. No matter how popular a candidate was in his home ward, he could not be elected to the council unless he could also manage a city-wide plurality. The Chamber of Commerce backers of the amendment hoped that the system would eliminate the worst aspects of ward politics. All councilmen would have to appeal to the city as a whole.

In order to ensure that their structural reform was successful, some influential businessmen gathered in the Chamber of Commerce suite in the Tremont Hotel downtown and organized the Galveston Good Government Club. Despite its solid business credentials, the group had difficulty securing acceptable candidates. Its biggest enemy was apathy, but it was also handicapped by the fact that being an alderman brought little prestige and even less monetary remuneration to an honest man. The best the members could do was a ticket of typical middle-class businessmen and a physician. But even that was a decided contrast to the incumbent council of longshoremen, bartenders, small businessmen, and a drayman.

The opposition organized an ad hoc slate known as the People's Ticket. One of its candidates characterized the Good Government Club, the influential Cotton Exchange, and the Chamber of Commerce as the "unholy Trinity." Another suggested that the club consisted of lawyers, millionaires, and their petty clerks. The People's orators pitched their appeals to laboring men, including the island's numerous blacks. They stressed that the Good Government slate had no Negroes on it while, in contrast, they endorsed the black incumbent from the eighth ward. Incumbent Mayor A. W. Fly was not officially on the Good Government Club ticket, but he was closely identified with it. The People's campaigners continually attacked Fly's antilabor stance.

The Good Government partisans made a point of avoiding class-oriented rhetoric. Stressing the importance of business procedures in government, they proclaimed a community of interests between labor and commerce and produced testimony to that effect from workers and prominent blacks. Judge M. E. Kleberg, the club's president, counseled the voters to "go among men who have successfully administered their own business and get them to represent you in the management of the city, and you will get men who will make good aldermen."[8]

Both the charter amendment and the efforts of the Good Government Club paid off for the business forces in 1895. Ten of the twelve candidates on their slate, including two who also had the People's endorsement, were elected. The at-large provisions worked as the Chamber of Commerce drafters had probably hoped. Five candidates who won election in the city-wide totals had lost their wards of residence. Four of these councilmen who would represent wards that they failed to carry were members of the Good Government slate. One of the Good Government men managed to carry his own ward but lost overall. Without the dual endorsements and without the at-large system, the Good Government Club would have elected only five councilmen.

As some black leaders had anticipated, the at-large feature of the 1895 charter effectively terminated Negro office-holding in Galveston despite the fact that the race comprised 22 percent of the city's population in 1900. The black incumbent whom the People's Ticket endorsed carried his district but fell victim to city-wide prejudice in the total vote. Shortly after the city inaugurated the commission plan, changes in Texas' election code made Negro political impact even less likely.[9]

The 1897 race did not produce a working man's slate similar to the People's Ticket, but the organized business forces reappeared under the new name Citizens' Club. In this election they overwhelmed the independent candidates and a rival slate of businessmen who were pledged to grant a franchise to a local railroad. All eleven Citizens' Club candidates won, although one of them failed to carry his home ward.[10]

The council in office at the time of the devastating storm of 1900 emerged from the three-ticket race of 1899. In this case the real contest was between the Citizens' Club, still carrying the business banner, and the Greater Galveston Ticket, purporting to represent the common man. A third slate chose the likely winners from the first two lists. The Citizens' Club members had been so dissatisfied with the performance of the 1897 council they helped elect that they dropped four incumbents from their endorsement list. Most of the interest focused on the race for mayor. Fly was running for the fourth time, and Police Chief Walter C. Jones offered formidable opposition. Again Fly's antilabor actions, which included allegedly firing shots at picketers, were a major issue.[11]

Jones claimed a decisive victory with over half of his margin coming from four heavily working-class wards. In the council races the Citizens' Club elected only six candidates on its own—one of whom had lost his home ward. The Greater Galveston Ticket placed four, and two winners had been on both lists. The business forces did manage to place C. H. McMaster, the Chamber of Commerce's executive secretary, on the council.[12]

In the three elections using the Chamber of Commerce's at-large system, eight aldermen won seats despite losing their own wards. In six of those cases the candidates who benefited represented one of the business-supported good-government slates. The politically active businessmen of the city had learned that structural reform and good organization could aid their efforts to dominate local government; but full control eluded them. Soon after the 1899 council assumed office, it became clear that the members elected with dual endorsements would line up with Mayor Jones to oppose the six Citizens' Club representatives.

Although it is unlikely that a complete restructuring of Galveston's municipal system would have come without the impetus of the storm and the consequent necessity for strong leadership to promote recovery, neither was the commission born of a city unfamiliar with charter amendments aimed at reform. The city on the eve of its destruction was ripe for some sort of change. Throughout 1899 the council was late in its payrolls. By the summer of 1900 dissatisfaction had increased. Neither the July nor the August salaries had been paid, and the demand for capital improvements was high. The daily *Tribune* asserted, "The people have lost confidence in the integrity of public officials." The issue at hand concerned streets, but the implications were broader. The editorial continued, stating that "present conditions make it obligatory for radical remedial action" to be taken.[13]

Some action was already under consideration. Late in 1899 Alderman McMaster successfully introduced a resolution directing the city clerk to obtain copies of other city charters so "that we may profit by their ideas and experiences."[14] Even Mayor Jones conceded that "the early revision and compilation of the Charter and Ordinances of the city is a matter that demands immediate action."[15]

Without the storm nothing might have come from the rumblings of 1899–1900, but the disaster was the catalyst for action. With the blessings of hindsight a Galveston broker explained the situation to an out-of-town client: "I cannot say the storm is responsible for all the bad conditions now existing, for it is a fact that our town was, to say the least, very badly governed for some time past, and it only required a calamity like the storm to precipitate a state of municipal bankruptcy almost."[16] A few months after the water receded, an editorial expressed similar sentiments: "Long before the storm unwisdom and recklessness—not to use stronger terms—in municipal administration had well nigh bankrupted the corporation of Galveston. It was plain many months ago that a more businesslike system must be adopted."[17] At that very time, a group of wealthy Galveston business elites known as the Deep Water Committee had begun to lay the groundwork for just such a "businesslike system."

The Galveston Deep Water Committee was organized in 1882 to promote harbor improvements. It was especially concerned with removing the sand bar that hampered access to the city's wharves. Its lobbying paid off, and the federal government helped finance Galveston's new deep-water port. If the devastation left by the hurricane had caused the trade of the city permanently to decline, the Deep Water group's efforts would have been in vain. Although many warehouses and other commercial buildings near the docks lay in ruins, the piers themselves remained sound and the water stayed deep. Rebuilding was clearly possible, and prosperity along the waterfront could return.

The committee had only fifteen members and a few auxiliary confidants, but "among them," wrote the *Galveston News*, "are men whose names are synonymous with the prosperity, advancement, and most material interests of this community."[18] The heads of both daily newspapers were members of the group; thus, in Galveston, as in many of the later commission cities, the press was both an actor in and a chronicler of the change-of-government struggle. A visiting journalist estimated that the Deep Water men "represented in one way or another nearly half the property of the place."[19] An opponent of the commission plan testified that those promoting the scheme owned "nearly every big corporation" in town.[20] Although these contemporary estimates no doubt exaggerated the economic predominance of the committee, they were not far wrong. Analysis of the holdings of the members confirmed that the fathers of the commission plan did indeed comprise Galveston's commercial elites.

The Deep Water Committee and its close family and business associates dominated three key elements of Galveston's economy: banking, corporate directorships, and large property ownership. The city's banks were almost the committee's private domain. There were eight institutions in the local clearing house, and Deep Water men held influential positions in six. Four banks, including the two largest ones, had members as presidents. Two others had vice-presidents and directors that belonged to the committee. Of thirty-five directorships or partnerships in all eight banks, members or their close relatives held sixteen. None of the nineteen other directors openly opposed the plans of the Deep Water Committee. Naturally, the banking connections of the members and their associates gave them a financial stake in many other Galveston enterprises in which they played no direct role.[21]

Corporate directorships reveal a pattern similar to the committee's dominance of banking. The city directory for 1901 listed seventy-eight local corporations conducting business in Galveston. Members or close associates of the Deep Water Committee sat as directors on the boards of twenty-seven of the seventy-eight. Although in terms of number of companies this was only about a third of the city's corporations, the Deep Water–connected businesses had more capital stock than the rest of the enterprises combined. The fifty-one corporations with no Deep Water representation capitalized at just about $5 million, whereas the committee-related firms had total capital stock of nearly 8 million. Only two incorporated businesses in Galveston had directors that were openly hostile to the committee's commission government scheme, and the stock of those two companies was valued at only just over a million dollars.[22]

Besides controlling the city's banking and corporate systems, the Deep Water group owned most of the town's choice real estate. Excluding property owned by absentees and women not related to the committee, the municipal tax rolls for 1900 listed forty-six assessments in excess of $50,000 value. Corporate or personal ownership connected twenty-nine of the forty-six with the committee. The dominance in number of holdings was impressive, but in dollar value the committee's wealth was even more evident. The seventeen assessments not owned by Deep Water members and associates carried a combined valuation of $1,613,155; on the other hand, the Deep Water–related properties had a total assessment of $4,855,584. The largest single levy was on the Galveston Wharf Corporation's land and improvements. Committee members controlled the management of this firm, and the company in turn dominated the island city's shipping trade. The value of the wharf company's holdings alone was almost as much as all the non–Deep Water–related properties in the entire over-$50,000 grouping. No known opponent of the commission idea owned any of the properties assessed at $50,000 or more. In fact, none of the anticommission people even appeared on the list of those owning property assessed for at least $15,000.[23]

The bank, corporation, and real estate figures demonstrated that members and associates of the Deep Water Committee overwhelmingly dominated the economy of Galveston. When they made plans for the future of the city, those were the plans of the island's elite. The smaller businessmen in the Chamber of Commerce fell in line and resolved to "give hearty cooperation and assistance in any way that the deep water committee may desire."[24] No significant disagreement developed among the elites and subelties of the city. Those that did oppose the Deep Water group's efforts had virtually no control of the key elements of Galveston's economy.

Thus, in the fall of 1900 there were three groups concerned with Galveston's future. The Central Relief Committee was concluding its immediate recovery work, and the city council assumed that long-term rebuilding and the return to normal would be its obligation. But the Deep Water Committee was preparing to deny the council that responsibility. The committee felt that it could not afford to leave Galveston's future in the hands of a government in which it had no confidence and over which it had little control. "What converted businessmen into civic reformers," emphasizes James Weinstein, "was the increased importance of the public functions of the twentieth-century city." And seldom have these functions been more important than in the months after the great hurricane in Galveston.[25]

There was nationwide speculation that the city would cease to be an important port. Galveston Island was little more than a large sand bar, and detractors claimed that another storm like the September 1900 one would finish the job of destroying the town. Nearby Houston's boosters hoped that a planned ship channel would make it the major port along the Texas coast of the Gulf of Mexico. They knew that their sprawling city was far enough inland to be well protected from killer hurricanes. Deep Water members and associates urged the city council to rebuild the business district streets so that freight could be hauled and commerce restored. By the end of the year the Wharf Corporation had to acknowledge a "loss of revenue caused by the great storm of Sept. 8." The committee members hoped that a sound and cooperative municipal administration could help save their millions of dollars in capital investment. No doubt those that had made their fortunes in Galveston also had a civic pride in the community and wanted it to retain its place as the state's most important port.[26]

Having decided to change the municipal government, the Deep Water Committeemen had to do three things. First, they had to draft a city charter that would accomplish their goals; second, they needed to create popular support for their proposal; and, third, because Texas did not allow home rule, they had to obtain legislative approval for their plan.

The initial task, drawing up a plan of government, began shortly after the storm and continued through January 1901 when the committee submitted its document to the legislature. As soon as a week or ten days after the disaster, some businessmen had suggested putting Galveston's administration in the hands of a commission, and the Deep Water Committee appointed a subcommittee to draft a charter embodying this idea. The committee also prepared bills asking the state and federal governments for tax breaks and other aids to help rebuild the city and protect the island from future hurricanes. The subcommittee in charge of drawing up the commission charter included bank president and former city attorney R. Waverly Smith, brewery lobbyist and wealthy ex-congressman Walter Q. Gresham, and prominent attorney Farrell D. Minor. Judge M. E. Kleberg, former Good Government Club president, and others helped during the months of almost daily considerations.[27]

Progressive Era municipal reformers would look to Galveston as an example in later years, but the drafters of the first commission charter had no clear-cut precedents. One of the three lawyers on the subcommittee told Charles Beard that they had "little guidance." A later eulogist went further and called the plan "entirely original."[28] But the men designing the Galveston system were definitely aware of some municipal precedents for commission-type institutions. Only a fortnight after the storm a headline introduced "The Plan Memphis Once Used," referring to a commission which governed that city during an 1878 yellow fever epidemic. The committee also studied the accomplishments of the appointive commission that governed Washington, D.C., and "thoughtful citizens were watching with interest and growing favor the experiment of Dallas, Austin, and other cities in the administration of police, fire, health, and street departments under a commission appointed by the governor."[29] The subcommittee looked to these appointive boards rather than to the good-government tactics of the 1890s because "they had lost faith in democracy," according to a Wisconsin professor. He noted, "All efforts at electoral reform had failed. . . . Despairing of ever being able to gain control, the property-owning classes turned to the governor."[30] Ballot box methods were inadequate, wrote a Deep Water member, because after an apparent victory the businessman "lapses into his old indifference."[31]

More important to the drafters of the charter than municipal precedents were their own business experiences. One contemporary account noticed that Galveston businessmen viewed their city as a "great ruined business,"[32] but in late 1900 those drafting the charter emphasized "ruined" as much as "business." Galveston was a corporation but a bankrupt one in their eyes. A vigorous debate developed over whether the city was, in fact, truly broke. The record did show unmet payrolls, unpaid taxes, and enormous debt, but the actual figures mattered less than the widespread impression voiced by a well-known citizen who believed that "bankruptcy is staring both city and county in the face, and some wise plan must be adopted in order to stave it off."[33] It was natural that experienced businessmen would suggest that the insolvent municipal corporation go into receivership. Shortly after the storm, the *Tribune* could "see no solution of the municipal situation but a receivership."[34] A few months later when a commission opponent told legislative hearings that the charter was "a receivership in disguise," a Deep Water spokesman gladly admitted the fact because he believed that such an arrangement was just what Galveston needed.[35] Thus, from the receivership principle, municipal precedents, and a businesslike desire for centralized responsibility, the Deep Water subcommittee evolved the proposed charter calling for the governor to appoint five men to manage Galveston. Each would be responsible for one department, and together they would make policy decisions as a commission or council.

Having drawn up a plan designed to improve municipal government, the business elites faced their second task of cultivating public backing for their behind-the-scenes work. The Deep Water Committee wanted to go before Texas' lawmakers armed with both local and statewide support. They got a chance to stimulate enthusiasm when the Fort Worth Board of Trade called a convention to discuss the needs of the state's main port. Realizing that to a great extent Galveston's problems were those of the entire state, about eight hundred delegates gathered in November 1900 in the north Texas city. Although the gathering concentrated primarily on questions of reconstruction and future protection, the Deep Water leaders took the opportunity to introduce a rough outline of their commission plan. Financial matters, questions about constitutionality, and other details forestalled complete agreement at the meeting, but the Galveston delegation returned home "well pleased with the results of the convention."[36]

The nurturing of local support would await the beginning of the third Deep Water objective—getting the legislature to ratify their proposals. On January 30, 1901, Representative Thomas H. Nolan of Galveston introduced the Deep Water group's commission charter bill, and the House referred it to committee. But the incumbent city councilmen did not intend to surrender without resistance. They drafted their own new charter, and Nolan courteously submitted it for them in mid-February. Unlike the commission bill, the council's plan envisioned no sweeping changes. Its main objective was to preserve the elective system that the Deep Water appointive proposals would abolish.[37]

Each side was determined to show the legislature that the people of Galveston supported its plan for charter revision. In defense of the council's plan, the assistant city attorney argued that the people of Galveston would vote down the commission if given a chance. To support this contention, the opponents of the commission bill scheduled a series of "mass meetings," but the tactic backfired. Within ten days in February 1901, the council-centered opposition conducted three meetings, but reporters for the procommission *Tribune* claimed that none of them attracted over two hundred people.[38]

Although the Galveston experience did conform to the theses of some influential historians inasmuch as business elites initiated and led the efforts to change city government, the struggle in Galveston did not develop the fairly clear lines of class cleavage that some of these studies found.[39] Anticommission elements charged that the new charter would usher in a rich man's government, but they were generally unsuccessful in arousing the kind of class antagonism that characterized Galveston's elections in the 1890s. The backers of the Deep Water plan apparently won the battle for hometown support among all classes. "From all accounts," reported a newspaper in the state capital, "there is no local opposition except from a small class of officeholders and political bosses, whose occupation will be gone under a strictly business rule." There was no referendum on the plan and no scientific pollsters existed to canvass Galveston systematically; but a number of unsophisticated attempts tried to gauge the state of opinion. Several members of the legislature initially opposed the measure because they had been told that a majority of Galveston's citizens did not favor the plan. However, upon visiting the city, some of them changed their minds. One state representative thought 90 percent of the people favored the bill, while another member declared on the house floor that his visit had discovered 95 percent support, excluding the blacks among whom he did not inquire. A third solon thought that the measure had the flood-swept city's backing "almost to a man."[40]

To encourage the public to back its commission idea, the Deep Water Committee and its allies in the press and business community vigorously attacked the incumbent administration. One editor-member charged, "Certainly no set of public officials ever seemed so indifferent to the welfare, safety, and health as the ruling majority of those now in office."[41] The committee itself proclaimed, "We believe that municipal government, as it has been administered in this community for the past twenty years, is a failure."[42] Similar charges were common at the various meetings in favor of the commission and in the testimony of change-of-government advocates before the legislative committees.

Worried that the opposition was being heard more in Austin and alarmed by the temporary defection of Galveston's junior representative, W. H. Tarpey, the friends of the commission intensified their efforts. An overflow mass meeting in Galveston attracted more than two thousand supporters according to the papers, and the gathering laid plans for a show of force in the state capital. The Chamber of Commerce sponsored a special train, and about six hundred amateur lobbyists converged on Austin wearing buttons which read: "FOR THE GALVESTON COMMISSION BILL." The group caucused at the Driskill Hotel with the Deep Water Committee's liaisons and cornered lawmakers in the marble halls of the capitol. Many of those who remained in Galveston sent to the legislature hastily drawn petitions totaling over five thousand signatures.[43]

The fathers of the charter took special delight in the surprising labor sentiment for the business-oriented scheme. The three-thousand-member Galveston Labor Council endorsed the charter, and the council's secretary testified to that effect before the legislative committee. Furthermore, the *Galveston Journal*, a union newspaper, backed the bill in its editorials.[44]

Partisan politics played only a minor role in the commission fight. Because Mayor Jones was the 1900 Republican congressional nominee from the Galveston district, the Democrats saw the termination of the old government as a chance to discredit a partisan foe. Both the county Democratic executive committee and the Jefferson Democrat Association formally endorsed the commission charter. On the other hand, a Negro weekly had supported Jones in November, and his Republicanism may have led some loyal Grand Old Party blacks to oppose the incumbent mayor's ouster by a new system.[45]

Such overwhelming backing indicated that middle- and lower-class Galveston favored the measure along with the elites. But, because of the emergency nature of the situation, Galveston's adoption of commission government presented a special case in determining why people supported the change. Three causes accounted for much of the favorable sentiment. First, many people believed that such an arrangement was the best, or only, way to obtain the state aid and local stability necessary to repay bonds, rebuild the city, and protect against future hurricanes. Second, there was a sincere feeling that appointive government was palatable because of its temporary nature. Third, and more generally, the lower- and middle-class public may have been simply willing to trust the judgment of the leading businessmen in time of acute crisis.

Some sort of state aid appeared essential if the struggling island community was to afford the cost of reconstruction. In the Texas House of Representatives, John Nance Garner attributed the bulk of public endorsement of the charter to fear that Governor J. D. Sayers would not allow state assistance without it. Had there been no such threat, Garner predicted, "there wouldn't be 100 men in Galveston who would ask for the passage of the measure."[46] This prediction may have had some validity. To pressure the public, the island city newspapers gave page-one coverage to the governor's ultimatum: "I will never consent to placing funds of the State in the hands of such city councils as the city has had during recent years."[47] But Marsene Johnson, whom the *News* called "the ablest representative of the anti-commission faction," replied that not even threats could move him to abandon elective democracy. "I for one," Johnson declared, "would not sell my birthright for a mess of pottage" in the form of state aid.[48] Both in the legislature and in Galveston, proponents continually referred to the temporary nature of the denial of suffrage, although they resisted writing a terminal date into the charter. One observer summarized the feeling by saying, "Of course, no one expects the commission to be permanent."[49] Later events modified this expectation.

Procommission testimony had a characteristically progressive ring with one advocate declaring that the new government was designed to "restrain the political bosses in Galveston."[50] On the other hand, opposition witnesses emphasized technical objections, used personal attacks on the motives of the bill's sponsors, and made the most of appeals to democracy. The only issue seriously to threaten the charter's chances was the charge that an appointive commission was tantamount to the disenfranchisement of the citizens of Galveston. Mayor Jones called it "government without the consent of the governed."[51] Many opponents, especially those associated with city hall, no doubt used the local self-government issue as a smoke screen to obscure their own self-interest in the continuation of the existing council and its patronage. But some legislators were more detached and sincere in their refusal to countenance the disenfranchisement of the city's voters. One flatly stated, "I care nothing for the Mayor of Galveston, whether he wants this bill or not, it is not a question of whether the laboring men or the rich men want it; it is a question of the sacred rights of government."[52] Two house members had their impassioned statement of opposition entered in the *Journal*: "We can not chloroform our consciences by voting for the commission feature of this bill, which disfranchises free citizens of Texas, destroys the right of local self-government, violates the Constitution of the State, holds in derision the Declaration of Independence, tramples underfoot the fundamental principles of a free republic, and repudiates the teachings, traditions and sentiments of the democratic party."[53]

Disenfranchisement was the argument that caused Galveston's own Representative Tarpey to turn against the proposal despite his admission that nine out of ten people in his district favored the bill. The Deep Water Committee and Representative Nolan brought Tarpey back into the fold by convincing him to introduce a friendly compromise amendment which made two of the five commissioners elective. For Garner and some others, disenfranchisement was not a matter on which to compromise, but Tarpey's amendment swung enough votes that the bill passed easily in April 1901.[54]

Since the act did not include an emergency clause, ninety days had to elapse before it could take effect. This meant that the date for the normal spring council election would fall before the commission could take over. Since a victory by Jones and the other anticommission incumbents would have discredited the new charter, the commission supporters sprang to action. Realizing that they could not abandon the electoral tactics of the 1890s, they formed the City Club along with the lines of the old Good Government and Citizens' clubs. They prepared a procommission slate that would ensure a smooth transition of power, but for political reasons Mayor Jones and the council refused to call the election. The procommission forces decided not to press the issue, and, consequently, the existing city council continued to rule in the interim.[55]

Table 1. Results of Galveston's First Commissioner
Election, September 10, 1901
(Electors could vote for two candidates)

Candidate	Votes Received
William T. Austin (City Club)	3,660
A. P. Norman (City Club)	3,344
W. F. Stewart (independent)	673
Charles L. Davis (independent)	544
W. H. Laycock (independent)	375
Martin Byrne (independent)	203
Total ballots cast 4,338	
Total registration 6,022	

Source: *Galveston Daily News*, September 11, 1901.

However, the City Club members did not disband. They maintained their organization in order to prepare for the September 10, 1901, election of the two nonappointive members of the first commission. In theory, argued the club, the office of commissioner should seek the man and not vice versa; but finding ideal candidates who were willing to run proved difficult, just as it had in the 1890s. Many leading businessmen shunned politics and were unwilling to make the sacrifices of time demanded of even a parttime commissioner. The club finally convinced Judge William T. Austin and livestock dealer and former Alderman A. P. Norman to carry the procommission standard. The club's announcement proclaimed that the ticket was "entitled to the support . . . of every business, laboring, and professional man in our city; irrespective of race, color or creed."[56]

Incumbent Alderman W. F. Stewart and three other independent candidates challenged the City Club. While all the independents claimed that they would uphold the new law, each one of them was in fact on record against the change of governmental form. Thus, the election was tantamount to a referendum on the new charter. When the returns were in, it was obvious that all strata of Galveston society were willing to give the new plan a fair trial with friendly officers. The City Club candidates easily carried every ward in the city on the way to rolling up four times as many votes as their combined opposition (see table 1).[57]

Once the election was complete, Governor Sayers turned to the selection of the three appointed members of the commission. He consulted with the "best citizens" of the city in making his choice. Again, some prospective commissioners declined to serve before the governor settled on real estate broker V. E. Austin, young financier I. H. Kempner, and wholesale grocer Herman C. Lange. He surprised many observers by designating one of the elected commissioners, Judge Austin, to be the board president or mayor. E. R. Cheesborough, who had been a major figure in organizing the business campaigns of the 1890s and who would continue to be the backbone of the City Club, praised the governor's selections. "Politics cut no figure in these appointments," he contended. "Merit alone was considered."[58] Although Kempner had served on a Deep Water subcommittee and would become the new government's strongest and richest figure, no official member of the Deep Water Committee consented to be a commissioner.

Thus, Galveston had her new government in operation almost exactly a year after the terrible hurricane. The change had not been quick or easy; but those who wished to secure upper-class business control of the important functions of the municipal corporation were never in real danger of losing. Neither in Galveston nor in Austin had class antagonism been a major impediment to the invention of Progressive Era business elites' favorite municipal innovation.

The citizens of the recovering city were quite satisfied with the new system from the start. The work of rebuilding, getting the city's finances in order, raising the grade of the island, and erecting a sea wall against the Gulf proceeded apace with generous state and federal aid eventually forthcoming. The county government, not the city commission, was in charge of the magnificent engineering feat that made the long narrow resort town secure from future hurricanes. The commission set about to clean up vice in the beachside dives, and a group of Negro clergymen praised the "commission's efforts to bring about a better moral condition of the affairs in the city."[59] Galveston soon attracted extensive national attention for her accomplishments—financial, physical, and moral. But the businessmen of other cities would not want to emulate a semi-appointive government except in similar dire emergency.

The courts of Texas deserve the credit for transforming a specific remedy into a viable general option for those who admired Galveston's record. Anticommission attorney Marsene Johnson persuaded a drayman to test the constitutionality of the partially appointive government. Arrested for emptying privy vaults at an unauthorized time of day, the old black man refused to pay his fine and went to jail. Meanwhile, his lawyer argued for a writ of habeas corpus on the grounds that local government by an appointed body violated the Texas and United States constitutional guarantees of self-government. In *Ex Parte* Lewis, the Court of Criminal Appeals ruled on March 23, 1903, "that the special charter violated the principle of local self-government embodied in the Constitution, and hence an ordinance passed by the board of commissioners was void." However, soon thereafter, the Texas Supreme Court of Civil Appeals disagreed and ruled that a municipality was merely a creature of the state and virtually any charter the legislature might grant was valid. In direct contradiction to the highest criminal court, their unanimous *A. A. Brown et al.* v. *City of Galveston* opinion found that "no inherent right of municipal self-government can be implied from the history or traditions of the State."[60]

The conflict of opinions possible under the Texas judicial system might have resulted in the unprecedented case of a city with civil but no criminal powers had not the legislature been in session at the time of the first case. The lawmakers already had before them a bill asking for minor amendments to the 1901 charter; and, upon the request of Galveston's city attorney and others, the legislature unanimously approved further charter changes providing for the election of all five commissioners. Since the *A. A. Brown* civil ruling came after these amendments had been passed, it was only a moral victory for the original commission plan backers who still supported gubernatorial selection of commissioners. "We regretted to give up this feature of our charter," wrote Mayor H. A. Landes, who had become mayor upon the death of Judge Austin, "because we believed that the very best material could always be had by the appointive clause it contained." Although a judicial challenge of the innovative charter was probably inevitable, the late judge's daughter blamed the entire episode on Johnson, whom she called a "keen-eyed, unscrupulous lawyer [who] saw a chance to make trouble in a peaceful camp."[61]

Eventually, the loss of the three appointive positions did lead to a decline in the organized business interests' influence on city government, but at first they continued their control. The court decision and consequent charter amendment forced an election on April 28, 1903. The City Club endorsed the incumbents, and the people returned the entire commission by a comfortable margin.[62]

As early as 1905 some resentment of the City Club's domination of local politics had developed. E. R. Cheesborough had been so active since the mid-1890s that one journalist called the influential bookkeeper and City Club director "the boss of Galveston." Cheesborough wrote a cousin that he was "as well known in Galveston as any man." He confided to her that when he read the account calling him a "boss" he "had to laugh"; but he immodestly added, "To a certain extent it is true." In 1906 Cheesborough told a commission supporter in another city that the City Club was "composed mainly of citizens who during the past ten yeards have been striving for better city government."[63] But by 1909 the group's grip was slipping. That year two of the five commissioners were elected without the club's endorsement. A few years later original commissioner and City Club candidate A. P. Norman turned against the slate-making organization because he believed that all its efforts had been designed "to aid a few millionaires." The club still had enough influence to keep Norman's charges out of the papers.[64]

Despite this incipient dissatisfaction, Galveston, on the whole, continued to be enthusiastic about the commission for at least a decade after its founding. The city received hundreds of inquiries about its municipal innovations. Dozens of visitors came to see the pioneer commission government in action and to witness the ambitious grade-raising and sea-wall projects. These observers reportedly went away unanimously impressed. The *Galveston Journal* continued to praise the new government to its trade union readers; and Father J. M. Kirwin, one of the town's most popular citizens, carried on his advocacy, testifying in 1907 that all classes of people retained confidence in the system. Even Marsene Johnson, the lawyer who initiated the suit declaring the appointive positions unconstitutional, proclaimed around 1910 that "no sensible tax payer" would want to change from the fully elective commission.[65]

Such local enthusiasm helped account for the extensive national attention that Galveston received for her governmental accomplishments. Only three months after the "emergency government . . . by commission" began operation, a Galveston writer praised its performance in *Harper's Weekly*. But it was not until the governing body eliminated its appointed members in 1903 that the country began to take wide notice of the new plan. In 1904 the *Independent* praised the efficiency of the "businessmen" on the board. Later in that year *Gunton's Magazine* enumerated the many apparent advantages of the commission form of government. In the next two years general-interest periodicals, such as *Outlook, Nation, Review of Reviews*, and *Reader*, carried articles describing and praising the activities of the board of commissioners. "The results they have achieved," according to a writer in *World To-day* in 1906, "mark a new era in the recent history of American municipalities." About the same time a southern trade journal claimed: "After five years of trial and experience with this system it is the verdict of those qualified to speak with authority on the subject that Galveston is now the best governed city on the American continent." Many newspapers around the country echoed the praise of the magazine press.[66]

Specialists in municipal government also soon undertook investigations of the Galveston plan. From 1904 onward, the annual meetings of the National Municipal League discussed the new idea. At the 1906 conference the league's secretary, Clinton Rogers Woodruff, spoke of the plan's "remarkable achievement," and the enthusiastic and ubiquitous Cheesborough presented a paper on the operation and success of "the Galveston Experiment." By the next year commission government was the hit of the convention. Woodruff said, "Dr. William Bennett Munro's paper, which occupied over a year in the preparation, represents the most thoughtful study of the now famous Galveston plan which has thus far been made." *Outlook* magazine noted that Munro's presentation and one on separating municipal from state and national elections "easily attracted the most attention at the meeting."[67]

Other organized municipal interest groups also heard of the commission's supposed superiority to the traditional mayor-council format. Walter Gresham of the Galveston Deep Water Committee wrote about the plan in the *Bulletin of the League of American Municipalities* in 1905, and this league later became one of the leading advocates of commission government. Also in 1905 *Midland Municipalities* told its readers in Iowa and the Midwest about the new scheme for urban government. About two years later *Municipal Engineering* praised the plan, marking an increasing interest in the commission concept by professional city officials.[68]

By far the most influential early piece concerning the commission was "Galveston: A Business Corporation," in the October 1906 issue of *McClure's Magazine*. George Kibbe Turner, whom S. S. McClure's biographer called "perhaps the most effective of the muck-rackers," wrote the article after the more famous Lincoln Steffens declined to do the story because of his suspicion of businessmen. Turner spent about three weeks in Galveston learning about the commission from Cheesborough and others. The magazine received a remarkable response requesting reprints. Seattle wanted 20,000; Topeka already had the plan under consideration and asked for 500; Philadelphia good-government forces turned the article into a pamphlet; and numerous writers drew heavily from Turner's account for their own stories about the Galveston plan. The *Des Moines Register and Leader* published most of the piece as soon as it appeared, and many other newspapers followed suit. Eventually the number of pamphlet and newspaper reprints reached an estimated twelve million. The *McClure's* office for a time was a major source for the dissemination of information on the plan. Turner was soon in demand as a speaker on municipal reform, and he continued to write on the subject. In the spring of 1907 he penned an indictment of Chicago's municipal government, and an editorialist for the *Independent* wrote that Turner's praise of Galveston and attack on the Illinois metropolis comprised "two articles which may unhesitatingly be described as the most illuminating studies of municipal corruption and the one possible way to achieve decent municipal government which have as yet been made."[69]

By 1907 the Galveston plan had received even more national exposure in the popular and municipal press. But the innovation was no longer the exclusive property of its island city inventors. Cities all over the country had begun to discuss the scheme's application to their own governmental situtions.

CHAPTER TWO

THE TEXAS IDEA

CITIES learn about governmental innovations from each other, and the major portion of that social learning usually occurs within the boundaries of the state.[1] Thus is was that the first cities to follow Galveston's example were the pioneer's neighbors in Texas—Houston in 1905 and five other cities in 1907. These towns proved that, although the plan had been designed in the wake of a great natural calamity, its use did not have to be limited to such circumstances.

Railroads tied Houston to its hinterland, and riverboats and trains connected the city to deep-water commerce fifty miles away at Galveston. The two cities had long been rivals for the commercial leadership of Texas. In the nineteenth century Galveston had been the more populous, but by 1900 Houston had a population of 44,633, almost 7,000 more than her island competitor. Ten years later Houston's population had doubled Galveston's, and the larger town had nearly completed the ship channel that would eliminate its rival's monopoly of the ocean-going trade. By 1920 Houston had three times as many people, and the battle for dominance of the Texas Gulf coast was over. Despite Galveston's impressive recovery from the storm of 1900, Houston had combined geographical advantage with political and business aggressiveness to surpass her challenger and become one of the nation's leading ports.[2]

The rivals watched each other closely, so it is no surprise that observers in Houston soon began to notice the development of Galveston's new city government by commission. As early as 1902 some Houstonians wanted to study the plan with an eye toward removing "the evils of the present system." The city's newspapers told of fiscal improvement under "strictly business methods," and the *Houston Post* proclaimed, "Galveston's example in municipal thrift is a lesson which all cities should learn."[3]

The patterns of support and opposition which appeared in Houston foreshadowed the electoral cleavages in many later commission charter struggles. The Business League, which, according to the *Post*, "embraces in its membership about all the business concerns of the city,"[4] spearheaded the procommission forces. They praised Galveston's experience, attacked the present system, and lauded the businesslike efficiency that a small board with full responsibility could bring to municipal government. The driving force behind the opposition to the charter change was the incumbent city administration. Its members claimed that the current structure of the city's government was adequate and could do even better if given a chance. The city hall crowd found allies among much of the laboring class, which was suspicious of the downtown businessmen's motives. They believed that they would lose representation under an at-large electoral system, and they charged that government by a commission of so few men with such great power was undemocratic.

The first official effort to acquire commission government for Houston came in July 1904 when Alderman J. Z. Gaston introduced a resolution calling for the council to investigate the plan. The motion died, but in October he tried again. This time he suggested a binding election on the question of whether the city should adopt the method that he said had "proven so satisfactory in Galveston." Again the city council opposed the idea and defeated the call for an election.

The forces that the *Houston Chronicle* called the "business element" were friendly to any change that might improve municipal finances and services, and the defeat of the Gaston resolutions inspired them to action. The Business League, of which Alderman Gaston was a member, organized a meeting of the Commercial Club, Freight Bureau, Manufacturers' and Merchants' associations, "and all similar organizations." The influential gathering endorsed the commission plan and threatened to go directly to the legislature if the aldermen would not call an election. Under this presure the council relented and finally called a commission plan referendum for December 10, 1904.[5]

The Business League and the newspapers immediately launched a campaign to convince the voters to give the Galveston plan a trail. The *Chronicle* lashed out at the local administration and contrasted its incompetence with its neighbor's efficiency. In Houston, one editorial pointed out, "expenses exceed receipts [and] the city has to borrow money to meet current bills." Meanwhile "poor storm-swept Galveston, under a commission, gets interest on balances in bank and pays her bills on the first of every month."[6] Many citizens were worried by the fact that Houston had a floating debt of over $400,000. The municipal warrants sometimes issued to pay city employees circulated at a considerable discount. "No individual or particular administration is blamable for this condition of affairs," concluded the *Post*, "but the system under which it exists is damnable and should be wiped out."[7] In its place they wanted to substitute the Galveston plan. As Gaston explained it, "My idea is to have a body that can be looked to to take charge of the affairs of the city and handle them on a business basis."[8]

The opposition campaign argued that the Galveston experience was not a valid example, because the apparent success derived more from the community spirit and government aid that the storm inspired than from efficient governmental methods. Other charges were more direct. One letter writer charged that the commissioners and boosters of the island city had juggled the figures to make debts disappear so the administration would appear remarkable. A councilman claimed that the best jobs went to relatives of commission members and that most of the improvements centered in the downtown area where the commissioners and their rich friends had heavy investments. Clearly, they implied, Houston would not want to copy such a system.[9]

Current officeholders, of course, had a vested interest in the continuation of the old aldermanic structure, and they defended its operation. Conceding that city government had not been perfect, they argued that the method for improvement lay in better administration, not in a restructuring of the entire municipal system of Houston. The city assessor and collector claimed that, "if the city is economically managed during the next year under the present system, there is no reason why the floating debt cannot be reduced from $400,000 to $50,000. An example can be set that it will be difficult for a commission to exceed." In short, he concluded, "Houston is not in such a deplorable financial condition as the hue and cry that has been raised would indicate."[10]

Electing only five men from the city at large and giving them sole authority over the entire administration was patently undemocratic, commission opponents charged. "I am opposed to the commission form of government all along the line," wrote one alderman. "I don't think it is democratic and I know it is centralization." He was unknowingly prophetic when he added a partisan jab that it was "the sort of government Roosevelt would advocate."[11] In an attempt to appeal to neighborhood politics, one group of councilmen argued that what the city needed was more wards and a larger council not a concentration of power in five men elected at large. A journalist visiting Houston a few years after the election summarized the contest by writing that the businessmen "met with the bitter and determined opposition of the old political ring."[12]

That "determined opposition" was not enough to defeat the commission proposition, and on December 10, 1904, the voters of Houston declared their preference for a municipal government based on the Galveston plan. The turnout was only about a third of the registered voters, which, in turn, was only a third of those eligible had they paid their poll tax. As the press had predicted, most of the support for the proposal came from the large and affluent Third and Fourth wards. The Fifth Ward, according to the *Post*, contained mostly laboring men, and it voted heavily against the business-backed resolution. Also two of the three smallest wards that stood to lose the most representation under an at-large scheme went against the commission plan. In the city-wide total there were 1,262 for the new system and 815 against. The city council canvassed the returns and passed a motion establishing a committee to prepare a new charter.[13]

The charter committee was composed of Gaston, two other aldermen, and the city attorney. Councilman Robert L. Jones began his work declaring, "I am inclined to track the Galveston law as closely as possible," but the charter that finally passed differed from the original commission plan in some important aspects. For one, Galveston's charter did not contain any direct legislation devices, such as initiative, referendum, or recall; and the demand for these tools motivated some of the support for Houston's change of government. Local single taxer and subsequent mayor, J. J. Pastoriza, circulated a petition urging the inclusion of direct democracy in the commission charter, and even the *Chronicle* endorsed such a move. In the course of deliberations, the Houston charter framers decided to make the mayor a stronger administrator, thereby incorporating unknowingly some parts of the National Municipal League's strong-mayor concept. Furthermore, Houston's commissioners would be expected to be full-time officials, whereas their Galveston counterparts were part-time overseers.[14] But the city did not easily agree on such a charter, and the writing of the document sparked much local controversy.

Alderman Jones of the council-appointed charter committee suggested that the mayor appoint a body of citizens to review the proposed charter section by section. The motion carried and in mid-January 1905 the chief executive selected a group of a dozen men, two from each ward, to look over the document. Six of the twelve appointed were members of the Business League. The Citizens Committee and the council's charter committee conferred for about two weeks, compromised on a few issues, and submitted a completed charter to the full council on February 6, 1905. The citizens and the original drafting committee agreed on all points except the effective date of the new government. The city council had directed its committee to prepare a document that would initiate the commission plan in April 1906 when the current terms expired. The citizen group recommended that the sooner the new system could be launched the better, so they stood for an April 1905 beginning date. Actually Gaston and the city attorney favored the earlier date, but their official submission had to call for the current terms to run their course. Mayor A. L. Jackson and Alderman James A. Thompson also favored immediate initiation of the new charter.

The effort to legislate them out of office so embittered the majority of the city council that they refused to meet with the Citizens Committee. The council scrutinized the charter, as jointly submitted by its own committee and the citizens, and made a number of changes reducing the power of the mayor and weakening the utility control sections. After a solid week of work, they directed Alderman Jones to take the revised measure to the legislature, which was in its regular biennial session.

Meanwhile, the Citizens Committee, Aldermen Gaston and Thompson, and the city attorney met in Mayor Jackson's office to seek a compromise with the council majority. When the council refused to hear their report, they decided to make a separate submission to the state lawmakers. The Citizens Committee dispatched the mayor and city attorney to Austin to present their version of the charter. The scene for conflict was set.[15]

Two Houston-area legislators told Alderman Jones that both sides should try to compromise—advice the council did not heed. In the meantime, the Citizens' charter gathered influential backing. The Business League officially endorsed the Citizens' version by a unanimous vote of its board of directors. The league sent a delegation to Austin headed by wealthy ex-Mayor H. Baldwin Rice. Other commercial organizations, including the Cotton Exchange and Board of Trade, soon followed suit. By February 20, 1905, many business-men and all but two aldermen were at the state capital lobbying for one or the other of the two charter drafts.[16]

The opponents of the Citizens Committee charter included the public ser-vice corporations because the document required open records. Others at-tacked the Citizens' version because it gave the mayor too much power. The appointment prerogative was such that one witness told the legislature that the plank "would facilitate the building up of a political machine beside which Tammany Hall would pale into insignificance."[17]

The strength of the mayor, the regulation of utilities, and other specific sec-tions of the charter inspired much debate, but the most important issue was the effective date of the new government. This was the crucial difference between the council's charter and that of the Citizens Committee. Most of the municipal officials from aldermen to city scavenger testified against the Citi-zens' version because it would remove them from their jobs. The *Post* con-tended that such opposition defied the will of the people: "The legislature should not overlook the fact that the majority of the aldermen were opposed from the beginning to the commission idea which the people declared for at the ballot box, and in framing their charter they have sought to weaken the new system from the start. If the legislature desires to please the great ma-jority of Houston's citizens, it will enact the charter drawn by the friends of the commission and reject that prepared for the most part by men who are interested in continuing in office for another year."[18]

A minority of the incumbents, including the mayor, city attorney, and two aldermen, declared that they would gladly consent to being legislated out of office in order to bring better government to Houston. The press reported that the city attorney believed the charter "was the outgrowth of a feeling that better results could be obtained by changing the present form of govern-ment, and that the quicker the change was made the quicker the good results would be obtained." The mayor added that he hoped the legislature would pass the Citizens Committee charter because, "I am sure the people desire it."[19]

Mayor Jackson got his wish. The House Committee on Municipal Corpora-tions gave the Citizens Committee bill a favorable recommendation, and it was soon passed and, following some minor adjustments, signed by the gov-ernor. The courts had to settle the legal issue of whether the incumbent ad-ministration could be ousted by the new charter, but they soon ruled in favor of the new plan and local interest could turn to the election of commis-sioners.[20]

Although the leading daily newspapers had been united in their call for a change to the commission plan, that unity vanished as the first election under the new charter approached. The *Post* endorsed ex-Mayor Rice and called him "the candidate of the genuine commission advocates." The *Chronicle* backed retired printer A. Franklin Sittig, whose platform declared, "No man or set of men can usurp the exclusive right to be called 'commission men'"[21] A member of one of Houston's most prominent families, Rice led the so-called Straight Commission Ticket. The procommission aldermen, Gaston and Thompson, earned places on the basis of their advocacy of the Citizens' charter in defiance of the old city council. Thompson, a printer, and J. B. Marmion, a blacksmith, of the Straight Commission Ticket were union members as well as employers and businessmen. This gave the slate some appeal to the working man. The other member of the ticket was a retired railroad employee and cotton broker, James Appleby. Since all of the men on the Rice-led slate, except Appleby, had previously held public office, opponents charged that it was a politicians' ticket. Friends of Rice defended him, saying that the ex-mayor was "more of a businessman than a politician." He responded to charges that he was procorporation by promising to resign his directorship of the street railway company if elected. He would, however, keep his banking, lumber, and brewing interests.[22]

The May 29, 1905, Democratic primary was tantamount to election, and the entire Straight Commission Ticket won. Gaston, already known in Houston as "the father of the commission plan," led the ticket with a 434-vote plurality. Rice's margin over Sittig was only 125. Significantly, Rice lost the same three wards which had voted against the commission idea in the December referendum. Apparently many of the working men who concentrated in the First, Fifth, and Sixth wards were suspicious of the business orientation of the new government and its mayor.[23]

On July 5, 1905, the outgoing mayor administered the oath of office to the new city fathers, and Houston officially became the second commission plan city. The early results under the new administration appeared almost as rewarding as Galveston's. "Upon assuming control of the city's affairs," Mayor Rice wrote in the first annual report, "we found that the city, financially, was in deplorable condition." In the first eight months of commission government, he boasted, the floating debt of over $400,000 was "virtually cancelled."[24] The Business League claimed that the new system had ushered in "a notable area of economy without niggardliness." Cautiously, the editor of the *Houston Chronicle* wrote that some of the city's claims were "extravagant," but on balance he admitted that the accomplishments were indeed significant.[25]

The praiseworthy results continued throughout the first few years of commission government as the city made many capital improvements while actually lowering the tax rate. Besides its financial improvements, the commission set about to clean up the city. The police suppressed gambling in open houses and limited the hours during which saloons could operate. Apparently such action met with the approval of the voters. In the spring of 1906 former Congressman Thomas H. Ball asserted, "The commission form of government for Houston has satisfied its friends and largely reconciled its former opponents." A year later the election results confirmed this assertion when Rice and his ticket received about three-fourths of the vote.[26]

The new government immediately began to attract attention. The Civic Improvement League of St. Louis wanted a copy of the charter even before the commission began operation. The Business League announced in 1906 that the city had received inquiries about its innovative system from every section of the United States as well as from Europe, Asia, and Australia. A Pittsburgh newspaper extolled the Galveston plan and Houston's adoption of it, and a Chicago charter-reform group asked for copies of the document and information on the government's operation.[27]

In April 1907, when only Galveston and Houston were actually operating under commission governments, *Outlook* magazine dubbed the plan the "Texas Idea." A long article described and eulogized the municipal administrations at Galveston and Houston, and an editorial declared that the plan was "a practical and successful method which, in our judgment, ought to be widely followed throughout the country."[28] But before the Texas idea could diffuse over the nation, it had to spread across Texas itself. By the spring of 1907, five more Texas cities were in the process of beginning operations under the new format.

Proximity is an important variable in the diffusion of any idea, and Houston's nearness to Galveston was certainly a crucial factor in its early adoption of the commission form. Other cities of the state soon began to notice the new system too. As early as 1903 and 1904, newspapers in many Texas cities reported on the outstanding record of the new government in Galveston. By 1907 the entire state was alive with the news, and the *Fort Worth Record* concluded, "These are facts which cannot be disputed and which unanswerably prove the superior efficiency of commission government."[29] In both Dallas and Fort Worth the city councils went on record in favor of the plan. Early in 1906 the former acknowledged that the system was "in successful operation in both Houston and Galveston, under broad and liberal charters granted by the legislature," and the latter resolved that "municipal government under a commission has proven an undoubted success."[30]

Dozens of observers from all around the state visited the two original commission cities to make firsthand observations. Reporting on such trips, a Denison newspaper remarked, "Every delegation or representative that goes to Houston and Galveston to investigate the commission form of government comes away a firm believer in it and an enthusiastic advocate." In addition to actual visits, the two cities were swamped with letters of inquiry about the new form of government.[31]

In anticipation of the 1907 biennial legislative session, groups interested in promoting new special charters had to begin work in 1906. The first official action came in Dallas. In January the *Morning News*, owned by the same company as the *Galveston Daily News*, called for a "complete reorganization of the municipal government, modelling after the Galveston elective commission." By April the voters had answered two to one in favor of drawing up a Galveston plan charter.[32]

Fort Worth was not far behind its larger rival. The commission plan had been the subject of a city hall meeting in 1905, and during the next two years both daily papers, the Board of Trade, and other business organizations joined the agitation for the change of government. Consideration of the plan was an issue in the 1906 legislative campaign, and the procommission candidate won. Even the incumbent aldermen went on record that year as favoring the system, although they later dragged their feet when faced with the imminent possibility of a new charter establishing an all-powerful board of five men. A committee prepared a commission bill, and the citizens of Fort Worth voted on it in April 1907. The document received their approval by an astonishing five-to-one margin.[33]

El Paso actually began using its commission charter before Dallas or Fort Worth did although it began consideration of the plan much later. The first meeting of the El Paso commissioners was on April 12, 1907, whereas the Fort Worth and Dallas bodies did not convene until May and June, 1907, respectively. In December 1906, El Paso's city attorney reminded the city council that any charter amendments desired in the next two years would have to be presented to the legislature early in January. The council then directed him and a committee to investigate what changes the city's organic law might need. By mid-January the committee had prepared an entirely different document. The *El Paso Herald* immediately endorsed it saying, "First and foremost among the improvements the new charter aims to bring about is the adoption of the commission form of government, such has been found so successful in Houston and Galveston." The incumbent council was in favor of the move, and it voted to submit the charter to the lawmakers in Austin without first conducing a local election on the matter. The evening paper and many citizens opposed such a high-handed action, but the legislature granted the charter anyway.[34]

Two smaller northeastern Texas cities also adopted the commission plan in 1907. Denison showed some interest in the Galveston plan in early 1906, and by December discussion of the Texas idea had become more general. The Board of Trade called a "mass meeting" that urged the city council to consider adopting a commission-type form of organization. The citizens at the meeting were virtually unanimous in their praise for Houston's and Galveston's advances in municipal administration; they hoped that the fresh idea could do the same for their community of somewhat more than 12,000. Some opposition to the plan emerged in a second Board of Trade–sponsored public gathering, but the body still passed a resolution favoring the holding of an election to decide if Denison should indeed experiment with the new system. The idea proved to be a popular one, carrying the city by more than a two-to-one margin. A joint city council and citizens' committee drew up a charter, and in March 1907 the legislature approved the document in less than a week.[35] That same month a charter breezed through the legislative process making Greenville, with a population of about 8,000, the smallest commission city.[36] Thus, by the spring of 1907, there were seven cities governed by the "Texas Idea": Galveston, Houston, Dallas, Fort Worth, El Paso, Denison, and Greenville.

In each of the cities the patterns of support and opposition to the changes of government were similar but not identical. Invariably the business community and/or the daily press initiated and supported the new charters. The Deep Water Committee was primarily responsible for the initial commission plan in Galveston, and in Houston a coalition of commercial organizations headed by the Business League managed to push their commission charter through. In Fort Worth and Denison the Boards of Trade coordinated efforts to secure the new plan. Businessmen in Dallas and El Paso joined the agitation that the leading newspapers started.

The organized business community also generally led the commission forces in those Texas towns that assumed the system after 1907. Austin, of course, was the stage for the Galveston and Houston legislative fights to obtain commission charters. A few urged that the capial city considered the plan itself, but in 1905 on representative observed, "The idea of a commission is not setting the town on fire."[37] About two years later Mayor I. H. Evans began pushing for a commission charter in speeches to the Business League. The letters he read from his counterparts in Galveston and Houston praising their administrators may have impressed his listeners, but still they took no action. Finally, on September 4, 1908, the majority of a committee of the Austin Business League reported, "We are led to believe that Austin would take no risk in changing her system of government to that form generally known as a commission."[38] The league organized a procommission campaign and in December the voters approved the charter with only one ward showing a heavy majority for the alternative proposal. From the commission's adoption until 1919, Mayor A. P. Wooldridge served as the head of a "business men's government."[39]

Sherman, twin city to commission-ruled Denison, initially rejected the Galveston plan. But the Business Men's Club and its allies did not give up. They secured a commission charter in 1910 and exchanged it to become a leader in the city manager movement five years later.[40]

In Beaumont, wealthy lumberman George W. Carroll and his business-oriented allies in the press continually championed municipal reform, in general, and the commission system, in particular. In 1905 and 1907, commission-like charters met defeat at the polls. By 1909 the leading businessmen were forced to accept a mild reform charter that did not include the essential features of the commission plan.[41] Clearly, then, the Texas idea was consistently endorsed by businessmen who wanted to improve their city governments by initiating a municipal administration that five men elected at large would control. It was hoped they would be men of sound business judgment.

Not quite as consistent as business support for the plan was working-class, especially organized-labor, opposition. An exception was Galveston where, faced with the emergency, labor served as part of the united community front that supported the Deep Water Committee's proposals. Union spokesmen continued to endorse the pioneer commission in the early years of Galveston's new government. Another exception was Fort Worth, where the business leaders anticipated the likelihood that organized labor would oppose their efforts. They avoided such a possibility by including working men in the change-of-government movement. Unions participated in the drafting of the charter, and, according to a Trades Assembly leader, labor got everything it wanted included in the document. Initiative, referendum, and recall, in particular, were among the workers' demands. The assembly resolved to "use our best efforts in behalf of the new city charter and work for its adoption."[42] Official union support even continued through the first commissioner election when the Fort Worth Trades Assembly endorsed the business-dominated Citizens' Ticket. The business leaders gave labor one spot on the ticket and chose a member of the International Brotherhood of Electrical Workers to run. Apparently the official labor endorsement for the commission charter, and later for the commissioners themselves, extended to the rank and file because both the charter and the Citizens' Ticket carried every ward in the city. The union representative on the new municipal governing board wrote to a reformer in another city that all classes of Fort Worth favored the commission.[43]

The scenario was considerably different in other Texas commission cities, In Houston, for example, opposition centered in the incumbent officeholders, but they had labor as allies. The Labor Council refused an invitation to attend a fall 1904 meeting of commission supporters, and the wards that the press identified as labor dominated voted against the commission idea. Much of the union suspicion of the Business League–led municipal reform disapated when the first commission included two members of organized labor.[44]

The Trades Assembly of Dallas did its best to prevent the city's adoption of the commission plan with its attendant at-large elections. The assembly pressured the city council to word the ballot so that the Galveston-type plan was only one of a number of choices. The *Dallas Morning News* reported that "labor leaders have been busy urging qualified voters among the unions to vote against any commission form of government." The effort, however, was unsuccessful, for the commission idea gained the approval of nine out of ten wards.[45] Failing to block the charter, labor leaders attempted to ensure that it was written in a way satisfactory to their desires.

A wide range of citizens participated in the convention that produced the first draft of the Dallas charter. At the legislature, labor spokesmen testified in favor of direct legislation and other sections that the unions especially wanted, and eventually got, in the final version. Unlike their counterparts in nearby Fort Worth, the Dallas Citizens' Association did not select a union-related candidate to run on their business-dominated slate. According to campaign organizer Philip Lindsley, "all the walks of life were represented," in planning the ticket; but, he admitted, "the conservative business element was in the majority."[46] Citizens' Association literature appealed to "those who have to depend upon their labor for their support" but stressed that their candidates were "men who have made a success of their private affairs." They promised that such businessmen could provide "an honest, efficient, and progressive administration." The vocal labor opposition was ineffectual at the polls, for the Citizens' Association easily won every seat.[47]

In Denison the Trades Council was on record as being "unalterably opposed to the commission form of government." They proclaimed that the concentration of so much power in the hands of a few men elected at large was patently undemocratic. Suspecting a plot to dominate city hall, they questioned the motives of the commission's backers. The *Industrial Record*, a labor-oriented newspaper, argued that Denison could elect good men to the council under the existing aldermanic system. Supporters of the change feared that the working-class Third and Fourth wards would vote against the Board of Trade–promoted plan, but the commission idea carried easily in all four of Denison's wards. Apparently labor's charges that the Galveston plan was undemocratic did not convince the people of Denison.[48]

El Paso opponents of the commission plan tried to arouse that city's working men by reporting that labor in other cities was against the system. But since El Paso never had the opportunity to vote on its commission charter, the extent of labor opposition is unclear.[49]

The businessmen of Sherman blamed the initial defeat of their commission proposal on worker opposition. One speaker said that the Business Men's Club had not made enough effort to cooperate with the working classes in drafting and explaining the charter. Others felt that the plan lost in the less-affluent wards because workers feared that a tax increase would accompany a new government.[50]

This general tendency of labor opposition to or suspicion of the business-supported charges of government in Texas was often repeated as the commission idea diffused across America. According to some studies of Progressive Era municipal reform, the charters of large heterogeneous cities of low socioeconomic status were less susceptible to structural alteration by commission or by manager than were small and medium-size cities cities.[51] The lower classes correctly perceived that the at-large election of a small board would make it difficult for people of limited means to be elected. They expected that governmental schemes devised and promoted by business interests would be run for the benefit of those same interests.

Because there was not a model commission plan charter for cities to follow, not all of the commission charters were alike. In fact, Houston's system was noticeably different from Galveston's, and the other Texas cities each had unique documents. The unifying feature, and the definition of commission government, was the election of a small board at large and the assignment of specific departmental responsibilities to particular members of the board of commissioners. There were few, if any, other elected officials; the commissioners were fully responsible for the running of the city. The departmental assignments varied somewhat from city to city, but Houston's were typical. The mayor, elected separately, supervised general administration, and there were commissioners of finance and revenue; police and fire; water, light, and health; and streets, bridges, and public grounds. In Galveston the commissioners were overseers rather than actual department heads, so they were expected to give only part of their time to city affairs. Houston's charter required full-time service, and each commission member participated more directly in the management of his department's business. Although Galveston defended its system as allowing prominent men to serve without great sacrifices of time, the Houston system became more typical in Texas and the rest of the country. Only Denison among the early commission cities joined

Galveston in permitting the commissioners to spend less than half time on their municipal functions. Of the original seven charters, only Greenville's provided that candidates run for specific seats on the commission. In the other cities the departmental allocation among the commissioners was made by the mayor or the commission itself. As commission government developed, the practice of selecting commissioners for specified places became more common.[52]

The most controversial provisions of the new commission charters were direct democracy devices. Galveston's system did not provide for any such checks. Houston's original commission charter allowed for franchise referendums only, although the city added the initiative, recall, and a general referendum in 1913. The *Dallas Morning News* opposed these devices: "It is time to drop this foolishness and a lot of other fads, and to return to the plans tested by Galveston and Houston."[53] But in both Dallas and Fort Worth, laboring groups demanded and got initiative, referendum, and recall included in the commission charters. Any petition had to have the signatures of 15–35 percent of the voters to activate the checks; thereby the charter framers made the use of direct democracy unlikely. In 1910 Fort Worth's commissioner of public works said, "The strength of the initiative and referendum lies more in its existence in the organic law than from its actual exercise by the masses."[54] El Paso, Greenville, and Denison resisted direct democracy planks in their charters except that all three provided for franchise referendums, and Denison made the mayor subject to recall. As commission government moved around the country, initiative, referendum, and recall became generally associated with the movement although they were never essential parts of the new form of government.

The results of the new plan in the first seven commission cities were uniformly satisfactory—at least for the initial years. Galveston made a remarkable recovery from the devastation of the 1900 hurricane, and Houston managed to pay off the accumulated debts of previous administrations. The five cities adopting the system in 1907 also reported significant accomplishments. Just before the new Dallas commission took over, the outgoing mayor asserted, "I believe that the record made during the past twelve months by the entire administration will be hard to duplicate, even under a Commission form of government." But during the first two years of the new government, according to the finance commissioner, "the board of commissioners maintained these departments at a net saving under the cost of the former administration." An overdraft had been eliminated, and the city had a cash balance on hand.[55] In 1910 the *Morning News* wrote that the Dallas commission was still "producing results which seemingly are highly satisfactory to a majority of the people."[56] There was still a sharp difference of opinion over the merit of initiative, referendum, and recall, but most commentators agreed that Dallas was proud of its commission during the first few years.

"The people of Fort Worth," declared one commissioner in 1910, were "satisfied with their form of government. . . . More and better results have been accomplished under the commission government in three years than would have been realized in ten years under the old aldermanic regime. I know of no one in Fort Worth who would advocate a return to former conditions."[57] The reasons for the satisfaction included more streets paved, an improved water system, modern accounting and purchasing procedures, and expenses that were less, in the words of one local newspaper, "than they would have been under the old aldermanic form."[58]

Gradually the story of the success of the Texas cities with the commission plan filtered out to municipalities nationwide. Numerous observers, famous and obscure, came to see the commission in action. For example, Charles W. Eliot, president of Harvard, told an audience, "So much interested have I become in the question of municipal reform that I went down to see the plan on the quiet—to see the men in charge of these Texas cities, governed under their charters by commissions of five." He was uniformly impressed with the results he found in Dallas, Houston, and Galveston.[59] Another Harvard professor, Albert Bushnell Hart, had made a trip to Texas before Eliot, and he cautiously reported that "the Texas commissions are so far distinctly successful and are likely to last a considerable time."[60] The Illinois General Assembly sent a special subcommittee to Galveston, Houston, and Dallas to study the "Texas Idea." They reported: "In every city we visited, we found the almost unanimous sentiment of the citizens favoring the commission form of government. We sought the opinion of bankers, merchants, laboring men—in fact all classes of citizens. The enthusiasm of the people for this form of government is hardly describable. . . . Without doubt there has been a marked improvement in the conduct of affairs of these cities under this plan of municipal government."[61]

As the commission form spread beyond Galveston, media notice continued to increase. Aside from the dozens of magazine articles on the commission plan, many big-city newspapers began to take notice of the municipal experiments in the Texas cities. Papers in Boston, Philadelphia, Pittsburgh, Baltimore, Memphis, and Indianapolis praised Galveston and Houston in 1906 and 1907.[62]

In 1907 and 1908 the Texas idea even attracted international notice. Houston reported worldwide inquiries, and the British government took official notice. Ambassador James Bryce's charge that corrupt city government was the one notable failure of American democracy was widely known, and he maintained his interest in observing municipal developments in this country. The ambassador reported to the Foreign Office: "The so-called 'Galveston-plan' of city government by a small elected commission instead of by a large municipal chamber is growing in favour. . . . Reports now say that in all cities in Texas in which it has been adopted it has proven uniformly successful." Other dispatches noted that the idea was spreading beyond Texas.[63]

The favorable publicity that the Texas-idea cities received for their municipal innovations would be the envy of any chamber of commerce, and the business elites were quick to capitalize on it. A spokesman for El Paso's chamber of commerce declared that the border town was "one of the best governed cities in the country."[64] Dallas and Fort Worth made similar boasts.

Not to be outdone, one journalist expanded Galveston's claim to governmental superiority to cover the entire continent. A Denison newspaper reminded its readers that "should we make a success, it is going to be a splendid advertisement for Denison."[65] The *Houston Post* ventured, "The Houston system will redeem any city that adopts it from the curse of spoils, politics, graft, extravagance, bankruptcy, and waste," and *Progressive Houston*, city hall's own organ, announced that the city was governed according to "business principles."[66]

Even by 1909, when many states had made some provisions for their cities to adopt the new plan, the Texas experience was still crucial to the idea's diffusion. "Naturally," a Galveston paper wrote, "people of other states who have taken an interest in the matter still turn to Texas, where the test has been most thorough for information on the subject." By 1909, Austin, Waco, and three smaller cities had joined the original seven Texas-idea towns, and the state legislature had passed a general law permitting cities of under 10,000 to adopt the commission plan by simple referendum. In 1913 and 1914 the enabling act was amended to expand its coverage.[67]

The three Galveston attorneys who prepared the pioneer commission charter did not know that they were writing an item for the nation's progressive reform agenda. Even later the businessmen in Houston, Dallas, Fort Worth, Denison, and Greenville probably did not envision themselves as part of a national mood, although their reform rhetoric often had a progressive ring. The Dallas Citizens' Association was composed of conservative businessmen whose campaign documents called for "an honest, efficient, and progressive administration" to help the city pass "from the antiquated government composed of a mayor and aldermen to the modern system made up of a mayor and four commissioners."[68]

Texans became jealous when their progressive idea had spread so far across the country that it was no longer as closely identified with the Lone Star state. In 1910 the *Dallas Morning News* complained of municipal plagiarism: "Organizations at Des Moines, Iowa, have very persistently and widely advertised what they term 'The Des Moines Plan of Municipal Government,' oft-times forgetting to say that the Des Moines charter is based upon that of Galveston, and always failing to explain that the charter of the Iowa metropolis is copied almost literally from the Dallas charter. . . . It does not seem amiss to say that Des Moines is using the commission form of government largely for advertising purposes, and without regard to its authorship."[69]

To a certain extent the paper was right in its bid to establish a commission copyright. Des Moines as well as other cities and states did draw heavily on the Texas experience. Without it they probably would have never thought of adopting a plan of government that abandoned the separation of powers in favor of municipal rule by a small body of men exercising both legislative and executive functions. Iowa and Des Moines' main contributions to the commission government were, first, proof that it was not merely a provincial southern idea, and, second, attachment of direct legislation so closely to the plan that initiative, referendum, and recall henceforth seemed to go hand in hand with the new system. Of course, as the Dallas press pointed out, their city had even beaten Des Moines to these devices—"if it is anything to brag about."[70] The idea had appealed to many people in Texas but especially to businessmen because it allowed them to have a better opportunity to influence municipal policy. Galveston's success impressed these Lone Star reformers, and they wanted the same efficiency for their own city governments. Their accomplishments in turn were responsible for demonstrating the workability of the Texas idea to the rest of the nation. But it was up to the capital of Iowa to prove that the concept was not only workable but also acceptable.

CHAPTER THREE

THE DES MOINES PLAN

ACCORDING to the 1905 state census, the capital of Iowa had a population of 75,626; and by 1910 the city had grown to over 86,000 with its boosters, naturally, claiming more. Des Moines was a relatively homogeneous midwestern city with native whites of native parentage comprising 62.3 percent of the population. Those persons of foreign or mixed parentage brought the native white total up to almost 85 percent. The balance of the populace consisted of 12 percent foreign born and fewer than 4 percent Negro. Obviously any municipal woes the town might have encountered did not originate from a stereotypical immigrant-based political machine.[1]

With an area of fifty-four square miles, Des Moines was a low-density city larger in territory than Minneapolis, St. Louis, or any city of comparable population. But Des Moines was almost two cities. The fundamental political cleavage of the municipality had long been the Des Moines River, which runs just east of downtown. On the west side of the river were the central business district, Drake University, and most of the better residential sections; the east side had the state capitol complex and tended to be more working-class oriented. The few black and foreign-born citizens were distributed fairly evenly throughout the city, so that native whites of native parentage constituted the largest ethnic group in every ward.[2]

Aside from the east-west division, the most important specific political issue in the capital's municipal politics for twenty-five years had been the public service corporations which controlled all of the small metropolis' utilities and mass transportation. As in many cities, charges about franchise-related corruption were common, and many voters tended to be pro- or anticorporation on general principles without regard to the specific case.[3]

The system of municipal organization in Des Moines prior to its adoption of the commission plan consisted of a mayor and nine aldermen, two of whom were elected at large. Also chosen on a city-wide basis were the treasurer, auditor, police judge, and solicitor. Much of the executive power, however, was in the hands of the Board of Public Works, which the mayor appointed subject to the council's approval. Quasi-independent boards also conducted the business of the fire and police departments, placing many of the municipality's functions beyond the direct control of the voters. For years this complicated arrangement had failed to satisfy many of the city's leading citizens.[4]

Open disgust at the existing government and active efforts to change the system began in 1905. Late in the year the city's leading newspaper, the Republican *Register and Leader*, commented that "a general feeling of dissatisfaction over the present management of municipal affairs has been manifest for some time." In preparation for the upcoming spring council election, a so-called scratcher movement started to organize a "list of candidates backed by a fusion of business interests regardless of party lines." Unsure of the success of this movement, the dominant commercial element stood clear of the predominantly Democratic ticket. The slate lost most of its races in March 1906, but the press remarked that its surprisingly good showing was symptomatic of citizen unrest at the state of municipal affairs. At the same election a non-binding referendum, which the Socialists had initiated, found that the voters were ready to accept city ownership of the public franchises. But attempts to try to capture city hall through the ballot box and the present system were not enough.[5]

November 1905 had already marked the beginning of serious consideration of the commission plan for Des Moines. The "father of the Des Moines plan," James G. Berryhill, reported to the city's businessmen about the wonderful accomplishments of Galveston's new idea in urban government. The man who brought his city to leadership in municipal reform circles was an ardent Republican whom Iowa's progressives characterized as a "standpatter." He had been a leading Republican member of the state general assembly but had lost a bid to represent the capital city in Congress. His business endeavors were decidely more successful than his political activities. As a wealthy lawyer and real estate developer, Berryhill had often visited Galveston on business and reportedly was in the island city when the original commission form began. On subsequent trips he became interested in the workings of the new system. In the course of events, Berryhill mentioned his observations about Galveston to Harvey Ingham, editor of the *Register and Leader*. This was the starting point of an eighteen-month agitation that Ingham's paper spearheaded. The editor suggested that, on his next trip to Texas, Berryhill should gather solid information about the plan so that the newspaper could publish it for general consideration in Des Moines.[6]

Berryhill spent about two weeks in Galveston, obtaining data about the commission's operation. When he returned, the Commercial Club called a public meeting for November 17, 1905, to hear his report; it was a glowing account. He recounted the alleged misdeeds of the prestorm administrations, lauded the public-spirited efforts of the Deep Water Committee, described the workings of the arrangement, and praised the commissioners' business methods. According to Ingham's paper, Berryhill's audience was "the most important congregation of business men Des Moines has witnessed in many years. . . . There were represented in the meeting the brains and financial backbone of the city."[7]

The speech and the *Register and Leader*'s agitation led to the organization of a committee to promote the commission idea. About two weeks after the report, over fifty business and professional men, "representative of the very best citizenship of Des Moines," met at the Commercial Club and launched a drive to get the general assembly to allow use of the Galveston plan in Iowa. Throughout December the commercial element met to discuss the idea, and the evening *Capital* and *Daily News* joined their morning rival in advocating the fresh governmental concept. The newly organized Committee of 200 appointed Berryhill and attorneys W. H. Baily and John Read to draw a commission charter for presentation to the legislature. The subcommittee submitted its draft to the 200 and called for quick legislative action so that the voters could decide at the regular March municipal election if they wanted the new form of government. Although based on the Galveston charter, the Des Moines version that went to the legislature in late January included nonpartisan elections and direct legislation not in the pioneer plan.[8]

The commission suggestion quickly attracted opposition, and one city official went to Galveston to gather arguments against the plan. Resistance to the change of government centered in the incumbent administration and other politicians. The bill came up at a joint meeting of the House and Senate Committees on Cities and Towns, and the *Register and Leader* reported that it was "practically laughed out of the legislative committees."[9] In 1911, Professor Benjamin F. Shambaugh, head of the State Historical Society of Iowa looked back and made a similar analysis: "Among the legislators the scheme was regarded as decidedly visionary and impracticable."[10] and the committees of the general assembly killed the bill without even taking a roll-call vote. Even though the proposal would have been an enabling act applying to seven Iowa cities, it became clear in the hearings that the lawmakers tended to regard it as special legislation for Des Moines, and the lack of local harmony and agreement within the capital city was the primary reason that bill died. As Berryhill later commented, "public sentiment had not been sufficiently aroused."[11]

The commission plan forces refused to regard the February 1906 defeat as final. The morning paper called the legislative action "a temporary setback" and vowed that it would not give up. For the first few weeks after the commission defeat, concern for local politics concentrated on the upcoming council election, and the plan received little attention in the press. All three daily editors refused, however, to let commission plan references disappear entirely from their columns. By early fall 1906 the Galveston plan was again in the news, and the change-of-government effort became involved with a massive city-boosting movement.

When the Commercial Club met to launch its booster drive, many agreed that "the diseases of the city government . . . have been Des Moines' worst handicap."[12] They wished to include municipal reform among their goals for a better city. To lead its city promotion efforts, the Commercial Club organized the Greater Des Moines Committee, composed of the commercial and professional elite. Officially, the new committee stayed out of municipal politics, leaving such matters to the larger and more broadly based Commercial Club; but, behind the scenes, members of the new group pushed the commission plan.

Even those who favored a major change in Des Moines' charter disagreed on the advisability of the Galveston method. Soon after the 1906 legislative defeat of the commission bill, newspaperman John J. Hamilton came out in favor of the strong-mayor plan, which he argued would "make the mayor in this way the business manager of your city."[13] Discussion of this so-called Indianapolis plan continued through the rest of 1906, and a substantial number of businessmen and community leaders came to favor it. W. H. Baily, former city solicitor and one of the attorneys who helped draft the defeated commission bill, drew up a full proposal based on the Indianapolis charter. The Civic League also endorsed such a plan. The state senator from Des Moines suggested that a strong-mayor format might stand a better chance of getting through the general assembly than another commission bill would. Governor Albert Baird Cummins' called for an Indianapolis-type municipal reform bill strengthened this contention.[14]

Those favoring the strong-mayor concept emphasized that it would retain the traditional American separation of executive and legislative functions that the commission plan would abolish. The principal arguments in favor of the commission arrangement were the specific point that the strong-mayor plan constituted one-man rule and the general conviction that Des Moines needed a totally new system. The *Register and Leader* acknowledged that the Indianapolis charter could be a great improvement but emphasized, "The Galveston plan is not in appearance a mere modification of what we have, while the mayor and council plan, however strengthened, is after all the mayor and council plan."[15] Berryhill agreed that the Indianapolis plan was little more than patchwork upon the present system. On the other hand, some politicians critized both systems, claiming that they concentrated too much power and authority in one body or one man elected at large.

The businessmen and editors calling for substantial change in the machinery of municipal administration realized that if they approached the legislature without a united front both the Galveston and the Indianapolis proposals would probably lose. In an attempt to reach a consensus, the *Register and Leader* polled 120 business and professional men, and 117 favored a change in the municipal system. Of those taking a specific stand, 62 favored the commission choice and 26 declared for the strong-mayor alternative. The *Capital* conducted a wider opinion survey and found 606 for the Galveston plan, 412 on the side of the Indianapolis method, and only 23 against any change.[16]

Meanwhile Hamilton suggested that a public debate between Baily and Berryhill in front of a jury of prominent men decide the matter. The panel of judges would listen to the two sides and vote for the better plan. The dissenters would agree to support the victorious proposition. Hamilton thought that such a meeting and decision "would carry enough moral weight to unite the great body of well-meaning citizens." He submitted a list of 100 judges including representatives of all parties, races, and factions.[17] The two principals quickly agreed to present their alternatives to such a meeting as long as the people would consider it a "discussion" and not a "debate." The Greater Des Moines Committee and the Commercial Club endorsed the idea and added 200 more names to the original jury. This established a Committee of 300 similar to the 1906 commission group. One alderman prominent in the opposition to all major charter revisions refused an invitation to address the gathering because it was packed with antiadministration businessmen. Reportedly, a large audience attended the January 31, 1907, meeting; but only 133 of the over 300 appointed judges came and voted. They favored the Galveston alternative 106 to 27. In his speech against the Texas idea, Baily promised, "If it is decided that we must have the Commission System, I will be ready as I was a year ago to help." The meeting took him at his word and chose him to be among those selected to draft a charter. Berryhill and Read from the 1906 subcommittee along with S. B. Allen, vice president of the Commercial Club, and I. M. Earle, an insurance company lawyer, joined Baily in writing a new commission bill to submit to the thirty-second general assembly. In an attempt to dispel opposition from the incumbents, the new version would not allow the commission to take over until existing terms had expired. Also, the 1907 bill expanded the direct legislation provisions to include a general referendum and initiative in addition to the recall and franchise referendums included in the first measure. Aside from these elements and a few other minor changes, the 1907 commission proposal closely tracked its predecessor.[18]

To tie the municipal reform efforts closely to the city-boosting movement, the drafting committee and press began to refer to the bill as the "Des Moines plan," and the name stuck. The *News* said, "It was a happy thought in the framers of this legislation to call it the Des Moines Plan. If adopted it will not only bring about a great reform in municipal affairs, but will advertise Des Moines far and wide as a city that 'does things.'" The *Capital* agreed, writing, "If the plan is worked out successfully here, it will be adopted all over the United States and will be called the 'Des Moines Plan.' Thus Des Moines would be advertised from ocean to ocean."[19] The Committee of 300 became known as the Des Moines Plan Committee, and they laid plans for their two objectives. First, they had to secure legislative approval of the optional charter bill, and, second, they had to see that the people of Des Moines would adopt the system when given a chance.

On February 6, 1907, the charter committee handed its work to the Polk County legislative delegation, who would present the bill to the general assembly. The area lawmakers, I. M. Earle of the drafting subcommittee, and some others met with Governor Cummins and went over the proposal, making a few minor changes. Cummins suggested the use of a double-election run-off system and wrote the appropriate section. Although his annual message a few weeks earlier had called for a strong-mayor format, the press reported that the governor now supported the commission bill.[20]

The Iowa League of Municipalities, composed of city officials from across the state, also had a reform bill pending. It proposed to eliminate some independent boards, strengthen the city engineer, and enhance the mayor's appointive powers. The previous year the league had obtained from the assembly a uniform municipal accounting act, and the editor of the organization's journal had commented, "I am willing to go on record that this bill is a greater reform measure than the pet Galveston plan and all other plans and theories advocated by the capital city reformers, and will do more to improve municipal conditions that would ten dozen Galveston plans."[21]

The league believed that "the better way to secure needed reforms is to work for the necessary changes in the present laws without trying to change the entire system."[22] To make matters even more difficult for the Des Moines Plan Committee, the mayor of Des Moines was the current president of the state league. In face of the *Register and Leader*'s alleged threat to attack the League of Municipalities bill if members of that group testified against the Des Moines plan, sponsors of the two measures agreed not to interfere with each other. Since the league's reforms were mandatory and were not inconsistent with the commission form, commission backers were willing to let the half-a-loaf revisions pass in case the legislators or the voters defeated their pet plan.

A special legislative committee of members from districts with cities of over 15,000 that the enabling act would affect heard testimony on the Des Moines plan in early March 1907. Besides attacking the commission form and defending the present system, opponents claimed that the Iowa League of Municipalities bill was sufficient to correct any shortcomings that might exist in current urban governmental methods. Although the proposed commission law would apply to a number of cities and the state press seemed interested, all of the witnesses were from Des Moines. Some legislators opposed the measure because they feared that their cities might vote to adopt the new system. This apprehension led to an amendment which limited the bill's application to Des Moines and the half dozen other cities with populations in excess of 25,000, which included Burlington, Cedar Rapids, Council Bluffs, Davenport, Dubuque, and Sioux City. The lawmakers resisted all attempts to confine the measure to Des Moines alone.[23]

The senate committee favored the bill, but the house group voted for indefinite postponement. Although the legislation could have still reached the full house through passage in the senate, the Des Moines Plan Committee members had expected both reports to be favorable, and they were afraid the vote to postpone might prejudice the bill's chances. To influence the lower house committee to change its mind, about fifty prominent businessmen made last-minute calls at the statehouse. Furthermore, the proposal's sponsors increased the number of signatures required to call a vote on commission adoption to pacify legislators who feared easy special elections. The combination of pressure and amendment prompted the committee to reconsider its postponement of the bill and to send it out of committee without recommendation. The senate soon passed the commission measure without much debate, and the house followed a few days later. On March 29, 1907, Governor Cummins signed the act into law.[24]

The next hurdle facing the Commercial Club–appointed Committee of 300 and its various subgroups was to obtain enough signatures to force an election on whether the city would actually adopt the Des Moines plan. They had to gather nearly 3,000 names (25 percent of the 11,564 that had voted in the last mayoral election) to ensure an election, but they set their goal even higher and met it. Campaign workers circulated petitions throughout the business district, and some representatives even carried them into the factories on the east side to seek workers' signatures. The subcommittee in charge planned a Good Government Day to cap the effort, and by April 20 they had secured 6,032 names—twice the necessary number.[25]

Several groups had already held numerous meetings to discuss the Des Moines plan, but it was not until after the mayor called the special election for June 20, 1907, that the Committee of 300 organized a coordinated campaign. A special campaign committee planned precinct and neighborhood meetings and opened a well-equipped downtown headquarters with two telephone lines and a staff. Democratic ex-Congressman Walt Butler served as the most prolific orator on the list of half a hundred procommission speakers. Sidney J. Dillon acted as secretary. He carried on the group's correspondence and sent out form letters to answer specific objections to the plan. The prosperous and hard-working secretary took time off from his own affairs to solicit testimonials from municipal experts and officials in Texas-idea cities. He was careful to obtain endorsements of commission government from labor leaders in Galveston and Fort Worth. The campaign committee issued handbills announcing its meetings and published pamphlets containing copies of the commission law and arguments for its adoption.[26]

Meanwhile, the opposition to the Des Moines plan was far from dormant. Essentially the same forces that opposed the 1906 version stood united against the resubmission of the commission charter. The leading forces for the opponents were the Trades and Labor Assembly and the Polk County Republican Club, both of which were headed by members of the city council. The *Register and Leader* described the Polk County Republicans as "the mouth piece of the present city administration."[27] Several ward-based political clubs also went on record in opposition to the Des Moines plan. Drake University Professor of political science F. I. Herriott suggested theoretical arguments against the new governmental arrangement, but most of the attack revolved around organized labor and the incumbent administration.[28] The local Socialists added their active but ineffectual oppostion. They resolved that the commission system was a "capitalistic and corporation measure . . . opposed to working class interests."[29]

The nature of the background of the pro- and anticommission forces became an issue. Just before the election the morning paper charged, "As it stands now, the forces arrayed against the plan include the city hall politicians, the [Congressman J. A. T.] Hull leaders and politicians, the saloon interests and the gambling element, together with some excellent and misguided citizens."[30] The *Daily News* contended that only the ward politicians opposed a change of government. Late in the campaign the paper ran a bright red headline that proclaimed, "A CORRUPT CITY MACHINE IS FIGHTING DESPERATELY TO SAVE A CORRUPT CITY GOVERNMENT."[31] The *Cedar Rapids Gazette*, observing the Des Moines situation, reported that the "bosses" opposed the new plan and that such opposition was in itself a good recommendation for the idea.[32] On the other hand, the procommission forces claimed that they represented the leading citizens. They asserted that their camp included leaders from the east side as well as the west side, from both the Republican and Democractic parties, and from the two factions—"progressives and standpatters." Even Hull, who remained officially noncommittal, admitted that the "best people of the city seemed to be for it."[33] Hull's supporters among the commission advocates tried desperately to get the congressman to endorse the plan. Just four days before the election, they wrote him, "Nothing has so aroused the feelings of the leading citizens and better classes, as this movement for a nonpartisan, business government for Des Moines."[34]

The anticommission forces did not regard the Des Moines Plan Committee of 300 as "leading citizens and better classes" but as "silk stocking aristocrats." The main organ for such attacks was the newly founded *Des Moines Tribune*, an east-side daily established for the express purpose of opposing commission government and presenting a view different from that of the three west-side dailies which were united behind the change of government. The Commercial Club, the Greater Des Moines Committee, and, of course, the 300 were the main targets of the *Tribune* and other commission opponents. To emphasize the elite nature of the Des Moines plan backers, some unknown party had thousands of cards printed with the simple question "Are You a Member of the Committee of 300?" Antibusiness campaigners charged that the Commercial Club had imposed a "gag rule" to prevent its members from questioning the wisdom of the commission proposal, and they questioned the motives of several backers of the Indianapolis concept who were now in the forefront of the Galveston–Des Moines plan drive. W. H. Baily, John J. Hamilton, Walt Butler, John MacVicar, and Governor Cummins were all on record against the theory and principles of the Galveston plan. But in the interests of community harmony all but Cummins became active supporters of the commission system. The governor's endorsement was lukewarm to keep from offending his followers among the commission opposition.[35]

In addition to charges that corrupt bosses favored the existing arrangement and that silk stockings backed a change to the commission format, there were a number of specific issues to debate. The most important of these were, first, the abandonment of the separation of powers; second, the interests of organized labor and workers versus those of businessmen; third, the role of public franchises; fourth, the efficacy of direct legislation provisions; and, fifth, the wisdom of concentrating all municipal power and authority in a small board that would appoint all other officers.

The task of assailing the plan's theoretical shortcomings fell primarily upon Professor Herriott. The cornerstone of his attack was the commission idea's necessary fusion of executive and legislative functions. He acknowledged in one speech that "many—alas too many—[are] opposed because they have a sordid interest in the maintenance of the *status quo*—personal, pecuniary or political attachments that make them resist this or any other change." But he insisted that his opposition was different. The professor admitted that the capital city was in dire need of municipal reform, especially in reference to the spoils system and the lack of good central control of budgeting and administration, but the Galveston plan was not his solution. He found four basic problems with the Texas format. First, he denied that the precedents were authoritative, because of the emergency in Galveston and the island city's unusual influence on nearby Texas cities. Perhaps, he charged, when the novelty wore off, these cities would return to their old ways. Second, the Drake teacher questioned if the plan could indeed provide businesslike efficiency since it was unlikely that experts in administration would be elected. Besides, he emphasized, municipal government is more than business despite the utterances of groups like the Commerical Club. The third argument, the "crux of the present debate," involved a violation of the mechanics of good government and democracy through the investing of the commissioners with both legislative powers as a council and executive responsibility as department heads. His final attack concerned the possible unconstitutionality of a state-imposed commission. Some opponents whose motives were less academic than Herriott's were happy to appropriate his arguments for their own use against the ominous Des Moines plan.[36]

To answer the arguments of Herriott, the plan's sponsors obtained a statement from the president of Drake University that four-fifths of the faculty and virtually all of the board of trustees disagreed with Herriott and endorsed the commission system. The *Register and Leader* countered Herriott by quoting a Des Moines College professor of history and political science who favored the governmental change, unlike his counterpart at the rival institution. The Des Moines plan's campaign committee also secured testimony from nationally recognized experts on municipal reform. At the closing meeting of the drive one speaker read letters from Brand Whitlock and Louis Post of Toledo and Chicago, respectively.[37] Seth Low wrote the city editor of the *Des Moines Capital* that he hoped "very much that the plan may be adopted and be given a trial; for it has many very interesting features that are well worth trying out." He closed with "best wishes for the success of the plan and for the City of Des Moines." Commission proponents made the most of this letter from the prominent New Yorker.[38] Other letters and favorable comments came from Delos F. Wilcox, publisher of Detroit's *Civic News*, and Secretary Clinton Rogers Woodruff of the National Municipal League, who wrote the campaign committee that his league would conduct discussions on the Des Moines plan at its next annual conference. James M. Head, a former mayor of Nashville, told John MacVicar that the Des Moines proposal was the best charter he had ever seen. If such appeals to national authorities failed to convince voters of the theoretical soundness of commission government, the sponsors hoped that analogies to school boards, state boards of control, and the District of Columbia Commission would be more persuasive.[39]

The second important issue concerned the relative interests of the business and worker classes. Clearly, the commission act had been the direct outcome of a business-and-press-dominated effort. The Commercial Club and the Greater Des Moines Committee were composed of the city's elites. Unions were not included in the procommission coalition; and, speaking for organized labor, the *Iowa Unionist* complained that the "unionwreckers who drafted the bill ignored organized labor and other classes, drafted a bill to their own liking and railroaded it through the legislature." The paper contrasted the situation in Des Moines with that in Fort Worth, where union men were included in the charter reform movement from start to finish. Another reason that labor detested the Des Moines plan movement, besides being left out in the formation of the charter, was that some of the leaders of the all-important 300 headed nonunion establishments and had some connections with an antiunion group of previous years. In general, the commission issue got tied up in the open-shop controversy, and labor was understandably suspicious of a plan which its economic enemies spearheaded.[40]

Many working-class citizens also believed that specific provisions of the charter were inimical to their interests. They objected to technicalities that weakened the direct democracy provisions, and they disapproved of making all city officials except the commission itself appointive. However, their main argument against the structure of the plan was the effect of at-large representation on governmental responsiveness. A widely distributed pamphlet containing an unfavorably annotated version of the commission law attacked the at-large provision because it "removes ward representation, thus departing from the true theory of representative government."[41] A minor city official told the legislative hearings that ward representation kept government close to the people since the alderman could personally know his constituents. Many workers felt that at-large selection of commissioners would ensure that the entire body would come from the more affluent west side. The existing system that mixed at-large and ward representation guaranteed that east-side voices would be on the council. One of the earliest commission proposals back in 1905 had proposed electing five commissioners at large but with the requirement that two of them reside on the east side of the Des Moines River. This suggestion got lost in subsequent drafts. In a last-ditch effort to inspire anticommission sentiment, the city council voted to create two new wards in areas of the city that had long desired their own councilmen, but the move was apparently ineffective. Union labor thus felt snubbed in charter preparation, threatened by open-shop advocates at the head of the commission movement, and angered at a potential loss of representation in at-large elections. The Trades and Labor Assembly, under the direction of Alderman W. S. Staly, became one of the primary focal points of anti–Des Moines plan agitation. Staly estimated that 90 percent of the working men opposed the charter, and the editor of the *Unionist* vowed that he would deliver the anticommission votes at the June 20 special election.[42]

A third crucial consideration throughout the commission fight was control of franchises. Each side tried to tag the other with the onus of public service corporation associations. One opponent called the plan's sponsors "foxy franchise grabbers",[43] another wrote, "The 'leading citizens' of Des Moines, members of the '300' club, are owners and stockholders of trolley lines, water works, gas and electric light plants, etc."[44] Except for gas, home capital did control the utility and transportation franchises, and members of the 300 no doubt did have some financial interests in the corporations; but the Des Moines plan was not necessarily favorable to franchise holders. The charter expressly provided for mandatory referenda on all but the most inconsequential uses of public rights-of-way. Detractors charged that the wording of the law might allow some future council to evade this provision, but the bulk of legal opinion doubted that a loophole existed. The city engineer and a state legislator, as well as the *Register and Leader*, asserted that the public service corporations were actively opposing commission adoption. They implied that franchise money helped finance the well-organized and costly Citizens' Committee campaign against the Des Moines plan. Solicitations at city hall, they claimed, were only a cover for more sinister sources of money. A street car company lawyer did testify against franchise referenda before the assembly committee, and other subordinates of various utilities showed up at anticommission gatherings. Naturally, the west-side press made special efforts to discover such associations that might discredit the opposition.[45]

After the voters had safely adopted the Des Moines plan at the June 20, 1907, special election, Sidney J. Dillon, who had been the hard-working secretary of the campaign committee, felt more candid in discussing the commission fight. Responding to questions from members of the Chicago City Club, he blamed the opposition on the "political machine," on Des Moines' "strongly organized" labor, and on the public utilities.[46] So much did the sponsors of the measure fear franchise holders' opposition that they arranged a last-minute deal with them to prevent any more effort against the plan. In preparation for the first Des Moines commissioner election, John MacVicar wrote Walt Butler, John J. Hamilton, and city treasurer John B. Lucas, a MacVicar ally and one of the few city officials who had openly favored the commission adoption. In these letters MacVicar told of alleged negotiations. Writing to Lucas, he claimed: "I have absolute proof that [*Capital* editor Lafe] Young and Ingham called on certain of the public service corporations the day before the election for the Des Moines Plan and by means of threats got them to lay down their fight against the plan, which fact accounts for the large majority it received at the election. I have a curiosity to know just what these two newspaper men promised in return for supporting the fight. I believe I know, but am not absolute sure."[47]

The ex-mayor then asked Lucas to look into the charges. He was less veiled in the letter to Butler, strongly implying that, since candidates on the Ingham-Young slate had to be "acceptable to the public service corporation," the deal must have involved promises and threats about the make-up of the commission personnel. The Butler and Lucas replies are not available, but Hamilton wrote MacVicar that he had accosted Ingham with the story and that the editor had "denied it in the most unqualified manner, quite a lot of fire and brimstone thrown in."[48] The key to the arrangement was apparently an agreement to keep MacVicar, who favored public ownership of utilities, off the commission. The franchise owners probably concluded that the reality of mandatory referenda was more palatable than the possibility of a municipal takeover that MacVicar might lead. Besides being a major power in Des

Moines politics, he was also executive secretary of the League of American Municipalities and editor of its bulletin. Such a man would be a formidable opponent to the public service corporations. Naturally, they would have liked to avoid both MacVicar and the Des Moines plan, but evidently Ingham and Young did not offer them that alternative. Eventually they had to face both; franchises and MacVicar were major considerations throughout the first decade of the city's commission era.

Fourth among the primary issues of the commission fight was the efficacy of the Des Moines plan's direct legislation provisions. It was the grafting of such planks onto the Galveston system that led the Committee of 300 to claim that it had produced a unique form of government—Dallas' accomplishments in the same vein not withstanding. Ingham's paper praised the 1907 commission proposal because it went beyond its 1906 counterpart in matters of direct legislation, and this would please the working men who had wanted such devices as the initiative, referendum, and recall for years. Throughout the campaign procommission speakers and writers praised the direct democracy sections, especially when addressing labor-oriented audiences. Upon closer investigation, however, workers found that the direct democracy proposals did not have much bite.

To secure a recall, initiative, or referendum election, except on franchises, the petitioners had to gather signatures equal to 25 percent of the number of electors in the most recent mayoral contest. Only in the most extraordinary cases, opponents argued, could one-fourth of the voters be induced to sign petitions within the alloted ten days. What sections 18, 19, and 20 provided, charged a local Socialist who had headed the Direct Legislation League of Iowa in the 1890s, were only the "ghosts" of initiative, referendum, and recall. A Citizens' Committee leaflet criticized the recall section, declaring, "As a practical thing it is valueless."[49] Another anticommission pamphlet implied that there must be a catch to the popular control devices since many of the current advocates of such provisions had only recently characterized recall advocates as "cranks, lunatics and socialists."[50]

Defenders of the Des Moines plan and its direct democracy inclusions pointed out that they had been able to secure signatures of the necessary 25 percent of the voters in order to force the very election that was causing the controversy. Others, they argued, could do it in the future. Furthermore, the secretary to the mayor of Los Angeles wrote Dillon explaining that his community's recall requirements were similar to those suggested for Des Moines and that they had already removed one alderman and forced some others to alter their ways. Lyman Abbott of *Outlook Magazine* wrote that such liberal popular control measures might hamstring municipal government, but the *Register and Leader* maintained that the charter framers had found a nice compromise between Abbott's insulation of officials and the constant elections that the paper claimed would result from low petition percentages. Commission proponents also implied that the politicians really opposed recall because they feared it—not because it was weak and ineffectual. One letter writer expressed what must have been the sentiment of many voters when he said that any direct legislation was better than the present system, which contained none.[51]

The fifth of the central issues of the Des Moines plan's adoption campaign concerned the wisdom of centering the bulk of the city's duties in a small commission. Opponents charged that the system "makes the council the absolute rulers of the city government and converts the city into an aristocracy with a supreme ruling body of five, three of whom possess all powers and authority whose will is as supreme as that of any ruler in an absolute monarchy." This would have the effect, they claimed, of creating a machine worse than any combination possible under the fragmented present system.[52] A one-time candidate for mayor wrote, "It is true, the council is elected by the people and to an extent accountable to the people; but here intervenes the most powerful political machine ever created or tolerated in our midst and created, too, by law. . . . The result is despotism."[53] Some of the attacks on centralization drew heavily from Professor Herriott's more theoretical dispute with the merging of executive and legislative functions in a single unit. A local newspaper, *Plain Talk*, concluded, "To give such enormous power to one body is obnoxious to all that is distinctly American in principle and in practice."[54] Of course, the implication underlying such assaults was that the wealthy elites of the Commercial Club and the Greater Des Moines Committee might dominate the all-powerful commission in order to secure downtown improvements and generally slight the common man's interests. A member of the Polk County Republican Club said that experience bore out such implications, declaring, "The Galveston commissioners favor the corporation."[55] Other opponents said that the business-dominated City Club of Galveston was virtually a political machine. They further pointed out that the Houston commission used its power to reduce workers' wages on city jobs.[56]

Sponsors of the Des Moines plan said that, far from creating an invincible anti-common-man machine, their system merely provided for efficiently concentrated businesslike administration. The commissioners would not be five, or even three, bosses; they would serve much as a board of directors carrying on the business of the municipal corporation. With each man in charge of a specific department, the voters could fix responsibility. The board was no despotic aristocracy, because the citizens had recourse to initiative, referendum, and recall. Ring control, declared the plan's defenders, was endemic to the mayor-council system—not to the commission idea. The revised administration, they hoped, would take politics out of municipal business.[57] Ingham was so confident he told the Greater Des Moines Committee that the adoption of the new system would make it "possible to eliminate breweries from politics." He added that, if Iowans had to drink, "it might as well be made here."[58]

In addition to the five most prominent issues (governmental theory, organized labor, public franchises, direct legislation, and concentrated power), there were a number of interesting peripheral concerns. Skillful antagonists of the commission charter fired a shotgun blast of technical objections at the wording of the law. They asserted that loopholes would allow the city clerk to refuse to certify initiative, referendum, or recall petitions regardless of their actual validity. This would leave the petitioners with no recourse. Proponents pointed out that there were legal remedies through writs of mandamus and other judicial actions. Orators and pamphleteers insisted that the plan's supposedly model civil service provisions could be evaded since the commission itself would be the appeal body, allowing the creation of an old-fashioned, spoils-based machine. That the commissioners would not have to post bond and could hold closed meetings under certain circumstances become standard arguments, despite the fact that the situation was much the same under the existing charter. Answering such attacks required considerable time and effort on the part of the campaign committee and its allies in the west-side newspapers. Most attacks of this nature were probably intended as diversionary tactics, and, to some extent, they accomplished their purpose. After the fight was over, Dillon conceded that the phraseology of the commission law probably could have been better.[59]

The forces aligned against the Des Moines plan even resurrected the bloody-shirt tactic so effective in Iowa politics. The *Tribune* cried that the Galveston plan was "a new illustration of the resources of the aristocracy of the South to dominate popular government by excluding the people from effective participation in the rule of themselves. This principle is identical with that which brought on the Civil War."[60] Appealing for the six or seven hundred black ballots in the city, an orator told the Trades and Labor Assembly, "This is no Des Moines bill. This is the Galveston system pure and simple to keep the so-called white trash and the colored vote of the south from exerting itself in participation of the affairs of the city."[61] Defending the plan, Walt Butler noted that it was state law and not the city charters that disenfranchised blacks in the Lone Star state's commission cities. A Des Moines judge wrote that "the commission is not, strictly speaking, a Texas idea, but an Iowa idea," referring to a 1903 report of the Hawkeye state's Bar Association that had recommended a municipal system very similar to the Galveston plan.[62] In fact, the suggestion may have had some influence on the drafters of the Des Moines charter law. The press tried hard to ensure that the Iowa commission would not be regarded as a southern invention, so, in addition to the city-boosting motive, the system's backers had other reason to call their charter the "Des Moines plan."

Naturally, the last few weeks of the agitation were the most heated. Handbills announced at least twenty-nine meetings around the city. The campaign got so hectic and bitter that one flyer accused the anticommission forces of posting false bills. Every street corner seemed to be the site of debate.[63] MacVicar returned from League of Municipalities duties and placed his considerable influence on the side of the Des Moines plan. Ingham, who, according to Butler, never ceased worrying about the outcome of the election, went to his sometime enemy's home to plead for him to aid the campaign committee. And MacVicar worked hard. Butler later wrote the controversial reformer

Table 2. Results of the Des Moines
Commission Election, June 20, 1907

	West Des Moines	East Des Moines	City total
For the commission	4,527	1,849	6,376
	69%	46%	60%
Against the commission	1,951	2,136	4,087
	31%	54%	40%

Source: *Des Moines Register and Leader*, June 21, 1907.

and politician, "No one helped more than you did." In addition to last-minute approaches to the public service corporations, desperate advocates also apparently contemplated similar meetings with the saloon interests who opposed the change.[64]

On election morning, June 20, 1907, the chairman of the executive committee of the Des Moines plan movement predicted in the *Register and Leader* that the commission proposition would come close to breaking even on the east side and would carry the entire city by a 2,500-vote plurality. It was a prognostication of which Gallup would be proud. Certainly it was far more realistic than Alderman Staly's earlier claim that 90 percent of the working people took exception to the Des Moines plan. The proposal lost on the east side by only 287 out of nearly 4,000 votes, and passed the whole town with a margin of 2,289 (see table 2). The heaviest working-class areas did cast their ballots against the change as all factions had expected, but over half the east-side precincts actually favored commission adoption. On the other hand, only one precinct on the more affluent side of town voted down the proposition. It was a great victory for the three downtown dailies, the Commercial Club, the Greater Des Moines Committee, the 300, and all those who had carried on the movement since Berryhill's November 1905 address. Nor was the outcome a result of apathy. Nearly as many people had voted in the special referendum as had in the previous November's general election that returned Cummins to the statehouse. About 60 percent of the voters favored the Des Moines plan's acceptance, and this majority included a surprising 46.4 percent of the east-side electorate.[65]

Before the new government was due to go into effect, supporters of the charter initiated a law suit to determine the constitutionality of the Des Moines plan. Intervenors who apparently were less friendly in their attacks also joined the suit. The plantiffs argued that the charter and subsequent election were deficient on technical grounds and contended that the whole concept violated constitutional guarantees of republican government, including a separation of powers. Both the district court and the state supreme court upheld the commission on every count, and by February 18, 1908, the Des Moines plan had overcome any foreseeable legal hurdles.[66]

The actual election of commissioners and inauguration of the Des Moines plan were not to take place until ten months after the favorable referendum. Some of the charter leaders had contended all along that, to make the new government successful, the city would have to select a commission composed of responsible businessmen. By October 1907 behind-the-scenes arrangements for presenting a slate of business-backed candidates for the March 1908 elections had already begun. In January the revived Committee of 300 heard from a small group of editors and business leaders about their unsuccessful efforts to arrive at an acceptable ticket of prominent citizens. This group then handed the task to a larger subcommittee that worked for four days to come up with a list of men worthy of office and willing to serve. They presented the five rather unspectacular prospective candidates to the enlarged Committee of 500 at a disruptive meeting that betrayed a lack of business-community unity. But the gathering did finally agree on a Citizens', or Des Moines Plan, ticket.[67]

Two considerations dominated the campaign. First was the very principle of the economic elites and daily press forcing a slate on the electorate. The second issue was the commanding presense of John MacVicar. The Citizens' Ticket conducted an aloof campaign refusing to appear with the other candidates, and soon the people were often referring to them as the "silk sox ticket." One participant in the fray later summarized the situation: "The mass of the voters . . . resented the assumption of leadership on the part of the committee of three hundred and early showed signs of deep-seated hostility to 'the slate,' as the group of candidates so championed came to be called."[68] Representatives of the *Daily News* participated in the early closed-door, candidate-seeking sessions but eventually broke ranks with its two west-side competitors and refused to endorse the slate. Although the three papers had been unified in support of the commission charter's adoption, the *News* now repeated accusations that Ingham and Young had sold out to the public service corporations by promising to present a ticket favorable to the franchise holders' interests. The Civic League had also actively nurtured the Des Moines plan, but it, too, declined exclusively to endorse the Citizens' Ticket. Altogether seventy-one office seekers took advantage of the simple filing procedure to vie for one of the five spots on the commission. Four of the five men on the "silk sox slate" made it through the March 16, 1908, primary, but in the runoff election two weeks later they all met defeat.[69]

The other important current of discussion was John MacVicar's candidacy. *McClure's* journalist George Kibbe Turner wrote that the influential politician, "by unanimous consent, is the ablest man active in city affairs in Des Moines, and has been for twenty years." MacVicar's confidant, John J. Hamilton, told the popular figure, "You don't need to make issues being a platform yourself." "I tell you," Hamilton wrote in another letter, "it is going to take a lot of hard, personal work by you to neutralize the hostility that has been worked up against you among the business and professional men."[70] Both the subcommittee and full meeting of 500 favored placing MacVicar on "the slate," but Ingham and Young prevented it. He was probably not disappointed, however, because he expected that the average voter would rebel at a slate. He made it clear that his primary goal was to become a commissioner: "As a student of municipal government I would like to be connected with Des Moines government under the Commission Plan in its experimental stages, for I think that I might aid in establishing the efficiency and desirability of that form of government that is to be tried out in American cities. The influence of the Des Moines Plan on City Charters is destined to have a far reaching effect."[71]

The Des Moines election is sometimes interpreted as a repudiation of the new system. "The voters," noted one historian of city reform, "swept into office a slate of anticommission candidates who now controlled the new commission government."[72] In fact, two of the successful candidates, MacVicar and Alderman John L. Hamery, had been active on behalf of the charter's adoption. The mayor and the two other councilmen were indeed opposed to the commission, but they certainly had not been among the open and active defenders of the old method. Only one leading opponent of the commission, Alderman W. H. Brereton, made the second election, or runoff, but he did not become a member of the commission. Even the elitist Greater Des Moines Committee thought it could live with the body. The minutes reported that one member "said that regardless of the control of the government by any set of politicians, . . . the new form was better than the old because it fixed the responsibility."[73]

Even before the commission began operation in April 1908, the Des Moines plan had attracted nationwide attention. The city's business organizations immediately started using the new form of city government to boost their town. The Greater Des Moines Committee issued a booklet, *Des Moines Means Opportunity*. It proclaimed, "The 'Des Moines Plan' of municipal government is the most advanced form of government by commission. It has attracted world-wide attention and its practical application will be watched by men of affairs in every city of the union."[74] The Commercial Club printed the charter with the comment, "Its adoption presents the most important as well as the most radical experiment in municipal government ever attempted in the United States and its many unusual features are attracting favorable comments throughout the country." To back up this contention, the pamphlet listed twelve specific magazine and newspaper references and quoted such well-known municipal reformers as Seth Low and Brand Whitlock.[75]

MacVicar kept the League of American Municipalities posted on the Des Moines plan with at least six articles in the *Bulletin* even before the commissioner election. One of these said, "This Charter has been pronounced the most advanced ever adopted in this country." As early as Christmas Day 1905, Des Moines newspapers argued that national publicity could be one of the best reasons to adopt a new city government.[76] By 1907 the capital city reformers were calling their version of the commission idea the "Des Moines

Plan," and the term prevailed. The dozens of press references to commission government began more and more to refer to the system as the "Des Moines Plan," and less and less did they speak of the "Texas Idea" or the "Galveston Plan," although the latter term did continue in use.

Getting the plan adopted was a difficult struggle for Des Moines' business and professional leaders. The agitation begun in November 1905 did not see the actual plan in operation until almost two and a half years later. The arguments and cleavages that emerged in this first northern city to incorporate the commission plan were a prototype for later struggles over the same issue, and this northern pioneer's success or failure with the new format would be a key in the ongoing commission government movement.

CHAPTER FOUR

THE DIFFUSION OF A

PROGRESSIVE IDEA

*A*s information about the Galveston–Des Moines plan spread, so did its adoption. "One might say, in fact," wrote Harvard Professor William Bennett Munro in trying to explain the movement's success, "that the commission plan made its way into the arena of municipal reform at the proper psychological moment."[1] That moment was during this country's Progressive Era. The city-to-city and state-to-state diffusion of the new format rode on the crest of slogans which promised modernization, honesty, responsibility, and, most of all, businesslike efficiency. The litany of praise for the accomplishments of the pioneer commission towns created a logrolling effect that eventually swept as many as five hundred cities into the movement.

The diffusion of the plan actually began well before Des Moines started her famous experiment in 1907–1908. The city of Topeka sent a study committee to Galveston in 1906, and the next year the Kansas legislature debated the commission idea simultaneous with its consideration in the Hawkeye state. Both states passed general statutes allowing their cities to try the plan. Leavenworth launched its new charter about the same time as Des Moines, but the larger cities of Kansas did not get their commission governments in operation until 1910.[2] North and South Dakota also passed optional commission plan laws, and Idaho granted a special charter of the Galveston type to the small town of Lewiston. Thus, by the end of 1907 four states in addition to Iowa and Texas had made provisions for at least some of their towns to join the commission movement (see tables 3 and 4 for a year-by-year summary of the commission plan's spread).[3]

Growth of the system was still slow in 1908 when only three more states signed up. Tulsa, Oklahoma, voted in a home-rule commission charter that would begin the next year and last until the present. Thus, Tulsa is not only one of the largest but also one of the oldest commission cities in the country. Mississippi's legislature granted its municipalities permission to try the novel format, but no city actually used the plan until 1910. In the most significant development of 1908, the Galveston–Des Moines idea broke out of the South and Midwest. President Charles Eliot of Harvard had visited Galveston, Dallas, and other cities to study the new form of government; and his eulogy of the Texas idea before a meeting of the men's church clubs of Haverhill inspired that city to request and receive a special commission charter from the Massachusetts General Assembly. Lynn, Lawrence, and Lowell soon followed, and the Commonwealth had become the commission innovation's

Table 3. Growth of the Commission Plan by Year, 1901–1922

Year of operation	Number of cities	Cumulative total	Cities over 5,000 only	
			Number of adoptions	Cumulative total
1901	1	1	1	1
1902	0	1	0	1
1903	0	1	0	1
1904	0	1	0	1
1905	1	2	1	2
1906	0	2	0	2
1907	7	9	6	8
1908	4	13	3	11
1909	27	40	25	36
1910	52	92	30	66
1911	92	184	72	138
1912	64	248	38	176
1913	89	337	64	240
1914	46	383	32	272
1915	40	423	25	297
1916	19	442	15	312
1917	15	457	13	325
1918	10	469	10	335
1919	6	473	6	341
1920	4	477	4	345
1921	5	482	5	350
1922	5	487	5	355
NA	33	520	11	366

Compiled from the Appendix; see notes to the Appendix for an explanation of sources.

eastern pioneer, although adoptions in that section of the country would continue to be rare.[4]

After 1908 the spread of the commission movement accelerated. Seven new states—one by general law, three by special charters, and three by home rule—joined the Galveston–Des Moines plan ranks in 1909. Berkeley, San Diego, and Tacoma brought the plan to the Pacific coast; and Memphis proved that the idea's appeal was not necessarily confined to smaller cities.

Nine more states provided for various types of commission adoption in 1910. The most important general law of that year came in Illinois. When the legislature sent a special committee south to study the commission plan in 1909, many observers and politicians expected the report to be hostile; but the group of senators and representatives returned from their visit to Galves-

Table 4. State Legislative Action Allowing the Commission Plan by Year, 1901–1915

Year[a]	State	Type of charter law[b]	Selected adoptions and special notes
1901	Tex.	Special	Galveston (1901), Houston (1905), Dallas and Ft. Worth (1907)
1907	Iowa	Optional general	Des Moines and Cedar Rapids (1908), Sioux City (1910)
	Kans.	Optional general	Leavenworth (1908), Wichita (1909), Kansas City and Topeka (1910)
	S.Dak.	Optional general	Sioux Falls (1909), Rapid City (1910)
	N.Dak.	Optional general	Mandan (1907), Bismark (1909), Fargo (1913)
	Idaho	Special	Lewiston (1907)
1908	Miss.	Optional general	Clarksdale (1910), Hattiesburg (1911), Jackson (1912)
	Mass.	Special	Haverhill (1909), Lowell (1910), Lynn (1911), Lawrence (1912)
	Okla.	Home rule	Tulsa (1909), Oklahoma City and Muskogee (1911)
1909	Wis.	Optional general	Eau Claire (1910), Superior (1912), excluded Milwaukee
	Calif.	Home rule	Berkeley and San Diego (1909), Oakland (1911)
	Colo.	Home rule	Colorado Springs and Grand Junction (1909)
	Wash.	Home rule	Tacoma (1910), Spokane (1911)
	W.Va.	Special	Huntington (1909), Parkersburg (1911)
	N.C.	Special	High Point (1909), Greensboro (1911), Raleigh (1913)
	Tenn.	Special	Memphis (1910), Chattanooga (1911)
	Tex.*	Optional general	Cities less than 10,000
1910	Ill.	Optional general	Springfield (1911)
	S.C.	Optional general	Columbia (1910)
	Ky.	Optional general	Newport (1911), Lexington (1912)
	La.	Optional general	Shreveport (1910), New Orleans (1912), Baton Rouge (1914)
	Oreg.	Home rule	Baker (1910), Portland (1913)
	Minn.	Home rule[c]	Mankato (1911), Duluth (1913), St. Paul (1914)
	Mich.	Home rule	Wyandotte (1911)
	Md.	Special	Cumberland (1910)
	Fla.	Special	Passagrille (1911), Pensacola and St. Petersburg (1913)

[a]Year of legislative action except for home-rule states, for which it indicates the earliest year a city of the state chose to adopt a commission charter. The date is for the first such action and does not take into account subsequent amendments to broaden or narrow coverage.

Year[a]	State	Type of charter law[b]	Selected adoptions and special notes
1911	Wyo.	Optional general	Sheridan and Cheyenne (1911)
	Mont.	Optional general	Missoula (1911), Helena (1915)
	Nebr.	Optional general	Omaha (1912), Lincoln (1913)
	N.J.	Optional general	Trenton and Passaic (1911), Jersey City (1913), Newark (1917)
	Ala.	Optional general	Mobile and Tuscaloosa (1911)
		Mandatory	Birmingham and Montgomery (1911)
	Utah	Mandatory	All cities, including Salt Lake City (1912)
	Nev.	Special	Las Vegas (1911)
	Ga.	Special	Marietta (1911), Rome (1914)
	Idaho*	Optional general	Boise (1912)
	Wash.*	Optional general	For small cities not eligible for home rule
	Calif.*	Optional general	For small cities not eligible for home rule
1912	Ohio	Home rule	Lakewood (1913)
		Optional model	Middletown (1914)
	Ariz.	Home rule[c]	Douglas
	Maine	Special	Gardiner (1912)
1913	Ark.	Optional general	Framed for the benefit of Ft. Smith (1913)
	N.Mex.	Optional general	Las Vegas (1913), territorial government allowed commission
	Mo.	Optional general	Joplin (1914), Springfield (1916)
		Mandatory	Certain small towns
	Pa.	Mandatory	Third-class cities, e.g. Reading, Wilkes-Barre, Erie (1913)
	N.Y.	Special	Beacon (1913), Buffalo (1916)
	Tenn.*	Optional general	For cities not under special commission charters
1914	Va.	Optional model	Not used, excluded Richmond
	N.Y.*	Optional model	Watertown (1918)
1915	Mass.*	Optional mode	Not used, excluded Boston
	Nev.*	Optional mode	Not used

*State has already appeared in the table under a different year with a different type of charter law.

[b]The five types are special charter, optional general law (some of which were very limited in scope), home rule, mandatory statute, and optional model charter.

[c]Minnesota and Arizona passed specific legislation to ensure that their home-rule provisions would allow the commission plan.

ton, Houston, and Dallas with a very favorable impression of the desirability of the plan. They recommended that their colleagues allow Illinois cities to do as well. With the governor's support the measure passed; and nineteen cities, including Springfield, chose to try the system as soon as possible.[5]

In 1911 eight new states arranged for commission adoptions and three others broadened the option to more cities. Alabama went so far as to require that its two largest cities, Birmingham and Montgomery, use commission charters. The most unusual development of the year, however, was the decision of Utah to force the Galveston format on all its cities.

Promoters of the commission plan in Utah had to try three times before they were successful in bringing the fresh form of government to their state. Forces opposing reform in the largest city buried a 1907 commission proposal in legislative committee, but the movement did not die. In the fall of 1909 the Civic Improvement League of Salt Lake City dispatched a committee to Des Moines to investigate the workings of Iowa's famous city hall. Following the delegation's favorable report, supporters again introduced a commission bill. This time the measure made it through the legislature only to meet the governor's veto. During this period an anti-Mormon party controlled Salt Lake City, and leaders of the church were looking for a way to reassert their dominance. At the same time, some other charter reformers wanted to change city government for nonreligious reasons. Thus resulted a legislative alliance between those who wanted efficient, streamlined administration for its own sake and those who merely wanted to see the Latter-day Saints continue their historical influence on Utah's major institutions. Afraid that the anti-Mormon party in Salt Lake City and elsewhere might be strong enough to defeat commission charters if they were submitted to the people by referendum, the Mormon leaders and the charter reformers decided to impose the new system from the top.[6]

But far more significant for the substance of structural municipal reform than the imposition of commission government in the scantily populated state of Utah was the passage of permissive legislation allowing the cities of New Jersey to adopt the commission system. Massachusetts and Maryland had already granted some special commission charters, but prior to 1911 no northeastern state had enacted general statutes providing for the adoption of the plan. Structural reformers hoped that New Jersey's example would pave the way for other adoptions in the East. "Until New Jersey turned 'progressive,'" Henry Bruere of the New York Bureau of Municipal Research remarked, "New York had regarded commission government, if not quite 'populistic,' as a more or less radical innovation likely to work out a brief career in the remote confines of Iowa, Kansas, and Texas."[7]

Only ten years had passed since Galveston tentatively began her commission experiment in the late summer of 1901, but in that time thirty-three states had provided for some of their municipalities to adopt the plan, and nearly two hundred cities actually had it in use. It was an auspicious record for an idea originally intended as a temporary response to a natural disaster. Clinton Rogers Woodruff, executive secretary of the National Municipal

League observed: "Without question, the most conspicuous single development of recent years in the realm of American municipal affairs has been the
continued, rapid, and widespread interest in the commission form of municipal government and in charter reform generally."[8]

After 1911 state action on the commission plan slowed considerably although individual city adoptions continued at a rapid pace for a few more
years. The most important state legislation of this period came in 1913 when
Pennsylvania responded to the wishes of many of its third-class cities and
made the commission format mandatory for that group. This action brought
a large number of middle-size cities, including Reading, Wilkes-Barre, Erie,
and Harrisburg, into the commission ranks en masse.[9] Except for amendments to and repeal of previous laws, state legislative involvement with the
commission movement was over by 1915. Also, the number of city adoptions
in that year dropped to about forty. The peak years for the commission innovation were from 1910 through 1915, when 384 cities, including 265 of 5,000
population or more adopted the plan. Only a half dozen states—Connecticut, Delaware, Indiana, New Hampshire, Rhode Island, and Vermont—remained completely out of the movement. All the other states allowed commission adoptions by one or more of the devices of special charters, optional
general laws, mandatory statutes, home rule, or optional model charters. No
Virginia city availed itself of the last option, so forty-one states actually had
commission cities (see the Appendix for a list of cities).

The facts of the rapid diffusion of the commission innovation are evident.
The statistics in tables 3 and 4 make it clear that the idea did indeed spread
from coast to coast in scarcely a decade. But, of course, the important question is why. What was it about the particular reform commission government
that made it so popular? The Galveston–Des Moines plan did not spread
purely on its own momentum. Similar plans had appeared before in Memphis, Sacramento, and elsewhere, but they were consigned to oblivion. The
Galveston version, however, had the good fortune to appear at a time when
the nation was seeking answers to problems of urban government. It was
lucky to become identified as a "progressive" measure at a time when that
elusive label guaranteed at least some support. As Professor Munro noted,
"the plan of commission government has proved popular, for the most part,
in those sections of the country where the so-termed progressive political
ideas have found it easy to gain a foothold."[10] One contemporary observer
laid the entire success of the Des Moines plan upon this progressive spirit:
"It is my belief that this movement for reform can only be fairly attributed to
the Iowa sentiment which has sprung up as a result of the reform legislation
inspired and created by Governor A. B. Cummins. For a period of three
years, prior to June 1907, Iowa was rampant with 'progressive politics,' almost everybody wanted nearly everything reformed."[11]

The interest was not confined to Iowa. In the summer of 1907 *Literary Digest*
reported that of all the possible solutions to the problems of municipal administration "the one which at present attracts the most attention is the Galveston plan of city government by commission."[12] Such agencies as the New

York State Library and the University of Wisconsin Extension Division received so many requests for information on the subject that they printed
standard responses. There were so many books and articles about the plan
that in 1913 the Library of Congress released a bibliography on the topic with
488 entries. Some of these were background readings, but the vast majority
concerned the commission plan directly. In 1917 and 1920 the library issued
supplements that totaled more than 100 additional entries.[13]

The commission plan even attracted attention from students of municipal
affairs in foreign countries, including Australia, Spain, Canada, and Great
Britain. Ambassador James Bryce kept the British government informed
about the progress of the movement in several dispatches. Perhaps the ambassador perceived that American cities were overcoming their most conspicuous failure. "In the capital of Iowa, Des Moines, which adopted it [com-
mission government] last year," Bryce wrote, "satisfaction at the result is
stated to be general except no doubt among would-be 'bosses' and 'graft-
ers.'"[14] A few Canadian cities tried the plan although it never reached the
popularity there that it had in the United States.

Not everyone who called himself or whom observers called progressive
supported commission government; and, conversely, by no means everyone
who did advocate the plan could be termed a reformer, but the list of leading
Progressive Era figures who championed the commission movement is long.
It contained mayors, such as Brand Whitlock and Seth Low; editors, including William Allen White, Lyman Abbott, and Albert Shaw; and educators,
such as Charles Eliot and Woodrow Wilson. Although he did not make the
plan a paramount issue in his campaigns, Theodore Roosevelt, whom many
regarded as the preeminent progressive, joined the chorus of praise. He told
a Birmingham, Alabama, audience in 1911, "Now I believe in the commission
system, and I am glad you are going to try the experiment." A few days later
in Texas the former president remarked: "I am greatly interested in the Commission Form of Government which you have tried here in Dallas. Now, I
claim to be a pretty good progressive, but I decline to give my adherence
to everything just simply because it is called progress. But I am bound to say
that I am more and more favorably impressed with the Commission Form of
Government."[15] Less eminent voices agreed. In 1912 a Winona attorney told
the Minnesota Academy of Social Sciences that the commission form "has
become a part of the progressive movement holding sway in this country at
the present time. . . . It does away with the evils of boss and gang rule and
places the reins of government in the hands of the people."[16]

Word about the alleged success of the Galveston–Des Moines scheme
spread because of the general political mood and the interest in reform that
the national press exhibited. But the active interest of organizations conc-
cerned directly with municipal affairs was perhaps even more crucial to the
effective diffusion of the plan. As already noted, the National Municipal
League gave the system careful attention. Specialized periodicals for municipal engineers and other officials watched all governmental developments, including the commission plan, very closely. Organizations that might ally

with commission advocates to secure short ballots, nonpartisan elections, or civil service reforms helped spread the commission gospel at least to the extent that it conformed with their own objectives. Of all such groups dedicated to the affairs of urban government, the League of American Municipalities and its secretary, John MacVicar, were the most active forces behind the commission movement. The league, founded in 1897, was actually a coalition of state leagues and most of its members were officials from small and medium-size cities.

Since it consisted primarily of a series of state and local agitations, the commission movement had no true national leader; but MacVicar was more active than any other single person in promoting the idea. The business elites of Des Moines were apprehensive but respectful of the "fine Italian hand" of this tireless organizer who had long been a power in local politics. He defied most of those elites to secure a position on the first Des Moines commission which he came to dominate. All the time that he was the commanding influence in the local politics of Iowa's capital, he continued his duties as executive secretary of the League of American Municipalities. He saw to it that his city's plan was regularly a topic at the the league's annual meetings. Under his guidance virtually every issue of the group's bulletin, *City Hall*, contained extensive material about the new form of government. "The League of American Municialities has been the greatest agency in building up public sentiment to a point where the commission form of government will be acceptable to the American cities," a Fort Worth commissioner declared before a session of the 1910 league convention. "Perhaps it is not amiss to say," he went on, "that in the evolution and development of the commission idea this league will be the most important factor."[17]

MacVicar traveled across the nation touting the virtues of commission administration to commercial clubs, chambers of commerce, boards of trade, and other civic groups in Kansas City, Los Angeles, Salt Lake City, San Francisco, Portland, Minneapolis–St. Paul, Cincinnati, Chicago, Atlanta, and many smaller cities. Eventually he ran into political troubles at home, and the League of American Municipalities began to decline because of a lack of big-city support for its wide-ranging program. By 1915 the league was gone, and its intrepid secretary had lost his national forum.[18] Interestingly, the careers of both the organization and the man began to falter at just about the time reformers were becoming more and more skeptical of the commission system that MacVicar had worked so hard to promote.

The Galveston–Des Moines system, for all its weaknesses, seemed to furnish the most complete answer to the structural reformers' indictment of American city government. "On the whole," Herbert Croly wrote in *Progressive Democracy*, "the popularity of the commission form of municipal government is the most encouraging expression of a desirable tendency to combine a simple, strong, and efficient government with a thoroughly popular government."[19] The key to that assessment was the plan's alleged businesslike efficiency. The machinery of the charters tried to promote efficient administration, and the plan supposedly could shift control of city hall to a more business-oriented class. The idea spread because in city after city it initially provided positive results and seemed to meet its promises. One recent work has dubbed the entire span of municipal reform from 1880 to 1920 as "the politics of efficiency."[20] Indeed, the aim of the structural reform tradition of municipal progressivism was to bring efficiency to city government, and the Galveston–Des Moines plan proposed to do just that. A statement by the Allied Civic Bodies of Pennsylvania captured the key arguments: "Commission Government is the application of modern business methods to the conduct of municipal affairs. It concentrates responsibility in the city government and exacts accountability from those elected to administer the public business, thereby making efficiency the principal requirement in civic rule."[21]

Most commission supporters who based their adherence on appeals for businesslike efficiency actually regarded municipalities as corporate creatures little different from a business. Of course, this way of looking at urban government was neither uniquely American nor new. British reform mayor and national leader Joseph Chamberlain wrote for an American audience in 1892 that the concept of the city as "a joint stock or cooperative enterprise in which every citizen is a shareholder" had for years been "the leading idea of the English system of municipal government." Chamberlain's belief that "the members of the Council are the directors of this great business" coincided with the views of American structural reformers.[22]

A subcommittee of the Denver Chamber of Commerce summarized this idea: "City government ought, within reasonable limits, to correspond to the corporation system of business administration, with which, in these days, every one is more or less familiar. The conception that the citizen is a stockholder in our public municipal corporation is deeply and justly rooted in the common intelligence. Municipal government, therefore, should undoubtedly combine business efficiency and the fullest regard for the welfare of the individual stockholder or citizen."[23] Charles Eliot was blunter. Speaking to the Boston Economic Club, he declared, "Municipal government is pure business and nothing else—absolutely nothing else."[24]

In hundreds of cities the commercial and professional element led the change-of-government movements that ushered in the commission plan. In Kansas City, Kansas, the secretary of the Mercantile Club wrote a typical analogy between the proposed new government and prospering enterprise: "Its plan of administering the ordinary affairs of a city is based on the theory that a municipality is largely a business corporation, and seeks to apply business methods to public service. The voters are the stockholders of the municipal corporation. The board of commissioners corresponds to the board of directors of an ordinary business corporation, and the commissioners are elected by a vote of the people or the stockholders."[25]

A committee of one hundred headed by a leading real estate and insurance man issued a campaign flyer asking the voters to judge the existing government by criteria of commerical efficiency. "Is there any big private business in the whole world conducted in the manner in which a public corporation such as that of Kansas City, Kansas is run? Could a railroad or a packing company pay dividends on such a basis? Why shouldn't the city's business be conducted on the same business principles as private enterprises are carried on? These are questions for the taxpayers to answer."[26]

Business groups posed similar questions in dozens of other cities. Commercial organizations, standing or ad hoc, dominated the local commission agitations in city after city, beginning with the work of Galveston's Deep Water Committee. The success of Des Moines' business leaders in obtaining a general commission law and local adoption inspired commercial clubs in other Iowa cities to study the plan. Capital-city business elites spearheaded the commission drives in Topeka, Oklahoma City, and Columbia, South Carolina. The Commercial Club of Peoria worked hard for Illinois' passage of a commission law. Business and professional men dominated the association that brought mandatory commission government to all third-class cities in Pennsylvania. Buffalo, the largest commission city, finally obtained a commission charter in 1915 after years of trying. Throughout the struggle the new plan had "the endorsement of every civic and business organization in town."[27]

The commission victory by New Jersey's progressives was the culmination of an effort that the Trenton Chamber of Commerce began. In charter referenda throughout the state, business elements often guided the change-of-government efforts. The progressive Republican *Jersey Journal* and its business allies brought the plan to Jersey City. Business and industrial forces pushed commission government in Passaic, and the movement's main spokesman was a real estate broker who served as secretary of the Board of Trade. In Newark, civic organizations worked to obtain enough signatures to force a vote and then waged a quiet and effective campaign for the plan's final adoption. Woodrow Wilson, who may have endorsed the commission plan partially to aid his presidential aspirations, found the widespread acceptance of the new format gratifying "because it again expresses the desire of the people of New Jersey to make their municipal governments more efficient and responsive."[28]

The procommission business forces were by no means always successful in New Jersey or elsewhere. During the first two years under his so-called Walsh Act, New Jersey cities held forty-three elections on the plan. Commission government was successful in only twenty-one cases. The total vote in all forty-three elections interestingly revealed the close-fought nature of the controversial innovation. Jersey voters had cast 104,089 votes for the plan and 103,780 against it. Business elites had eked out victories in Trenton, Newark, Atlantic City, and Jersey City.[29]

Men of "high civic standing" formed an organization that unsuccessfully tried to bring commission government to Louisville. The Commercial Club of Fort Wayne, Indiana, appealed to William Allen White in their futile agitation for the plan. Davenport, Iowa's leading merchant and professional organization gathered enough signatures to force a charter election, but the voters declined to imitate the capital's municipal experiment. A similar group in Peoria published a full report following a delegation's visit to Des Moines, but they were unable to translate their enthusiasm to the citizenry. The Scranton, Pennsylvania, Board of Trade heard a former resident of Des Moines glowingly describe the governmental efficiency of his former home town, but the city did not take up the plan. The Commercial Club of Rochester, Minnesota, and the Portland, Maine, Board of Trade also endorsed the plan in vain. Business elites in Pittsburgh did get some elements of the commission movement embodied in their 1911 reform charter, but, despite the endorsements of the Allied Board of Trade and the Chamber of Commerce, the city did not obtain the essentials of the Galveston idea. The Chamber of Commerce and the newspapers assumed leadership of Atlanta's commission campaign, but entrenched politicians and laborers fearful of a businessman's government combined to defeat a charter referendum. Business-dominated reformers in Los Angeles endorsed an eight-man commission plan proposal in 1912, but anticommission forces charged that the charter would insulate municipal government from the people and also argued that the Galveston–Des Moines plan was not suited to large cities like the southern California metropolis. In December the voters decisively defeated the commission charter and the four-year progressive ascendency in Los Angeles began to wane. These failures and many others like them sometimes resulted from specific opposition to the commission format and sometimes from suspicion of the motives of the proponents. But often commission defeats were merely the result of apathy toward and/or contentment with existing governments.[30]

New commission governments sometimes faced almost immediate efforts to restore the old system. In Denver leading businessmen who had fared well under the administration of Mayor Robert W. Speer led the successful effort to oust the three-year-old commission charter. On the other hand, procommission commercial leaders held off onslaughts in a number of West Coast cities. The Chamber of Commerce and the businessmen's luncheon clubs of Portland led the move to uphold the new plan they had helped initiate. In 1918 the voters sustained commission government by a 17,000 majority whereas the original adoption five years previously had slipped in by only a few hundred votes. There was a similar story in Sacramento.[31] Unless commission government hopelessly failed, became too enmeshed in personality, or faced a new alternative, such as the manager plan, business forces generally contined their support for the Galveston–Des Moines idea.

To some extent businesslike efficiency stood as a goal in itself. The principles of centralization and responsibility that rationalized and systematized municipal government were wise practices that many businessmen wanted installed at city hall simply because they were good for the city. The commercial elements took a certain pride in seeing their values accepted and used. They abhorred inefficiency and petty politics as immoral as well as unwise.

To a greater extent, however, efficiency was merely the best means to more definite public policy goals. Municipal administration had always been important to certain companies engaged directly in business with the city through franchises or contracts, but by the late nineteenth century businessmen were coming to realize that the expanding functions of the municipality affected the commercial community as a whole. Paving, water, sewers, lighting, police and fire protection, and even recreational facilities all had a bearing on the economic well being of the city.

One writer noted in 1907, "A strong and capable local government is a most valuable asset for the business interests of the city, and more and more are business men today recognizing this fact." Two years later a former president of the Pittsburgh Chamber of Commerce cautioned, "Allow the city to drift civicly upon the rocks and the commercial prosperity will soon follow."[32]

This rising awareness of the commercial importance of city government coincided with an era of continuing fragmentation in local government machinery. In cities that lacked informal means of overcoming such dispersion of authority, the confusing arrangement of wards, boards, and elected officials often led to inefficiency. If centralization occurred, especially in larger cities, it was generally through bossism and machine control. A disciplined political organization could serve as a broker between its vote-supplying lower-class constituents and the other elements and institutions of the city. Sometimes reform-oriented politicians, such as Hazen S. Pingree of Detroit or Samuel M. Jones of Toledo, mastered the art of machine politics, but structural reformers were not content to trust the electoral process to bring such leaders to the surface. Moreover, radical social schemes often tainted these popular reform mayors in the eyes of the business-oriented elements.[33]

What the structural reformers sought was not a political machine but an administrative one. They looked for some arrangement that would produce a government they could deal with. A plan that provided a different type of officeholder and gave him the power to accomplish something was what they wanted. Although the strong-mayor system leaned in this direction, the commission plan more nearly met their desires. One early account told how the Galveston charter fulfilled this objective: "The power of the individual voter is increased and the boss and his ability and opportunity to graft are disposed of more effectively than by any other system worked out. . . . A corrupt or inefficient commission could work as much injury to a community as an unfit board of aldermen, perhaps, but its election is much less likely."[34] Indeed, the commission plan centralized power in a few hands just as the boss arrangement did. "The commission government rests upon the theory that the governing few should be responsible, that municipal power should be concentrated," publicist Oswald Ryan admitted, "but," he emphasized, "not in an irresponsible Cox, Ruef, or 'Bathhouse John.'"[35]

The unique feature of the Galveston format that appealed to many disciples of efficiency was the provision which placed each commissioner in charge of a particular department of city government. In some cities, such as Galveston, each commissioner was only a part-time supervisor or watchdog, while in Des Moines and the majority of commission cities the members performed as the active administrators of their divisions. In some cities the commission itself decided on the allocation of departments, and in others the voters selected members to specific places. Regardless of method, the intended result was to make clear who was responsible for each part of the city's administration. This arrangement pleased the Allied Civic Bodies of Pennsylvania: "If there is failure in any department, the Commissioner responsible for that department cannot say that it was occasioned because the other Commissioners were negligent. . . . If there is failure, the failure is his, and every citizen of the municipality knows where to place the blame."[36] William Allen White told a correspondent how it worked in Emporia: "We find that responsibility is clearly defined, that authority is unhampered. . . . Responsibility is so clearly marked . . . there is no shifting responsibility."[37]

Procommission orators and writers often told true and apocryphal stories about citizens going from office to office seeking redress for a grievance under the old fragmented plan where officials could avoid responsibility. A former mayor of Fort Worth said that under the old system "it would have taken a search warrant to find out who was responsible." But under the commission form a citizen knew exactly where to go, and complaints were met with dispatch. A few days later a local editor noted that strict accountability was a two-way street. "The departments of the city are so ordered that every citizen may know whom to censure for evil and whom to applaud for good administration."[38]

Clear responsibility presumed that the commissioners possessed the full powers of the municipality. Virtually all the governing authority had to be centralized in the commission. The plan abolished the fragmented arrangement of boards, authorities, special commissions, and elected officials. One or two offices, such as an independent auditor or treasurer, might remain elective; but the philosophy of the plan presumed that these would be few. For example, because the voters selected a judge, assessor-collector, city attorney, city secretary, and board-of-water commissioners in addition to the five regular commissioners, some purists excluded Waco, Texas, from the commission club. The commission itself did not have full control of the city. A Kansas City newspaperman summarized the argument in *Outlook Magazine*: "The increased efficiency to-day may be traced directly to the simplicity and centralization of the new plan of government, in which the mayor and four aldermen elected at-large are left practically untrammeled to work out the city's salvation."[39]

Skeptics of the Galveston plan and charter reform in general often declared that good government depended on the quality of the elected officials and not on the administrative machinery. The *Kansas City Journal* charged that "the mere matter of the form of municipal government has little to do with good government."[40] But a Des Moines attorney answered such attacks: "Fiddlesticks, you may say. Good men can accomplish these things under any system. But they can't. Good men have tried here and elsewhere. Something has always been wrong with the system. Des Moines now has the proper system."[41] Much of the credit for Galveston's renaissance, for example, was due to the high-quality men who comprised the first few administrations after the storm. "But it is practically certain," asserted one eulogist, "that they could not have accomplished half as much had they been handicapped by the cumbersome aldermanic system."[42]

Not only would the commission plan work wonders when in the hands of able men, enthusiastic backers boasted that it actually would attract qualified candidates who would never run for office if faced with ward politics and fragmented administration. But with concentrated power and increased prestige, prominent and competent citizens might be induced to seek a commissionership. Oswald Ryan explained: "The increased power and importance which the commission charter confers upon the council, and the freedom of the candidate from the tyranny of the boss, have no doubt been responsible for the presence of a better grade of officials in the commission-governed cities."[43] Secretary Woodruff of the National Municipal League agreed: "City government by commission will undoubtedly facilitate the election of a higher type of men, for American municipal experience plainly demonstrates that small bodies with large powers attract a better class of men than large bodies with small powers."[44]

In many cases the new system did lead at least temporarily to administrations composed of well-known and substantial businessmen. This fact led many contemporaries and some historians to assert that commission government and later the city manager plan brought business and professional leaders directly to the council chambers. But more typically the key influentials who pushed for the changes of government were unwilling to enter the political trenches as candidates. Satisfied that the machinery of the plan would eliminate lower-class, ward-based representation, the elites left the actual office holding to small businessmen or acceptable politicians. None of the full members of Galveston's Deep Water Committee, for example, became a commissioner. The wealthy men of the Greater Des Moines Committee did not run themselves and could not even elect the slate of business candidates they did support.

Statistical analyses of the qualifications of commissioners were not comforting to the plan's advocates. The New York Bureau of Municipal Research compiled charts showing the previous occupational and political experience of the commissioners in ten cities. The study revealed that, of forty-eight members on the new governing bodies, thirty-eight had held other public offices prior to their election. Another researcher found that thirty-six of fifty commissioners in ten cities had previously been connected to their city governments. They were perhaps a better grade of politicians; they were probably more acceptable to community-wide business interests; but they were politicians just the same.[45]

The occupational backgrounds of commission members varied; but they came mostly from small enterprise and the professions with a smattering of blue-collar workers. With few exceptions they had not held executive positions of the sort that would prepare them to head a department of municipal administration. Even so sympathetic an observer as Professor Munro conceded in 1912 that "the class of men who hold office under the commission form of government is substantially the same as that which managed to secure election under the old order of affairs."[46]

But Munro and other propagandists were not ready entirely to abandon commission movement rhetoric. If the plan somehow had failed to generate first-rate officeholders, they were still confident of its success. The simplified, concentrated nature of the plan would facilitate the work of any class of men. "So effective an incentive has this centralization proved in commission governed cities," Ryan argued, "that politicians of mediocre ability have developed unexpected efficiency." Munro himself was emphatic: "It has permitted men of the same calibre to achieve vastly better results. . . . In a dozen or more cities the experience has been that a man who made a very ineffective alderman or councilor or administrative official under the old system of divided powers has succeeded in doing excellent work as a commissioner under the new frame of government." Ernest S. Bradford made a similar claim in *American City* magazine: "Even where the new commission has consisted largely of former councilmen or mayors, their action has been characterized by degrees of public spirit, promptness and efficiency not previously known. The evidence on this point is very clear."[47]

Even when the elites did not fill the governmental posts from their own ranks, they tried to maintain a close working relationship with the incumbents. The Oklahoma City Chamber of Commerce wrote of such an arrangement under the new commission form: "The wire-pulling and politics which were persistent obstacles a few years ago have been entirely eliminated. . . . As long as a proposition is based upon *good business principles* and in no way compromises the interests of the public, there has been no question of difference between the commercial organizations and the city officials."[48] El Paso's Chamber also boasted of intimate cooperation with city hall "which," according to an organization spokesman, "is of absolute necessity to obtain the greatest amount of good to a community as a whole."[49] In Des Moines and Omaha the Commercial clubs often directly consulted with the commissioners, and other cities made similar arrangements.

Having the commission plan was an asset for city boosters. Galveston, Houston, Dallas, Des Moines, and the other early members of the commission group took advantage of the publicity about their charters to advertise the cities, but the pioneers did not have a monopoly on such tactics. Henry Bruere found that it was "very common for commercial organs in commission cities to advertise commission government first among the city's claims to recognition as a superior place for industrial settlement."[50]

The desire to obtain such a commercial advantage helped motivate some cities, including Des Moines, to adopt the commission form of government. Along with appeals for clean and efficient government, a poster in Columbia, South Carolina, promised that a change to the Galveston system would make the city "Bigger and Stronger." The city attorney turned city booster and wrote in *American City*: "The new Mayor and Councilmen promise Columbia that their administration will make her as conspicuous among the cities of the Eastern States as Des Moines has been among those of the Midwest, and the feeling of city strength which has been inspired by the success of the movement for the best form of municipal government known is one of the most valuable assets that we have."[51]

The head of a large industrial firm warned that he would not locate a planned factory in Leavenworth, Kansas, if the commission referendum failed—it passed. Soon the business-dominated Greater Leavenworth Club was boasting of the city's honest and economical government under "five leading businessmen."[52] The Denver Chamber of Commerce was badly split over the plan, but one study group urged that the mile-high capital ought to adopt the new system for its city-boosting value. "There is an art of municipal as well as business advertisement, and it should be the continuing endeavor of all of us so to elevate Denver's name and fame as to assure, speedily and forever, its proper destiny as the inland metropolis of Western America. To this end nothing will contribute more immediately and conspicuously than the adoption of this thoroughly modern, efficient, business-like and popular plan of government."[53] So anxious were some cities to promote themselves that they claimed possession of commission charters when in fact they had done little but window dress standard weak-mayor administrations.

A question as difficult for historians as contemporaries to answer was whether the plan really worked as well as all the pamphlets, speeches, city documents, and articles claimed. Journalist John J. Hamilton of Des Moines sifted through many such reports and summarized his favorable impression of commission government's good works: "Every city has its own story of deficits wiped out, floating debts taken up, bonds retired, business methods introduced, long-standing nuisances abated, laws enforced, books better kept, streets kept cleaner, public works more honestly constructed, public buildings erected, additional parks and playgrounds acquired, economies enforced or taxes reduced—one, all or many."[54]

A city accountant from Columbus, Ohio, however, was more skeptical and sarcastic about the commission plan: "Information concerning it is eagerly sought throughout the country, and the cities using it are quick at recognizing advertising value. So they vie with one another as to which can make the most attractive statements in order to boom their own town. This information, so freely given, has evidently convinced many good citizens that a panacea for municipal ills has been found."[55]

If the Galveston–Des Moines system was indeed a panacea, cities wanted to know. And, of course, if its accomplishments were overrated, decision makers wanted to know that too. A number of publications and agencies tried to perform this service by systematizing their inquiries into the plan's operation. *American City* polled fifty mayors under all types of city charters to discover if commission-governed cities were actually making more real progress than those using the older forms. All the mayors replying told of important forward steps in their communities, but the commission cities placed much more emphasis on economy, lower tax rates, and improved credit. Typical of the responses was that from the mayor of Columbia, South

Carolina: "Under the commission form of government we have rehabilitated the city's finances so that in place of having a large floating debt which we found to be the case upon our accession to office May 11, 1910, we are now absolutely upon a cash basis, with no floating debt whatever." From Coffeyville, Kansas, the chief executive wrote that he had served in the same position under the old charter and was convinced that "the present system is by far the best in all respects, and particularly as a business proposition." In response to the survey Mayor Edward Hull Crump of Memphis declared, "The improvements made under the present commission system have been so many and so striking that it would be impossible for me to tell them briefly." So he told them at length in a booklet called *One Year and Eight Months under Commission Government* authored by two of his supporters.[56]

In another ambitious project, the Short Ballot Organization employed special correspondents to report on commission results in twenty-three cities. They found general satisfaction with the plan in nineteen of them. Two of the cities studied had not had their charters long enough to make any meaningful statement. The only unfavorable accounts came from Tacoma and Wichita where political haggling and weak personnel had hampered progress, but even there the reports were tinged with optimism. The Mayor's Second Annual Report in the latter city told of urban growth and concluded, "This prosperity, which is healthy and permanent, may have come to Wichita under some other form of government, but the truth is that it came in greater proportions under the commission plan than it did under the old plan."[57]

A small-town newspaper in Illinois conducted one of the most thorough opinion surveys on the success or failure of the new plan in the cities that had tried it. The *Quincy Optic* sent inquiries to mayors, merchants, and bankers in thirty-eight commission cities. In thirty-five of the towns all the correspondents were unanimous in their support for the new form of government. Negative replies came only from one bank officer and two small-town mayors.[58]

Looking more at facts and figures than opinions, Bruere's study of ten commission cities for the New York Bureau of Municipal Research cautiously conceded that the system's "superiority to the customary manner of city government is sufficiently apparent to make the conclusion safe that where cities are badly governed they may in all likelihood obtain better government by adopting the commission plan."[59]

In 1911 Professor Ford H. MacGregor of the University of Wisconsin focused on Galveston, Houston, Des Moines, Cedar Rapids, and Leavenworth and found: "The records of these cities, as indeed the record of practically all cities that have so far adopted the commission plan, show that the plan has invariably led to improvement over the old system. In some instances, the improvement has been marked, even phenomenal, but in most cases merely what might be reasonably expected from the introduction of better business methods. It has not always resulted in an actual reduction in the cost of running the city, but it has invariably resulted in an improvement in the services rendered. In all cases the city has been placed on a cash basis, and its credit raised to par or above. In no city has there been a deficit at the end of the year. . . . In no city has there been any suggestion of graft or dishonesty."[60] A more glowing endorsement of a municipal innovation would hardly be possible.

One of the most systematic and thorough early analyses of the plan's fiscal successes was the work of Ernest S. Bradford. As a fellow in political science at the University of Pennsylvania and later as an economist and statistician for the Department of Commerce and Labor, Bradford wrote many articles and one of the most comprehensive books on the subject of commission government. In 1912 he prepared a study on the financial results of the Galveston–Des Moines system. In the *National Municipal Review* study he set up five categories by which to judge the accomplishments of the commission governments: clearing up old debts, living within municipal income, rate of taxation, investing in new municipal property, and city planning. While noting occasional lapses and opportunities for improvement, Bradford recounted commission successes under each category, concluding, "The results so far secured under the commission form may be said to show in the field of finance a clear improvement over those attained under the former common type of municipal government."[61]

Cities reporting economies great enough to pay debts and eliminate deficits included, in addition to the more famous commission cities, such places as Parsons, Kansas; Gloucester, Massachusetts; Mankato, Minnesota; and San Diego, California. Cedar Rapids, Trenton, and Haverhill economized so well that tax rates could be reduced. A well-known Boston accounting firm reviewed the books of Haverhill and found that expenditures had been held well down. "Comparing this result," the accountants wrote, "with what happened in previous years when borrowing money for various classes of running expenses was the rule, rather than the exception, the achievement appears to be a notable one."[62] A similar accounting study of Trenton under its changed form declared that the city had shown "a decided decrease in the cost of operating city government."[63]

Other cities were content to state that, although there had been no decrease in expenditures, they were operating in a more businesslike and efficient manner. The mayor of Austin, Texas, explained, "We do not spend less than our predecessors under the old aldermanic form spent, but we believe we make the dollar go much further with better results."[64] The dean of Buffalo Law School spoke of similar practices in the largest commission city: "Buffalo has never before been so efficiently governed. Admirable results have been achieved through the simplicity and directness of operation which is one of the most striking merits of the commission form. The city's credit was never so good, our tax rate compares most favorably with other municipalities of the state, and there is a satisfying conviction among the taxpayers that their money is being wisely and honestly spent."[65]

Public improvements, many of which were directly for the advantage of the commercial community, were popular with the new commission governments. A wealthy retired meat packer who served as street commissioner

Table 5. *Comparison of Average Per Capita Financial Statistics for Selected Cities, 1913, 1915*

Per capita	Mayor-council form			Commission form			Mayor-council 1913 Commission by 1915		
	1913	1915	Increase	1913	1915	Increase	1913	1915	Increase
Property taxes	$14.73	$16.36	11.06%	$11.11	$12.31	10.80%	$10.08	$11.24	11.50%
Revenue receipts	22.78	23.68	3.95	19.53	20.84	6.70	15.69	17,80	13.44
General department expense	13.27	15.06	13.48	11.58	12.38	6.90	10.05	10.86	8.05
Net indebtedness	29.04	36.27	24.89	41.65	41.49	.39*	27.79	30.11	8.34

Source: U.S. Bureau of the Census, *Comparative Financial Statistics of Cities under Council and Commission Government*, 1916, table 1.
*Decrease.

"openly expressed his intention of favoring all reasonable privileges for big business interests in Dallas." His first major act in office was to pave Main Street from one end of downtown to the other.[66] Both Cedar Rapids and Des Moines turned seedy river-front property into attractive civic center showcases. Boosters in the Iowa capital made the dedication of their brand new city hall a national event. John MacVicar, as program chairman, invited numerous important Progressive Era figures to "attend an Exposition of Municipal Administration as Exemplified by the Des Moines Plan."[67]

Because of standardized reporting of municipal statistics, the Bureau of the Census was a very influential force for urban reform from the Gilded Age through the 1920s. In 1916 the bureau released a report designed to aid in determining the relative economic efficiency of alternative forms of municipal government. The study compiled financial statistics from twenty-four selected cities with populations between 30,000 and 300,000. In order to control for population size, which is the most important variable in explaining municipal expense, the bureau chose cities roughly equal in average population. Thus the results would be more comparable. The mayor-council cities selected were Indianapolis, Indiana; Hartford, Connecticut; Youngstown, Ohio; Troy, New York; Peoria, Illinois; Little Rock, Arkansas; Davenport, Iowa; and Charlotte, North Carolina—averaging 94,000 population. The commission cities included Birmingham, Alabama; Lowell, Massachusetts; Salt Lake City, Utah; Pueblo, Colorado; Topeka, Kansas; Montgomery, Alabama; Austin, Texas; and Des Moines, with a population average of 82,000. The report also analyzed eight other cities that had the mayor-council form in 1913 and the commission plan in 1915. The census officials did not draw any conclusions from their figures, but the tables were generally pleasing to commission advocates. No aldermanic city reduced debts between 1913 and 1915, whereas five of the Galveston–Des Moines system cities showed lower per capita debt in the latter year. None of the selected cities reduced taxes, but the levies increased less in the commission towns. General expenses also grew more slowly in the cities with the new charters (see table 5).[68]

Figures such as these and the chorus of favorable opinion from commission cities impressed progressives in the structural reform mold. Surely, they assumed, the positive financial results obtained under the plan were testimony to the efficiency of businesslike methods. Businessmen could understand municipal financial reports as analogous to profit-and-loss statements. They could relate to better paving, bigger and newer municipal buildings, and improved fire and police protection as tangible products produced by the municipal corporation. At first, the new plan seemed to be profitable not only for the municipality and the taxpayers but also for the businesses of the community.[69] The merchants, bankers, lawyers, industrialists, and other commercial and professional men who formed the nation's chambers of commerce did not merely push commission government for their own narrow self-interest. They had faith in modernization and efficiency as worthy goals in and of themselves. Of course, they hoped to stimulate business and maximize profit; but they also had a sincere feeling that what was good for Main Street was good for the entire city.

CHAPTER FIVE

DIRECT DEMOCRACY, AT-LARGE

ELECTION, AND THE SHORT BALLOT

MUCH of the impetus for the diffusion of commission government came not from the essential elements of the plan, but from the alleged advantages of reform devices usually associated with the new form. Des Moines Commissioner John L. Hamery wrote a friend, "the main feature of the plan, the election of all councilmen at large and the designation of the department they shall head, . . . is the entire meat of the coconut."[1] This merging of executive and legislative functions in a small body, and the consequent designation of conspicuous responsibility for each commissioner, was indeed the essence of the commission arrangement. But the movement involved much more than the essence.

Beginning with the charters of Dallas and Fort Worth, commission cities began typically to include various direct-democracy devices in their organic laws. Galveston did not incorporate any such features, but by the time of Des Moines' landmark document, initiative, referendum, and recall had become so closely identified with the plan that many observers considered them necessary parts of the system. "Since then," wrote one reformer in the *National Municipal Review*, "these three graces, the initiative, referendum and recall, the trinity of democracy, have usually gone hand in hand with the commission form of municipal government in its remarkable sweep from the gulf to the Great Lakes, and from ocean to ocean."[2] For example, in 1915 Oswald Ryan listed five planks of what he called "the straight commission plan as it is in effect today in American cities." They were a small body with both executive and legislative powers; at-large elections; each member in charge of a specific department; nonpartisan elections and the merit system; and direct popular control by initiative, referendum, and recall.[3]

The grafting of direct democracy to the commission plan significantly boosted its national popularity. Professor Munro observed in 1912, "The plan would scarcely have met with its present-day favor, particularly in the west, had its supporters not seized upon the machine of direct legislation and the recall." He also gave credit to nomination reform and the short ballot. Henry Bruere's extensive study of the new system agreed with Munro's observation that the popular-control provisions enhanced commission government's chances for wide acceptance.[4]

Some Progressive Era leaders would not have supported the Galveston innovation had it not picked up the so-called trinity of democracy in the course of its diffusion. William Allen White answered one inquiry with a flat statement: "The most important features of the commission form of government are the initiative and referendum and the recall. Without them the plan would fail." Robert M. LaFollette's secretary wrote that the senator was only in favor of the new form of government "provided it is accompanied by the enactment of the recall." Brand Whitlock favored the Des Moines plan with some modification. He limited his approval to city charters that included nonpartisan elections, the merit system, direct legislation, and recall. In short, he told an audience, "I like the Des Moines plan and I do not like the Galveston plan." Many of the magazine stories about the spread of commission government also argued that the use of direct democracy and other reform structures made the Iowa version more acceptable. *Arena* called the Galveston charter "unguarded," declaring that the "guarded" Des Moines variation was more democratic.[5]

Not only did initiative, referendum, and recall help adapt commission government to the progressive agenda, but the popularity of the Galveston–Des Moines format aided the spread of these devices in return. Author Robert Treat Paine credited the commission idea with giving "great impetus" to the direct legislation movement. It did not really matter which movement helped the other more. The point was that the merging of the two principles in the public's mind helped promote both concepts. "Let is here be clearly stated," wrote the editor of the *Equity Series*, "that while the initiative, referendum and recall are not necessary parts of nor accompaniments to the commission form of municipal government, a happy association of this democratic trinity and the commission idea has been formed."[6]

Besides promoting the general popularity of the commission form, direct legislation was sometimes crucial in securing individual adoptions. James G. Berryhill, father of the Des Moines plan, conceded, "We could not have secured a law in Iowa like the Texas law. The democratic features were essential to secure the support of public opinion." In Dallas and Fort Worth laboring groups demanded and got direct legislation included in the charters. At least on the surface, the Fort Worth businessmen behind the change of government were more willing to make the accommodation than were their Dallas counterparts. In Oklahoma City the business community was able to gather significant labor support by advocating a "progressive" form of commission government that included direct legislation along with municipal ownership and the eight-hour day. One union representative in Kansas City announced that the working men would withdraw their objections to centralized municipal administration if they were guaranteed that any new charter would provide for initiative, referendum, and recall.[7] In its appeal for adoption of commission government, the Allied Civic Bodies of Pennsylvania proclaimed that direct legislation and civil service "are the most important features of the new form of city government."[8] In such cases it is difficult to distinguish sentiment for popular-control measures from support for the basic elements of the proposed commission laws or charters.

Calmer heads and opponents of commission government strenuously pointed out that, while initiative, referendum, recall, nonpartisan elections, and the merit system might be desirable, cities need not adopt the entire Des Moines plan to obtain them. An unfavorable report by a subcommittee of the Denver Chamber of Commerce explained the core of the commission format and then cautioned, "Usually associated with this form of government are certain safeguards or adjuncts, which are not its essential or peculiar features, but which are largely responsible for whatever success Commission government has thus far had." In Des Moines' Berryhill-Baily debate between the commission plan and the strong-mayor system, attorney Baily made it clear that direct legislation could be included under either type charter.[9] Those arguing that popular control was merely incidental to commission government generally reminded their audiences or readers that Galveston had pioneered the innovation without any such devices. They also told of the many cities and states that did have direct legislation without tying it to the commission plan.

Although such observations were technically correct, the new system and direct democracy continued to go hand-in-hand. Of the states that had general commission laws only Alabama, New Mexico, and Utah failed to provide for the initiative. The latter two states plus Wisconsin excluded referendum from their enabling acts. Kentucky, Tennessee, and Pennsylvania joined New Mexico and Utah in not allowing recall. The majority of the special-charter commission cities provided for at least one and usually the whole package of popular-control planks.[10]

Sometimes opponents of changes to commission government contended that direct legislation was only a collection of relatively meaningless devices designed to make an autocratic business take over of city hall more palatable to the masses. They argued that the rhetoric of democracy surrounding initiative, referendum, and recall was merely a smokescreen. The verbiage lauding the devices was indeed eloquent. A Fort Worth commissioner declared, "The recall is the most effective and at the same time the most dangerous principle in the commission idea: it is a sword hanging over the head of the commission." But the Des Moines Citizens' Committee thought the sword a dull one. One of their leaflets contended, "As a practical thing [the recall] is valueless as no one unless actuated by malice will take the trouble to circulate a petition." They made similar complaints about the "almost impracticable machinery" which effectively nullified the initiative and referendum.[11] One anticommission treatise said that direct-legislation rhetoric made "more noise than a boy kicking a tin can on his way to school, and has about the same meaning." The author argued that, if the malfeasance was great enough to inspire enough signatures to force an election, the officer in all likelihood could be removed by impeachment or the courts anyway.[12]

The most typical recall requirement was a number of signatures equal to 25 percent of the total number of votes cast in the previous mayoral election. The specifications for initiative and referendum were generally similar. In Des Moines and some other cities the percentages necessary to call a special election were higher than those sufficient to place a question on the ballot for a scheduled election. The rationale for this was to limit the trouble and expense of numerous special elections on relatively unimportant matters.

While some people charged that direct legislation was a hollow accomplishment, others opposed it because it would be too effective. I. H. Kempner, the youngest and richest of Galveston's original commissioners, called initiative, referendum, and recall "populistic viruses." He regarded them as "the most dangerous and seductive brew that a municipality has ever been called on to quaff." Houston's wealthy mayor, H. Baldwin Rice, agreed that the recall was an inheritance of populism and declared that it "has no place in a business government." Those who opposed direct democracy, especially recall, believed that the measures would lead to a succession of costly and unnecessary elections. They feared that the threat of recall and the possibility that policy could be overturned would deter good solid businessmen from seeking commissionerships. Galveston publicist E. R. Cheesborough made this point repeatedly, as did many other writers. The Mayor of Charleston, South Carolina, argued that the elaborate popular-control provisions of the Des Moines plan would be more than a Sword of Damocles. He suspected they would "be a terror only to the very class of men a community wants in office."[13] Although many of the Texas commission charters did have popular-control planks, there was opposition to such measures. The Wilsonian progressives supported them, but conservative Governor Oscar B. Colquitt vetoed a charter for Texarkana because it included the populistic viruses of initiative, referendum, and recall. In Utah the governor vetoed the 1909 commission bill for the same reason. Backers of the 1911 version had to strike out direct democracy to avoid another veto.[14] According to a member of the Chicago City Club responding to a defense of the Des Moines plan, initiative and referendum were the socialistic products of dangerous "long hairs."[15]

If the business elites had been truly convinced that direct legislation would be ineffective and meaningless, as some contemporaries charged and as some historians have contended, there would have been no reason for them to show the apprehension and to exercise the opposition that they often did when the three devices were suggested. It is also doubtful that such prominent reformers as William Allen White, Brand Whitlock, John MacVicar, and Robert LaFollette would have endorsed municipal direct democracy if it were merely an opiate administered by elite businessmen trying to ram commission government down the peoples' throats.

In practice, initiative, referendum, and recall were neither as hollow as some argued, as dangerous as others charged, nor as useful as progressive doctrine portrayed them. Bruere did find that, where such provisions were in effect, officials seemed somewhat more respectful of their constituents. Similarly, a National Municipal League investigative committee found that initiative and referendum "have proved useful as provisions for allaying the time honored popular fear of entrusting large powers to single bodies." On the other hand, they went on to note that the actual use of the devices was not very common in commission cities. Furthermore, the committee found that the recall had not been misused and in fact had been put to good purpose in a few cities.[16] Los Angeles, although not a commission town, invented the recall in 1903 and used it to remove some aldermen and to influence the policy of others. A letter circulated to the businessmen of Des Moines used this example to prove the desirability of recall. Despite stiff provisions that required petitons with signatures equal to 35 percent of the total number of votes recently cast for mayor, the citizens of Dallas recalled their entire school board. Tacoma removed its mayor and two commissioners. Emporia used the initiative to settle a difficult street car question. Although use of direct democracy remained rare, there were enough examples of its successful application to provide advocates with a plausible case.[17]

In addition to direct legislation and recall, the commission charter reform packages sometimes contained other important devices. Grand Junction, Colorado, and other cities experimented with proportional representation and other novel ballot arrangements. Commission cities often joined the gradual but steady trend toward incorporating the merit system into municipal service. The most important of such incidental charter features for the commission movement was nonpartisan elections. Because commission advocates almost invariably argued that the new system would eliminate politics from city government, the actual removal of party designation from the ballots was a significant step in that direction. MacVicar told a Moline, Illinois, group that he believed the securing of nonpartisan elections was the greatest benefit of the Des Moines plan. In one-party, Democratic Texas, technical nonpartisanship was less important because municipal elections were often only nominally partisan anyway. But in other areas the separation of city politics from state and national considerations could mean a major adjustment. Mayor A. J. Mathis of Des Moines explained that such matters as the tariff which divided national parties had no relevance at the local level.[18] Advocates of municipal nonpartisanship, whether pushing for commission adoption or upholding the principle in general, often quoted Theodore Roosevelt's dictum, "The lines upon which national parties divide have no necessary connection with the business of the city."[19] Most commission cities followed Roosevelt's advice and provided for elections without party designation.

Opposition to nonpartisan balloting came naturally from those active in local party machinery. The prohibition of party labels, along with at-large representation, threatened the strength of many ward-based political organizations. Socialists also launched major attacks on the principle of nonpartisanship. A special committee on commission government reported to the 1912 national Socialist convention that "there is hardly a serious problem of municipal government that can be solved at all aside from the state and national movement." The report pointed out that home rule and general commission laws were state matters and, therefore, potentially partisan. Something ostensibly simple and local like the establishment of a municipal coal yard, for example, actually involved national issues, such as control of mining corporations and regulation of railroads. "Thus the most elemental problem of the city becomes a state and national problem," the report concluded. "To undertake to solve problems of this kind by limiting our efforts to local issues, and separating our cities from state and national issues is absurd." J. Stitt Wilson, the Socialist Mayor of Berkeley under its commission charter, tried to calm his party's fears by pointing out that, while commission government eroded regular parties, it strengthened ideological groups.[20]

Such features as initiative, referendum, recall, merit system, nonpartisan primaries and elections, and balloting reform were neither unique nor essential to the commission concept. On the other hand, much of the support for the new form of government derived from two of its necessary but not exclusive elements. Although it might have been technically possible to elect five commissioners by wards rather than from the entire city, the commission idea presumed at-large elections. The scheme also required that all municipal power be centralized in a small body, thus ensuring that commission cities would have a short ballot. Generally the five commissioners were the only elective officials, and their terms were sometimes staggered so that the voter had even fewer candidates on which to concentrate. Thus, at-large representation and short ballots were essential features of the basic commission plan. But while essential, these provisions were by no means unique to Galveston's invention. The island city herself had used at-large elections prior to the great hurricane. Cities could also secure the short ballot under the strong-mayor system by having a small council and a few other elective officials. Even a shorter ballot could be obtained by having the voter select only his ward councilman and a mayor.

Although the result could be obtained outside the commission format, the elimination of wards was one of the most ballyhooed of commission government's alleged advantages. MacVicar placed it next to nonpartisanship in importance, and others may have ranked it higher. Businessmen especially believed that the entire city should be considered a single entity. A person might live in one section, work in another, and own property all over town. Some Denver businessmen asserted, "The city is our common household. It should be thought of and treated as a unit." Mayor Mathis of Des Moines argued that it was possible for the five best candidates to reside in the same precinct. Editor John J. Hamilton agreed, proclaiming, "The philosophy which insists upon treating the city as an organic whole is unassailable."[21] Houston's Mayor Rice explained that election at large would result in better officials because a potential candidate must have "sufficient standing and reputation to be known throughout the body of the city as a fit man." Hamilton put it simply, writing that city-wide elections would cause "the elimination of the merely neighborhood candidate from public consideration."[22] Time and again reports on the success of the commission plan emphasized that the new governments served the people as a whole.

Attacks on the ward system were the stock in trade of commission advocates. For example, a Cedar Rapids commissioner wrote that at-large elections were "a great improvement over the old ward system under which vicious and undesirable citizens are frequently elected. While they may have been fairly representative of their constituents," he went on, "their power for evil in a Council is not to be underestimated." He pointed to the infamous examples of Chicago's "Bath House" and "Hinky Dink."[23] The *Chicago Record-Herald* endorsed the commission plan and agreed that the ward system guaranteed "a certain proportion of undesirable aldermen."[24] The log rolling and trade-offs characteristic of district representation attracted the special ire of reformers. A citizen of Haverhill characterized the system as "swapping a lamp post in ward three for a special policeman in ward five."[25] The Denver Chamber of Commerce's procommission subcommittee called ward representation a "universally acknowledged evil." They declared that it was time "to pronounce in favor of the subordination of local and private interests to the welfare of the city as a whole." Iowa Professor Benjamin F. Shambaugh made similar appeals, calling the ward concept "a hopeless failure."[26]

Despite such violent attacks, ward politics had many defenders, and not all of them were politicians. In recent years historians and political scientists have used extensive research and empirical data to demonstrate that city-wide elections tended to reduce lower-class and minority representation. Minority plaintiffs have recently used such evidence to secure federal court orders directing Shreveport, Louisiana, and Mobile, Alabama, to abandon the commission plan in favor of charters embracing ward representation. Progressive Era opponents of at-large balloting did not need elaborate statistics to tell them what was going to happen. Des Moines' east siders feared that the more affluent side of the river would elect all the commissioners. Cedar Rapids' large Bohemian population believed that they would lose representation on an at-large governing body. Because of commission government and at-large elections, a spokesman for Passaic's laborers complained, "The great mass of the working class of this city have been neatly eliminated from politics; businessmen are now completely in the saddle." Charles A. Beard summed it up in his 1912 city government text, saying that election at large "substantially excludes minority representation."[27]

Defenders of ward-based selection of aldermen argued that neighborhood districts kept the voters intimate with the government. A Des Moines attorney charged, "When the ward system is eliminated and representatives are elected at large without respect to any political division, control of affairs are [sic] removed too far from the people." He contended that, if district representation were good for state government, it should also be beneficial at the municipal level.[28] At a convention of the League of American Municipalities, one Chicago delegate upheld ward politics, declaring that he "would rather have a few Bath House Johns and Hinky Dinks, for they represent the people."[29] Some observers, such as Seth Low, who were well disposed toward commission government for small and medium-sized cities opposed it for large metropolitan centers because at-large election would prove unwieldy.[30]

In the smaller places the defenders of ward representation fought a losing battle. Even some large cities, such as Buffalo with the commission plan or Pittsburgh and Boston without it, moved to city-wide selection of their councils. Progressive Era structural reformers believed that bosses flourished in the wards, so at-large elections were the ideal tactical weapon against the machine's basis of support.

Like at-large representation, the short ballot could be obtained without adopting the entire commission package. However, because the plan's structure required fewer officeholders with greater powers, the new system necessarily provided for a shortened ballot. Many observers credited Galveston's accomplishments to this feature. As early as 1906 the *Dallas Morning News* said, "The success of the so-called commission is now attributed largely to the fact that the body is small—therefore it is possible for the people to select more wisely than if they were obliged to choose a large number of officers." Five years later, after the country had had considerably more experience with the plan, one investigation concluded, "The fact that the short ballot exists universally under the Commission Form of Government is undoubtedly fundamental in the success of that plan."[31]

Not only was the short ballot conducive to commission government's success, but it also generated much of the plan's popularity. The activities of Richard S. Childs and his Short Ballot Organization were very influential in spreading commission government doctrine as part of the short-ballot principle. Only twenty-six years old and four years out of Yale when he began the short-ballot agitation, Childs used his father's considerable fortune from the founding of the Bon Ami Company and his own brief experience as a New York advertising executive to launch the campaign for his pet solution to urban governmental woes. In 1908 the enthusiastic young reformer privately published a thirty-page pamphlet entitled *The Short Ballot: A New Plan of Reform*.[32]

The little booklet emphasized that even well-educated voters often had no idea about the relative qualifications of the aspirants for the dozens of minor offices typical of municipal government. His private poll of the "three-story-brown-stone-house vote" of Brooklyn in 1908 revealed that only 15 percent of the respondents could even name their aldermen much less describe his political stance. The overburdened voter, he argued, voted blindly, thereby increasing the power of the professional politicians who made up the tickets. "Thus the connection between the long ballot and misgovernment is established: So long as we intelligent citizens, by voting the long ballot blindly, continue to entrust large governing power to easily-contaminated organizations of political specialists, we must expect to get the kind of government that will naturally proceed from such trusteeship."[33]

Child's rule of thumb was that the average voter could follow only about five conspicuous races—any more and the slatemakers would dominate. Not only must the ballot be short, but also the officials voted on should be important enough to attract the electorate's attention. An "overdose of democracy," Childs warned, "creates oligarchy." The upper-class young reformer blamed the ironic travesty on "the wave of Jacksonian democracy [that] swept the country with a new and then unfeared doctrine of rotation in office." The short ballot was already in operation in England, Canada, and Galveston, he pointed out. Commission government could help overcome the Jacksonian overdose of elective offices.[34]

Childs mailed copies of his pamphlet to dozens of prominent and not-so-prominent students of municipal reform, asking, "Am I right? Comment, suggestions and criticism would be appreciated." Many replied with enthusiastic endorsements. James Bryce wrote from the British Embassy that the pamphlet contained "a great deal that is both true and opportune." He encouraged Childs to continue writing on the subject. General approval came from college presidents and educators, including Harry Pratt Judson of Chicago, Arthur T. Hadley of Yale, Nicholas Murray Butler of Columbia, and Charles Eliot recently of Harvard. Professors from Yale told Childs that they planned to teach the short ballot, and Charles E. Merriam wrote that the entire Political Science Department at the University of Chicago approved the concept. Men in the forefront of American municipal reform responded favorably to Childs' little booklet. Seth Low, Newton D. Baker, Frederic C. Howe, Frank J. Goodnow, and the heads of city clubs or similar groups in Chicago, Buffalo, Philadelphia, and Albany all penned their approval.[35]

A number of correspondents remarked that the short ballot was not, as Childs had called it, "a new plan of reform." Newton Baker wrote, "I trust that you will not feel that I am robbing you of any of your glory in saying that for a long time in Cleveland we have been ardent advocates and apostles of this doctrine." Bryce reminded Childs that *The American Commonwealth* had touched on the problem of America's lengthy ballots. And the president of Chicago's City Club explained that the municipal reform associations of the country were "already alive to the importance of the short ballot."[36]

Although reformers were already alive to the short-ballot idea, it was up to Childs to coalesce the wide support for the concept into a national movement. On April 22, 1909, Woodrow Wilson, Charles A. Beard, Lawrence Abbott, Clinton Rogers Woodruff, Childs, and a half dozen other men gathered at the City Club of New York to form the Short Ballot Organization. Through the balance of 1909 the group formalized its officers and advisory board. They unanimously selected Wilson as president and Childs officially became the executive secretary. In that post he made a few speeches and published an article in *Outlook*. Soon the organization began distributing preset press releases in two type styles, and the secretary's talents as an advertising man were proving their worth.[37]

Originally Wilson and others insisted that the Short Ballot Organization promote only the general idea and refrain from endorsing specific applications of the short-ballot principle. But from its very inception the organization was closely tied to the commission government movement. In his 1908 booklet that spawned the Short Ballot Organization, Childs attributed Galveston's accomplishments to the short ballot. He declared that widespread application of the principle would result in "cleaner, unbossed government as a normal condition as in England, Canada, Galveston, Houston, Des Moines, Dallas, etc., where they have 'Short Ballots' already." Late in 1909 Childs spoke to the churchmen of Mount Vernon, New York, on the eve of that city's commission referendum. He emphasized then, as he would for the next few years, that the vital feature of the commission plan was its short ballot.[38]

Wilson had expressed opposition to the commission plan for large cities and was less than enthusiastic about the format in general. To sooth these doubts Childs wrote him in January 1910: "Commission Government, despite its faults, is doing an enormous service in breaking up the crust of provincial conservatism that has so long balked progress." The secretary gave his suggestion for a general commission bill and asked if Wilson would endorse it for New Jersey. Although he did not immediately accept Childs' proposal, Governor Wilson did come to support the state's general commission legislation. Although his duties as governor and president necessarily relegated the short ballot to the background, Wilson maintained at least a passing interest throughout his administration and into the 1920s.[39]

Up to mid-1910 the Short Ballot Organization's commission advocacy was unofficial and consisted mostly of Childs' speeches and writings. But in July the advisory board resolved to make the group into a national clearinghouse for information concerning the Galveston–Des Moines movement. Childs argued that such a move would place the organization in "a splendid strategic position in relation to the movements which are going on in almost every city in the Union to extend the application of the commission plan." He wanted to keep before the public the proposition that the short ballot was the key provision of the Galveston–Des Moines scheme. His public relations campaign involved preparing a looseleaf collection of commission charters as well as sending out pamphlets and news releases extolling the plan. "Promoting the commission plan in small cities," Childs wrote Wilson, William Allen White, Ben Lindsey, and the others on the advisory board, "is following the lines of least resistance for this organization. . . . By making ourselves a clearing house for information on the subject of the commission plan, we can help the Short Ballot movement more than in any other way."[40] The organization purchased advertisements in *American City* in order to praise the short-ballot idea and the commission application of it. By the time the first *Short Ballot Bulletin* appeared in February 1911, promotion of the commission plan had become the main line of attack for the group. The *Bulletin* continued the argument that "the path of least resistance to a Short Ballot in cities of under 100,000 is at present unquestionably the Commission Plan of Government."[41]

Although Childs and his staff did most of the work, Charles A. Beard lent his name and prestige as editor of the *Loose Leaf Digest of Short Ballot Charters*. The collection sold 800 copies, mostly to charter revision committees. The Short Ballot Organization believed that the compilation had wide influence in standardizing the commission plan and preserving its short-ballot basis. The *Digest* offered the following definition:

A true Commission Plan is one which conforms to the Short Ballot principle which is defined by the Short Ballot Organization as follows:

First: That only those offices should be elective which are important enough to attract (and deserve) public examination.

Second: That very few offices should be filled by election at one time, so as to permit adequate and unconfused public examination of the candidates.[42]

In addition to abstracts of charters and reports from commission-governed cities, the *Digest* contained analytical articles. Not at all surprisingly, Childs entitled his piece "The Short Ballot—The Secret of the Success of the Commission Plan."

The Short Ballot Organization and the commission movement got a significant boost when Theodore Roosevelt endorsed the interrelated concepts. Lawrence Abbott, editor of *Outlook*, was on the organization's advisory board, and he interested the former president in ballot-shortening efforts. On tour in Birmingham and Dallas, Roosevelt praised the commission experiments. In the latter city he explained why: "If you have to vote for thirty or forty candidates or on twenty or thirty questions every year or so, I think you will agree with me the average man doesn't and cannot follow the details of the ticket he is voting."[43] The great protagonists of 1912 were both in the commission–short-ballot corner.

Childs and his supporters were not exclusively bound to the commission plan. They favored any charter that conformed to short-ballot principles, and some correspondents reminded them that the strong-mayor or federal plan could easily be adapted in their direction. For large cities the organization specifically endorsed ward representation so that the voter could concentrate on his own alderman and give municipal elections sufficient scrutiny. Thus, it is clear that the organization's real commitment was to the short ballot and not to commission government. The Short Ballot Organization also worked toward shorter ballots in state and county elections although the bulk of its efforts were in municipal directions. There was no nationally organized opposition to the short-ballot movement. Of course, almost every individual application of the principle was sure to attract vigorous local resistance.[44]

To this day Childs has never abandoned his attachment to the short-ballot principle. In 1946 he published an article entitled "The Ballot Is Still Too Long!" In the 1970s, well into his nineties, he sat daily at a cluttered roll-top desk in his office at the National Municipal League headquarters and argued that New York and many other cities still had too many unimportant elected officials. But the great work of his long and productive life was a spin-off of his short-ballot advocacy. Although at one time he considered the commission plan "the answer to the maiden's prayer," he soon became dissatisfied with the system's deficiencies. His promotion of the city manager plan was even more influential in the commission movement's decline that his agitation for the short ballot was in its rise.[45]

Galveston's simple plan of entrusting all city administration to a body of five businessmen had developed far beyond its fathers' wildest dreams. The claims of efficiency for the structure itself had been joined by a chorus of support for adjunct features grafted to the plan by Dallas, Fort Worth, and Des Moines. When Progressive Era municipal reformers thought of commission government, they also envisioned initiative, referendum, recall, nonpartisan primaries, civil service, at-large representation, and short ballots. But others saw different things when they analyzed the new form of government. They saw a troublesome merging of executive and legislative functions, log rolling and trade-offs among department-oriented commissioners, and other administrative fallacies. When businessmen and professionals considered the Galveston system, they perceived a municipal government analogous to a corporate board of directors. But after a few years of experience, more seasoned eyes saw that the analogy was less than perfect.

CHAPTER SIX

STRUCTURAL WEAKNESSES

AND UNMET GOALS

*D*ESPITE its remarkable spread and enormous popularity, the Galveston–Des Moines innovation had its detractors. In some cases municipalities embraced the plan virtually without opposition, but more often the movement faced stiff and sometimes successful resistance. In some cases commission charters came to a vote of the people and were defeated. In other communities the idea reached the stage of charter committees or similar groups only to be rejected in favor of the status quo or alternative reforms. In hundreds more towns the plan was the subject of extended but ultimately negative public discussion among civic groups and in the newspapers. There was scarcely a municipality that was not at least aware of the new alternative. Commission government's defeats attracted much less attention than its adoptions. This was particularly true in cases where communities turned down the idea before it reached a vote. Often the cleavage developed along class lines and had more to do with the nature of the antagonists than with the provisions of the charter in question. But the specific nature of commission government was still an important, if not the dominant, element in the long-term failure of the movement.

Opposition to the commission arrangement came from three general sources. Incumbent politicians and others who had a vested interest in the existing structure naturally resisted change. Second, many people, especially lower-class spokesmen, philosophically opposed the plan and its related reform devices because of the consequent centering of municipal power in unsympathetic business-dominated hands. Finally, some businessmen and municipal experts favored efficient, concentrated urban government but believed that the commission format was not the best way to achieve it. They identified structural defects in the new scheme and consequently favored other municipal reform strategies.

The members and supporters of incumbent administrations were the first, and often the most vociferous, points of resistance. Ward-based politicians, patronage-dependent civil servants, and favor-seeking businessmen typically comprised this faction. These people profitted from established procedures and traditions, and any change of government would probably upset their elaborate arrangements. Reformers directed the bulk of their rhetoric and action against these interests. In some cities the factions were well enough consolidated to form a political machine. Other towns, while spared a dominant machine, still had various groups that could cooperate and unite in order to preserve their interest in the maintenance of the status quo. Established politicians led the opposition to Galveston's initial commission idea, and the pattern repeated itself in most, though not all, subsequent adoption struggles. So-called bosses defeated charter referenda in Jersey City, Bayonne, and Hoboken. The alleged "political dictator" of Joplin, Missouri, blocked commission government in the state legislature.[1] But entrenched officeholders did not always oppose change. In some small towns and cities incumbents paved the way to new charters because the commission possibility seemed to embody principles toward which they were already striving.

Those who stood philosophically opposed to commission government's principles and purposes formed a second and significant source of opposition. This element could attract electoral support based on more than narrowly selfish motives. Included in this group were the sincere political leaders that some historians have called "social reformers."[2] A few such critics charged, as modern political scientists would prove, that the Des Moines plan's at-large elections and nonpartisan ballots would dilute the impact of ethnic and lower-class votes. Social reformers also lamented the limited vision of community service among most structural reformers who advocated the commission plan. Although more an advocate of efficiency than of humanistic concerns, Henry Bruere of the New York Bureau of Municipal Research nevertheless criticized the lack of social reform in the ten commission cities he studied: "You can count on the fingers of your hands the number of commission officials in the cities visited who definitely conceive a city government as an agency for promoting public welfare. None of them is actuated by a program which seeks to equalize opportunity among citizens for health, for economic welfare, for education, or for recreation."[3]

The social action motivation and the structural tradition clashed most directly over the latter's conception of municipalities as business corporations. Commerical-oriented charter designers asserted that city government was predominantly administrative and that cities should therefore be run like any other company. But to the mayor of Charleston, South Carolina, this claim had weight only "to those who put the dollar on a parity with humanity, or above it, and who find in the profit and loss column the *summum bonum* of life." He asked, "Wherein does the Government of a city differ from that of a state or county except in degree?" The municipal government "ordains laws that intimately concern the welfare of its citizens, their safety, their health, their comfort, their convenience [and] their recreation."[4] Other commentators also rejected the analogy between cities and businesses. One declared that the main goal of the latter was *"private gain"* while in city government "the *human* element, such as everyday well-being, schooling, hygiene, and the general happiness of a vast community of men, women, and children is ever present."[5] A West Coast newspaper woman emphasized that "a municipality must give weight to many considerations of social well being" with which a profit-making corporation need not concern itself.[6] At a panel discussion, the president of the Minneapolis City Council attacked commission government, condeming the treatment of municipal politics as business and concluding, "Service to the people is the primary object and not a credit showing on the ledger."[7] If a city's government had social service as its most important goal, efficiency and economy were only means by which to achieve that purpose and not ends in themselves as many commission supporters seemed to think.

In practice, commission governments did not ignore social reform to the extent critics feared they would. Historians have defined social issues to include aid to the poor, lower taxes for consumers, recreation, education, franchise regulation, municipal ownership of utilities, and related programs. In short, "the whole tone of the social reform movement was humanistic and empirical."[8] Although their motives may have been different, Galveston-plan administrators sometimes made policy decisions consistent with social reform objectives. More to save money than to improve services, Houston appointed a municipal druggist to dispense prescriptions. The city also fitted out a surgical room so the assistant health officer could treat indigent patients formerly sent to the hospital. The commissioners also extended sewers, built new schools, expanded the park system, purchased the water works, and made other community service improvements in the rapidly growing bayou city. All these measures involved human concerns, but Mayor Rice and his fellow councilmen were far from being social reformers.[9] Austin's Mayor A. P. Wooldridge was very much in the businessman's mold, but upon his reelection in 1915 the *National Municipal Review* commented, "His idea of progress does not include merely the idea of street paving, parks and playgrounds, but includes the immediate improvement of the conditions of the people along sanitary and humanitarian lines."[10] Recreational facilities were on the list of accomplishments in Des Moines, Cedar Rapids, and Dallas. Haverhill's commission secured lower rates for consumers by threatening a municipal takeover of the utilities. Public purchase of municipal franchises was a major goal of Memphis' commission administration under Mayor Crump. Utility companies initiated unsuccessful litigation against the new charter. Many cities joined in claiming expanded sewers, improved public health and education, reduced utility rates, and other accomplishments that benefited both urban boosters and the citizenry as a whole.[11]

Reports such as these obscurred the real philosophical differences between the humanistic social reformers and the economy-efficiency efforts of most commission administrations. Bruere was essentially correct when he wrote: "Commission government does not adequately reach out into the problems of its community. It has no marked social welfare impetus."[12]

In many cases labor interests and/or Socialists were among the most active ideological opponents of the Galveston format. Among the cities where Socialists worked successfully against commission adoption were Pocatello, Idaho; Manitowoc, Wisconsin; and Hartford, Connecticut. Their active resistance was fruitless in Des Moines, Passaic, Duluth, Oklahoma City, and Denver.[13] The new form was an important enough issue that the party established an investigative committee to report to the 1912 convention. While the tone of the document was decidedly cool to the new plan, the committee's questionnaire revealed much about Socialist opinion. Sixty-eight local chapters responded to the survey, and thirty-six expressed general or specific opposition to commission government. On the other hand, thirteen locals reported that they favored the Des Moines plan. Of the remaining respondents, four were divided among themselves, and fifteen had not yet taken a position.[14] Undoubtedly, Socialists tended to be skeptical of business-sponsored charter innovations. Over half of the responding locals did officially reject the commission concept, but, contrary to some impressions, Socialist opposition was not monolithic.

Much of the Socialist aversion to the plan focused on the devices of non-partisan ballots and city-wide elections that reduced the chances for minority representation. But underlying such specific objections was a general mistrust of business motives and a feeling that commission charters would bring, at best, only superficial changes to urban governance. "It has seemed to me," a Socialist complained during the consideration of Des Moines' charter, "that the emphasis has been placed upon the form of government rather than upon the substance."[15]

Organized labor tended to oppose the Galveston–Des Moines idea for much the same reasons, but labor's opposition was even less monolithic than that of the Socialists. The Short Ballot Organization published letters from union officials who endorsed the commission plan. In Oklahoma City the labor newspaper and the Trades Council maintained a friendly neutrality through the height of a long charter fight. Fort Worth commercial-industrial interests kept working men pacified by involving labor representatives in reform efforts beginning as early as 1900. Friends of Commission Government in Peoria published numerous letters of support from various labor leaders. A vice-president of the Kansas State Federation of Labor wrote that "the report that organized labor is opposed to the Commission Form of Municipal Government, is a great falsehood, so far as I know." The local Electrical Workers Union boasted that "the laboring men of Cedar Rapids were largely responsible for the adoption of the plan." The president of the Central Labor Union of Haverhill, Massachusetts, considered commission government the ideal form and declared that the city would not dream of returning to the aldermanic form. A similar statement came from his counterpart in Burlington, Iowa. The mayor of Emporia, Kansas, estimated that over 80 percent of the labor vote had gone in favor of the Galveston system.[16] Des Moines labor and its voice, the *Iowa Unionist*, had fought adoption, but by 1910 a poll at the union hall found only two of sixty-seven men ready to return to the previous system.[17]

Despite such examples of working-class support, in most cases the unions stood against the new type of centralized administration. Often even initiative, referendum, and recall could not shake their stand. Neither did such sops as representation on charter boards or token places on business-dominated slates always diffuse labor's opposition. As a member of the Denison, Texas, Trades Council said, "It is taking the power of running the city out of the hands of the laboring man."[18] Labor charged that city government by commission was undemocratic. It feared centralized power, especially when that power was centralized in upper-class hands.

Antagonists of Galveston's reformation launched a theoretical assault on the scheme's merging of legislative and executive, or appropriating and spending, functions in one small body elected at large. As early as 1905 a Texas critic called the system "oligarchial government."[19] A few years later a Chicago delegate told the League of American Municipalities: "The commission plan is un-American, and I want to tell you why I consider it so. Under the commission plan there is placed into the hands of five men executive power, legislative power and a certain judicial power, and I claim that any form of government that places the three cardinal powers into the hands of one set of men is un-American."[20] Whether such an arrangement would be an effective way to run a city did not seem to concern this delegate or many other critics. Thus fundamental fears that business-oriented government would ignore social problems and dedicate municipal powers to its own interests led most Socialists, many working men, and some students of government to stand in firm philosophical opposition to the principles of the commission government movement.

Whether because of class-oriented dynamics of support and opposition or on account of specific objections to the plan, commission cities had demographic characteristics distinctively different from those that did not adopt the form. Comparisons based on cities of 25,000 or more in 1913 indicated that commission cities were slightly less ethnic and more middle class than noncommission towns. Such findings are consistent with expectations of scholars of the Progressive Era. In a series of studies historians were unable to distinguish between progressive and conservative individuals on the basis of comparative biographical traits, but similar techniques do reveal noticeable, if minor, differences between Galveston–Des Moines–plan cities and their supposedly unprogressive counterparts. Although the comparative means and correlation coefficients show only associations and not causation, a casual relationship can be inferred. Ethnic minorities were rightly suspicious of at-large elections that ended their close association with ward politics. Such groups and other working-class elements reasonably feared that middle- and upper-class interests would have more influence in commission plan administrations (see table 6).[21]

The third locus of objection to Galveston's invention lay within the structural movement itself. Such opposition, coming as it did from their own kind, was devastating to the promoters of the commission movement. In fact this thrust soon led many proponents of the Galveston–Des Moines system to abandon that form and enlist in the city manager movement. But before this could happen on a widespread scale, the commission structure had to be shown to be wanting. Those political scientists, businessmen, and other students of municipal affairs who believed in efficient, economical, businesslike city government but refused to accept the Galveston dogma argued that both incidental and inherent defects kept most commission charters from constituting ideal structural reforms. A few observers were wise enough to make such observations early, but attacks from this point of view were not common until actual experience revealed the system's shortcomings.

Table 6. Means and Correlations[a] of Selected Social Characteristics of Cities of 25,000[b] or More by Adoption of Commission Form of Government, 1913[c]

	All cities	Commission cities	Noncommission
Mean population	179,097	93,646 (−.158)	241,760
Native white of native parentage	72.6%	73.0% (.034)	73.3%
Foreign stock[d]	48.6%	43.9% (−.179)	52.0%
Negro	7.1%	8.4% (.094)	6.1%
Protestant[e]	49.6%	52.8% (.118)	47.3%
White collar[f]	28.8%	29.5% (.103)	28.3%
Rate of population growth, 1900–1920	79.4%	83.6% (.049)	76.3%
Age of the city[g]	63.7	56.2 (−.242)	69.2
Mean age of population	31.0	30.7 (−.162)	31.7

Sources: U.S. Bureau of the Census, 13th Census, 1910, Population, vol. 1, General Report and Analysis, and vol. 4, Occupation Statistics; Abstract of the 13th Census, 1910; 14th Census, 1920, Population, vol. 2, General Report and Analytical Tables, and vol. 4, Occupations; Abstract of the 14th Census, 1920; Religious Bodies, 1906, part 1, Summary and General Tables; Religious Bodies, 1916, part 1, Summary and General tables.

[a] All correlations are Pearson's r.

[b] Includes only cities that had a population of 25,000 or more in each census, 1900, 1910, 1920.

[c] All data were interpolated to 1913. The form of government was determined from Beman, comp., Selected Articles, pp. 518–535.

[d] Foreign stock includes foreign-born and native-born whites of foreign or mixed parentage.

[e] Protestant was determined by subtracting Roman Catholic, Eastern Orthodox, and Jewish figures from total church membership.

[f] White collar includes workers in the professional, trade, and clerical categories.

[g] The age of the city is the number of years from the first census in which the place recorded a population of 2,500 to 1913.

Arguments of this nature fell into three interrelated categories. Critics leveled attacks on the inherent combining of legislative and executive functions in a single body. A second charge concerned the multiheaded—or, more precisely, the headless—nature of commission administration. The last argument assumed that the plan required experts to head the various departments but emphasized that experts could not be secured by popular election of commissioners.

The charge concerning the unification of executive and legislative powers was also widely used by working-class spokesmen, politicians, social reformers, and other commission opponents outside the charter-tinkering tradition. But where those attackers assailed the alleged undemocratic nature of the abandonment of the separation of powers, structural reformers emphasized its inefficiency. Philosophical charges of un-Americanism did not bother efficiency-oriented critics. "Yes, thank heaven!" exclaimed Richard Childs. "A city government in which graft is not even suspected is decidely un-American." However, soon Childs and others became concerned with the operational pitfalls of a government that placed expending and taxing powers in one set of hands. The plan's defenders, such as the Mayor of Buffalo, argued that "the combination of legislative and executive authority makes for efficiency and ease in administration."[22] But an Atlanta exponent of bicameral councils explained that such a government might be subject to efficiency of power and ease of corruption: "There is absolutely no check on abuse of power. If the tax rate is limited by charter, they can get more money by raising assessments. If some of their expenditures are irregular, they can appoint easy going auditors. If the ordinances put too many obstacles in the way of their political schemes, they can change the ordinances. If they want a wide open town, they can weaken the ordinances and put in a recorder who will nod on the bench."[23]

As early as 1907, Professor F. I. Herriott of Drake University identified the unification of powers as the "crux of the present debate," and John MacVicar believed that no other element of the Des Moines idea had aroused more discussion.[24] Virtually every list of commission weaknesses cited the violation of the doctrine of separation of powers. By 1913 even so friendly an observer as the secretary of the National Municipal League, Clinton Rogers Woodruff, admitted, "To the extent to which the commission form of municipal government mingles the policy-determining and the policy-executing functions in one and the same body of men, there is serious danger."[25] Some critics pointed out that such problems were already evident in county commissions whose members had both administrative and deliberative duties. It was not difficult to draw an analogy between the notoriously inefficient county governments and the similar arrangement called for under the Galveston plan.[26]

The absence of a single strong executive head was the second major weakness of the commission structure. This failing was actually a function of the dual executive-legislative duties of the commissioners. As a part of the council, a member made policy decisions for the whole city. Elected by an at-large constituency, he supposedly represented all the citizens and shared responsibility for the entire city government. On the other hand, as the head of a specific department of municipal affairs, the commissioner naturally became more concerned with his own particular area. Thus the head of public utilities would often be inclined to fight for appropriations with his counterpart who headed public works. In order to avoid conflict and interference in their own departments, commissioners developed a tendency to allow their colleagues to mind their own bailiwicks without effective coordination or leadership. In some cities the populace had simply traded the logrolling and political trade-offs of ward politics for similar tactics among semi-autonomous departments.

This lack of central responsibility and direction did not immediately appear in such cities as Galveston and Dallas, where public spirit and business concern led to the election of unified administrations. On the other hand, after only a few months of imitating the island-city pioneer, some cities suffered from the leaderless, multiheaded nature of their new governments. For example, the mayor of Wichita soon learned that he could not control his administration. Before a meeting of city officials he ridiculed the commission arrangement in a vivid analogy: "Think of running a ship with five captains. No marine insurance company would take such a risk, and the boat would in all probability drift on the rocks while the captains were trying to settle their differences as to how the boat should be run."[27] Well before Des Moines launched its commission ship, skeptics predicted the stormy wrangling and conflict that would soon shake the system. A local newspaper wrote: "A city administration is not and cannot be accountable if five men are in charge of executive work. Our old proverbs, 'Too many cooks spoil the broth,' and 'What's everybody's business is nobody's business,' are as true as Holy Writ in city government."[28] By 1915 Mayor James R. Hanna agreed with other studies that the major flaw of Des Moines' charter was the five-headed administration.[29]

When Denver's city commission took over the reins from Mayor Robert W. Speer, a leadership vacuum quickly appeared. The commissioners bogged down in disputes over appointments, expenditures, and priorities. Soon big businessmen were longing for the days of the strong leader. Three years' experience with the hydralike structure at city hall was enough for the mile-high city, and in 1916 it reverted to a strong-mayor form. The *Denver Times* commented, "The return of Mr. Speer may mean 'one man' power, but that is better than no-man power."[30]

H. S. Gilbertson, Childs' chief assistant at the Short Ballot office, hinted in 1913 that similar problems with leaderless administrations were causing dissatisfaction with new charters in Haverhill, Oakland, Oklahoma City, San Diego, "and Des Moines itself."[31] Even in Houston, where Mayor Rice had greater personal and charter power than most commission plan chief executives, departmental rivalry and jurisdictional disputes between the mayor and individual councilmen caused problems.[32] Sometimes conflict became so bad that commission majorities would, where charters allowed it, redefine departments in order to strip difficult members of all significant power. Most authorities agreed that the commission arrangement could lead to five (or three or seven) little fiefdoms rather than a unified and efficient municipal government.

The need for expert administration led to the third flaw in the new system. Since each commissioner was responsible for a specific facet of the municipality's business, he was expected already to be or soon to become something of an expert in his field. The original Galveston plan did not necessarily contemplate that each member would have special competence for his particular city department. Quite the contrary, the commissioners were to be men of broad business experience who could generally supervise their departments without directly running them on a day-to-day basis. Many defenders continued to argue the case for having part-time supervisory men serve with little or no compensation. Oswald Ryan was a major advocate of this view point: "The commissioner, being an elective official, cannot be expected to be an expert official. . . . The commissioner may be an efficient unprofessional, supervisory official, however, acting in the same capactiy as the English council committee: and in such a capacity he will reach his maximum efficiency. . . . This proposition, clearly understood, settles the crucial point in the problem of commission government."[33]

On the other hand, some authorities argued that the commissioners should be the active, full-time heads of their branches. Many cities paid good salaries to attract competent men to office. Unfortunately, often the amount was large enough to inspire many mediocre men to seek the position but not substantial enough to pull a prosperous businessman away from his own concern to devote his entire time to civic pursuits. Most early commission charters did not provide for election to specific posts. In such cities the mayor or the body itself made the departmental assignments after the election. Gradually, however, the policy of requiring candidates to stand for particular position came into favor in Oklahoma City, Denver, Colorado Springs, Salem, Massachusetts, and elsewhere. One Harvard professor wrote that election to specific departments was essential to preserve the "fundamental principle of commission government that the line of responsibility from member of the council to the people should be clear and sharp." He argued that the voters could make better decisions about a candidate's qualifications if they knew in advance what department the winner would head.[34] In some cases a de facto system evolved where candidates would run on a general ticket but with a particular position in mind. This was especially true when a commissioner was running for reelection and expected to retain the same department that he was currently serving.

Sometimes both systems worked, and competent administrators secured election on specific or random ballots. Denver elected an excellent engineer. Dallas selected a commissioner of streets and public property who was well known as an architect, engineer, and authority on paving. The city also chose a former police chief to direct the department of public safety. After one election boosters proudly asserted that "the city of Dallas has secured the service of men for the sum of $16,000 which no other corporations could secure for less than $100,000."[35]

Popular election, however, could not be trusted consistently to produce competent administrators. One National Municipal League release called the election of department heads "intrinsically absurd."[36] Even the argument that commissioners should be good businessmen with general supervisory ability failed to impress those who demanded nothing less than trained professionals in administrative positions. "We must abandon the idea that because a man is a successful lawyer, or merchant, he will therefore make a successful municipal administrator," a Colorado Springs attorney wrote. "No banker would imagine that because he has succeeded in managing a bank, he was fitted to conduct a railway."[37] Public administration studies blamed the absence of expert professional management and the rise of interdepartmental wrangling among commissioners for commission government's failures in Long Beach and Berkeley. Other students predicted the collapse of the whole Galveston–Des Moines movement because of this defect.[38]

Especially in specific-ballot cities, but also in other places, voters developed a tendency to make their choices on the basis of apparent expert qualifications. Thus, in a race for finance commissioner a mediocre banker might get the nod over a talented real estate agent with better general ability. In Dallas, for example, the people almost elected a man to head the water works because he claimed to be a hydraulic engineer. It turned out that he dealt in office supplies.[39]

A candidate chosen for legitimate talents at representation might possess no equivalent expertise for executive service. Efficiency advocates bemoaned such examples as the popular street laborer who sat on Wichita's commission. As an exponent of the working man's point of view he may have excelled, but he was a complete failure as a department head. Democracy may have been served but efficiency was not. Childs summed up the growing anticommission feeling among charter designers: "When you want representation, elect. When you want administration, appoint."[40]

Despite its three major structural weaknesses, most charter reformers had to admit that the commission plan often brought improved government to cities that had suffered under various shades of aldermanic charters. For example, a National Municipal League statement generally critical of commission efficiency conceded that "no one acquainted with the facts will deny" that the Galveston–Des Moines arrangement has improved both the political and business aspects of municipal government. Gilbertson was even more assertive in one article. Before he began assailing the new system's deficiencies, he included this admission: "No one can now seriously get up in a meeting and maintain with a straight face that commission government is not a vast improvement over the form in general use up to six or seven years ago."[41] Such references to the "old form" of government failed to impress some knowledgeable observers, because they knew that the prevailing system was not the same everywhere. A minor finance officer from Columbus, Ohio, explained: "It is frequently asserted by advocates, that the people of commission governed cities would not consent to return to the 'old form.' The impression left with many is that *the* old form is some definite, universal form resembling their own, whereas in fact it is only the particular local form, which may or may not coincide with forms prevailing elsewhere."[42]

Businessmen and reformers in some cities were satisfied with their charters. For example, one study group admitted "that the Commission Form in many instances improved the conditions prevailing under the systems of government supplanted"; but they went on to conclude that "it does not follow that the adoption of the Commission Plan in Denver would improve conditions prevailing here."[43] Undoubtedly, citizens in other cities who were contented with the municipal status quo reasoned along similar lines. Many commentators credited the new format's success not to its particular provisions but rather to a renewed public spirit and municipal interest that change-of-government struggles inspired.[44]

One of the most common explanations advanced by those who admitted commission advantages but stressed its limitations was that the new form was not well adapted to places of great population. Richard Childs posed the question, "Will commission government succeed in large cities?" and answered, "Yes, but not so well as in small cities." Others were not willing to make even that much of a concession. Admitting that "it has worked well in places ranging from 10,000 to 100,000," Seth Low declared, "I doubt whether the Commission form would meet the exigencies of a very large city." A commission of five, many argued, was too small to adequately represent all the factions and interests of a large community. One critic pointed out that Cleveland, for instance, had more people than many states, yet no one argued that entire state governments should be entrusted to as few as five men elected at large.[45] Indeed, Mayo Fesler, one of Ohio's leading municipal reformers, opposed the commission plan for big cities. As secretary of the Ohio League of Municipalities, member of the Cleveland Charter Commission, and active participant in the city's Civic League, he emphasized the Galveston plan's unsuitability for major cities.[46]

At-large elections were Childs' main objection to large-city use of the commission plan. In smaller municipalities, he contended, a candidate could carry his case to the people with an inexpensive personal campaign; but in populous centers, if the aspirant were not independently wealthy, he would have to seek backing from political organizations and/or interest groups. He correctly explained to short-ballot advocates that Woodrow Wilson would not endorse the plan for a large metropolis. Childs told his advisory board that the attempted application of the system to great municipalities might bring both commission government and the short ballot into disrepute; thus, the organization refrained from recommending the plan outside small and medium-sized cities. In reply to Childs, John MacVicar defended his Des Moines idea and contended that it would be applicable even to New York City. He was confident that metropolitan voters certainly could pick five or more prominent, efficient, and truly representative men to run the largest cities as well as the middle-range ones, such as his home town. S. S. McClure agreed that the plan could work in large cities, and in 1909 he proposed a hypothetical super commission to rule New York City. Former President

Roosevelt would be mayor and he would be supported by a list of luminaries including J. P. Morgan as commissioner of finance and Gen. Leonard Wood as commissioner of public safety. Public works would be entrusted to William G. McAdoo, and Elihu Root would handle the legal matters. Ever since George Kibbe Turner popularized the Galveston plan, McClure had been one of the system's leading proponents.[47]

The arguments against the plan's use in large cities were impressive. Although discussion of commission government principles did influence reform charters in Pittsburgh, Baltimore, and Boston, only a half dozen cities had over 200,000 residents when they adopted the system. About a dozen more between 100,000 and 200,000 experimented with commission charters.[48] In addition to being structurally ill-suited to the large cities, the business-oriented values of the commission movement were less likely to appeal to the heterogeneous and diverse populations and interest groups characteristic of major urban centers. The Galveston–Des Moines format was clearly more popular in smaller cities. In 1913 the mean population of all cities over 25,000 was 179,097; but the average count for commission cities in this grouping was only 93,646. However, noncommission municipalities were much larger than average, with a mean population of 241,760 (see table 6).

Many who recognized that commission charters generally brought at least temporary improvements to municipal governance were quick to add that the mere adoption of the new plan alone was not enough to ensure efficient administration. There were frequent caveats to the effect that the system was no "cure all" or "panacea" for urban woes. Such observers noted that for the plan to be effective the voters must select good men as commissioners, and the movement's most ardent champions were confident that the system would attract competent officeholders. Others, however, contended that quality administrative procedures were as important as top-notch officials.

Individual authorities stressed the importance of their particular aspect of municipal management. For example, a Census Bureau statistician declared that commission cities must employ modern and uniform budget principles to succeed. The secretary of the National Civil Service Reform League decried the fact that only about one-third of the commission cities had adequate merit systems as of 1911. He argued that civil service was especially important under the commission plan because of the extreme potential power of the governing body. Others emphasized the importance of modern accounting methods, advanced urban-planning concepts, and other pet procedures.[49]

The best example of this line of criticism was Henry Bruere's work for the New York Bureau of Municipal Research. The study's thesis was evident: "Modern progressive standards of municipal efficiency cannot be attained merely by the processes supplied by the commission plan." Bruere acknowledged that the format did "remove numerous impediments to good government," but his study warned that reformers would never find "some short cut from misgovernment to efficient government." The bureau's analysis of ten commission cities revealed that they were as slow as other municipalities in obtaining modern systems of accounting. Dallas exhibited progressive planning, but other commission strongholds lagged behind. In short, Bruere placed more faith in efficiency-oriented policies and procedures than he did in revised charter forms. In his view, charter tinkering and the Galveston–Des Moines plan were only useful insofar as they promoted the primary goal of scientific administration. "Obviously," Bruere noted, "the efficiency movement and the commission government movement, the two great forces now energizing American city progress, are not irreconcilable." He went on to note that efficiency programs could be applied to the plan's centralized structure, but he never lost sight of his central contention that commission adoption alone was not enough to ensure good government.[50]

If the city commission movement were to fulfill its promises, it had to provide efficient, boss-free government. Although in many cases the plan met this goal, in others it did not. Structural deficiencies and inadequacies began to appear more often. Soon there were enough cases of unsatisfactory administration to cause some questioning of the plan's benefits. In some cities already mentioned specific problems emerged. Writers often citied Wichita, Kansas, and Tacoma, Washington, as examples of the new format's collapse. In both cities voters recalled officials and exhibited a general dissatisfaction with the plan.[51]

Opponents delighted in attacking inefficiency and political squabbling in Des Moines. An Ohio municipal economist criticized poor debt management in the commission movement's showcase city.[52] W. W. Wise, who had been a major leader of the antireform forces in the Iowa capital, told Atlanta businessmen that the pioneer northern commission's first year had been marked by "bickering, strife, and political machinations."[53] By 1913 Houston's eight-year-old-government was the target of charges of extravagance, and the voters turned out the administration that had dominated city hall since the plan's inception. Critics also asserted that new charters had brought excessive expenditures rather than economical management to Lynn and Gloucester, Massachusetts. Gradually such negative impressions spread.[54]

A former commissioner of Spokane, Washington, described a classic example of the failure of commission-based reform. Charles M. Fassett was a typical progressive structural reformer. He owned a large assay firm, had served as president of Spokane Chamber of Commerce, and was a member of the study committee that drafted many charter reform alternatives before drafting a modern Des Moines–plan charter for Spokane. He helped lead the fight that got the new charter passed over the objections of local vice lords and politicians. While Fassett was out of the city, reformers drafted him to stand for election, and he became commissioner of public utilities. "Every member of that council," according to Fassett, "was thoroughly honest and determined to give Spokane the best government in its history." Indeed, the first few years did witness "a very marked improvement in civic affairs." But by 1920 the disillusioned commissioner could identify the problems that plagued the new structure in many cities. Enthusiasm waned and mediocre men took the reins. They were unable to provide the expert management that their dual roles as executives and legislators demanded. Their specific departmental responsibilities led to a fragmented approach to city administration. "In Spokane, and I believe in many other commission cities," Fassett wrote, "there has been a gradual but decided deterioration in the quality of the government following every election since the first."[55] He was right. In numerous cities the dreams of efficiency had not been fully realized, because of the inherent conflicts within commission administrations.

Another crushing blow to the commission movement's hopes was the growing awareness that the plan's structure could not always even eliminate boss politics, much less politics in general. From the very beginning of the commission movement, there were numerous cautionary statements to the effect that with bad men the new format could be even more injurious to the public interest than the old-style governments. In the spring of 1901 a Galveston editor recognized that the experiment's success would hinge "upon the character of men who constitute the first board of commissioners."[56] Mayor H. A. Landes cautioned, "With dishonest, incompetent and indifferent men in office, our plan would be more disastrous to both taxpayer and the people than the old plan . . . because a designing man would have a greater field to operate in, his powers being more concentrated."[57] Increased danger was the corollary of increased power.

There were like warnings in many adoption struggles. A Fort Worth sage foresaw the new charter making the political boss's task easier. He warned that the politicians would inevitably obtain dominance because "they are skilled in the art of vote-getting—an art that the 'good businessman' knows little and cares less about." The warning continued: "And when the machine politicians do get in control won't it be a beautiful machine for their purposes, with its fat salaries for the bosses, its unrestricted power as to appointment . . . and the naturally attendant power of self-perpetuation in office. Tammany would then perhaps have to lay down its laurels as an exemplar of ring rule."[58] Charges of this nature also came out in the Des Moines and Dallas considerations and continued to appear in municipal reform literature.

It soon became apparent that commission government did not universally escort a new breed of officeholders to the country's municipal buildings. Studies showed that the commissioners, with some exceptions, generally came from the same class of men who had served city government in prereform days. In fact, in numerous cases it was not only the same class of men but also the same men. Apologists for the Galveston concept were reduced to claiming that the system attracted a "higher grade of politicians" and that it allowed average and below-par men to perform superior service.[59]

Not only did "politicians" often capture commission governments, but also in some cases outright bossism could grip a Des Moines plan city. Critics of the format sometimes claimed that the system epitomized boss rule even when it worked right. There was no single, sinister, cigar-chomping personality; but the business-dominated, centralized political control was itself, in the words of one vocal enemy, "the very climax of Boss rule."[60]

Historians are well advised to avoid the oversimplified boss-reformer dichotomy. Some social reform leaders did employ bosslike tactics to perpetuate their administrations. And certainly commission government's success, like that of bossism, depended on central control.[61] In many ways the commercial-professional reformer saw the whole organic city, based on downtown interests, as his ward. But it should be remembered that the term *boss* had a particular and specific contemporary meaning in the context of the Progressive Era. He was an identifiable political personality, visible or behind the scenes, who used unsavory as well as legitimate methods to dominate a city's politics. To wreck the machinery of this type of ward-based boss was a major objective of the proponents of structural reform impulse. They proposed to destroy his machine by substituting one of their own—not a morning-glory-like reformer who, despite his political schemes, would be a transitory phenomenon, but a permanent change in the organic law governing the organization of city government. The commission plan would be the reform machine.

In some cities the scheme worked. Reformers ousted entrenched politicians and alleged bosses. In Trenton the previously dominant ward leader was reduced to coming before the commission to plead his case as did any other private citizen. At least that was the story according to an enthusiastic Short Ballot Organization press release. In the case of Denver, commission reformers ousted Boss Speer, but he scarcely had time to rest before the city called him back.[62] Unfortunately for commission advocates, the bosses sometimes learned how to operate the reformers' own tools.

Martin Behrman, the "easy Boss" of New Orleans, sensed the rising mood for reform and worked with civic and commercial groups to bring commission government to the delta city in 1912 as the newest municipal innovation. He knew that he could dominate a slate of respectable but acquiescent businessmen. Behrman placed himself at the head of the ticket. In 1916 the "boss of the fifteenth ward and of the city" outpolled President Wilson. At-large elections, the short, ballot, and commission government did not purge New Orleans.[63]

Unlike Behrman, the other most celebrated bosses of commission cities did not hold power prior to adoption of their cities' new charters. They were thus not in position to accommodate commission government to existing power structures, because they were excluded from those structures. Already established as an important ward politician, Frank Hague of Jersey City opposed commission government in 1911 when it first came to a vote under the provisions of the new Walsh Act. The referendum was unsuccessful despite a visit from Governor Wilson. Affluent wards wanted the change, but downtown Democratic regulars resisted. Because of local and state political developments, Hague decided that his electoral future was brighter as a progressive. Thus, he reversed his position and joined the progressive Republican *Jersey Journal* in advocating a resubmission of the commission question. With Hague's support the voters accepted the plan in 1913. Capitalizing on his new image as a reformer, Hague ran for commissioner and won. In his campaign the future dictator of Jersey City urged voters to elect him and other candidates who "will not submit to any political bossism." As head of the department of public safety, Hague compiled an impressive record. He cleaned up the notorious police department and made inroads on significant crime problems. But as he gained power and influence, his opportunistic progressivism waned. After his election as mayor in 1917, Hague gradually emerged as Democratic boss of not only his city but also the state. The supposedly boss-proof commission system had not prevented his rise. His machine mastered the technique of dominating the inherently fragmented structure of the commission plan. Ironically, after the Second World War when internal revolt and outside pressure broke Hague's power, his loyal lieutenants became vociferous critics of the outmoded charter system upon which their boss had based his power.[64]

The rise of Edward Hull Crump as commission boss of Memphis was perhaps not so crassly opportunistic but was just as effective. Crump allied himself with the commission government movement and authored a strategy to pit the newer progressive areas of the city against the old Democratic faction. A procommission slate of legislators under Crump's direction got a charter through the Tennessee legislature early in 1909. That autumn Crump became mayor and was on his way to power. In the space of a few months one major daily newspaper was calling the mayor a boss, and in the space of a few years he undoubtedly was. Crump's machine, like that of his Jersey City counterpart, extended beyond the city limits and well beyond the Progressive Era.[65]

As late as 1950 the National Municipal League credited "Crumpism" with Memphis' admittedly good government. While cautioning that "it is up to the people of Memphis to make up their own minds about the price of bossism," the league's assistant secretary nevertheless conceded that Crump "undoubtedly has made a group of commissioners look a good deal more like a real team than they do in many other cities. The fact is, of course," he went on, "that about the only way in which to inject anything like centralized responsibility and coordination into commission government is through a boss."[66] Reformers could recognize that tendency clearly by mid-century, but it was something of a shock to hopeful Progressive Era commission advocates who were suddenly faced with structural weaknesses and unmet goals.

CHAPTER SEVEN

A TRANSITION ROLE

*T*HE prime contribution of the commission plan to history," according to Richard S. Childs, "was the cracking of the assumption that the mayor-and-council plan was the only conceivable structure for a municipality."[1] Indeed, the Galveston–Des Moines idea did shatter the near monopoly that the aldermanic system had held on nineteenth-century city charters. But, contrary to some zealous predictions, the new format did not become the characteristic type of municipal organization. Today only 163 cities of 5,000 population or more retain the commission plan, and no new places have adopted it in years. On the other hand, the mayor-council system remains healthy, and about 47 percent of the country's municipalities of 5,000 or more inhabitants use this traditional plan. Another 43 percent employ city manager charters, and it was the commission movement that paved the way for the rise of this concept. Together the two reform structures, commission and manager, outnumber mayor-council cities in the 5,000 and over population class.[2] A *National Municipal Review* editorial explained shortly after World War Two, "Historically the commission plan has proved to be a transition device between the over-complicated check and balance system of the nineteenth century and the modern simple council-manager plan."[3]

The city manager idea is actually older than the Galveston plan. As early as 1899 a California reformer suggested that there should "be a distinct profession of municipal managers." In 1904 one small California town did appoint a chief executive officer although the council did not call him a "manager." The following year Professor Charles E. Merriam suggested a similar arrangement for Chicago. In 1907 Professor F. I. Herriott sarcastically but prophetically offered that if cities were merely businesses then Des Moines should simply contract with James J. Hill or some such corporate magnate to manage the city. Three years before statehood, the territorial legislature of New Mexico provided for a plan that allowed town councils to hire a "superintendent of city affairs . . . to take charge of all public matters."[4] But none of these suggestions or actions attracted significant national attention.

The first important city manager experiment was in Staunton, Virginia. Located in the Shenandoah Valley, Staunton had a 1910 population of just over 11,000 and was the birthplace of Woodrow Wilson. For 145 years a single council had governed the quiet little city; but in 1906 population growth brought it into first-class status, and state law required the establishment of a larger bicameral governing body. It soon became apparent that the new arrangement would be unwieldy, and a committee of councilmen recommended that the city employ a "manager or superintendent of the city's work" to "have the duties generally imposed upon the general manager of a business corporation." Some forces wanted to adopt the Galveston plan, and the city might very well have turned to it had not the Virginia constitution been a stumbling block. The final report went into effect by ordinance of January 28, 1908. It called for a "general manager" who "will discharge in general all of the executive and administrative duties now appertaining to the city council and its various standing committees, and will hold his office at the pleasure of the council."[5] Although the Staunton manager plan emerged from a committee that was sympathetic to the commission format, their plan did not, and constitutionally could not, contain the small at-large council essential to the commission concept. The experiment got some early publicity in the League of American Municipalities bulletin and elsewhere, but it did not start a wave of manager hirings.[6]

One of the people who read about Staunton's business-manager idea was Richard Childs. The scheme appealed to him immediately. As an advertising man, he knew that the manager concept would spread much more quickly if he could graft it to the existing popularity of the Galveston–Des Moines scheme. That is exactly what he did. In the summer of 1910 Childs published his first reference to the manager plan and directed his young assistant, H. S. Gilbertson, who was one of Charles Beard's graduate students, to draft a model city manager charter for the New York State Short Ballot Organization to advocate. But Elihu Root, Jr., Horace E. Deming, and the others on the governing board preferred to concentrate on New York City and statewide issues. A new plan of government for small upstate cities did not interest them, so Childs had to look elsewhere to find a sponsor for his manager idea.[7]

Like any good public relations firm, the Short Ballot Organization subscribed to a clipping service. Childs saw an item indicating that the Lockport, New York, Board of Trade was considering the Des Moines plan, and he decided to offer them "the latest thing in a commission charter." Convinced that Gilbertson's creation was an improvement over typical commission charters and induced by Childs' promise of free publicity, the businessmen of Lockport and the New York Commission Government Association embraced the city manager concept. The bill never even emerged from committee in the 1911 legislature, but the Lockport proposal became the model charter for the early city manager movement. The Lockport plan called for a council of five members elected at large and subject to recall. The person receiving the largest number of votes would become mayor, but he would have no veto and few special duties. There were to be no other elective officers. The only significant departure from the typical commission format was the provison for the appointment of an executive to manage the city. Although the Short Ballot Organization never officially claimed authorship, it wrote, printed, and paid for a thousand press releases and hundreds of pamphlets extolling the so-called Lockport plan.[8]

All of the publicity treated the Lockport scheme not as a completely new type of municipal government, but as a mere refinement of the tried and proven commission plan. In February 1911 the first issue of the *Short Ballot Bulletin* called it "a new development in commission government." A few months later, in an article in *American City*, Childs said the Lockport proposal was "an improved commission government plan." Also in 1911, Beard's *Loose Leaf Digest of Short Ballot Charters*, which sold over eight hundred copies, included an explanation of the city manager idea. In the *Annals'* special commission government issue a Lockport engineer outlined the plan and extolled its virtues.[9]

The publicity blitz was so effective that some people got the mistaken impression that the commission-manager plan, as it was usually called, was already in effect. The *Boston American* published an editorial and the Denver Chamber of Commerce released a report under that false assumption.[10] While on a western speaking tour Woodrow Wilson saw a press item about the Lockport suggestion and publicly endorsed it. Not until he was back in Connecticut playing golf with Childs some weeks later did he find out that the whole scheme was a creation of the organization of which he was president.[11] The campaign had struck a responsive chord with progressives.

Charter reformers in many cities read and considered the signed and unsigned propaganda that the Short Ballot office poured out, but the first town to take official action was Sumter, South Carolina. Although his published materials were the main source of information in Sumter's manager agitation, Childs was not aware of it; and he had no direct role in the adoption. But Sumter knew that he was the plan's intellectual father, and the Chamber of Commerce sent him a telegram announcing the legislature's approval of a commission-manager referendum. The proposition carried by a wide margin. Childs convinced Sumter to advertise nationally for an expert city manager, and he drafted the message.[12] A key line of his appeal concerned the professionalization of municipal management. The job would be "a splendid opportunity for the right man to make a record in a new and coming profession, as this is the first time that a permanent charter position of this sort has been created in the United States."[13]

The distinction between the city manager of Staunton and the commission-manager plan of Sumter was not trivial. The Staunton manager worked for an elected council that did not embody the commission principles of at-large election, concentrated responsibility, and, most important to Childs, the short ballot. "Staunton, in other words," the *Short Ballot Bulletin* succinctly wrote, "has a City Manager, but not the City Manager Plan." Childs and Gilbertson were actually less than satisfied with the Sumter version. The *Bulletin* declared that it was "crude and incomplete compared with the Lockport bill, which should remain the model of draftsmanship for other cities."[14]

Although the champions of the Lockport-Sumter plan deliberately called it the commission-manager idea to signify that it was based on a small council and to capitalize on commission government's favorable image with structural reformers, their objective was to eliminate the crucial flaws in the original Galveston scheme. First among those structural weaknesses was the combination of executive and legislative duties for each commissioner. Commission government had abandoned the separation of powers. The manager idea kept the unification of all powers in one small council, but it separated *function*. The commissioners would employ a manager to carry out the executive functions of government, but they would still retain responsibility for his actions.

Probably the most important argument supporting the commission movement was that the new plan would guarantee businesslike government. George Kibbe Turner's influential *McClure's* article about Galveston's government had called it "a business corporation." *Outlook* magazine had called the Texas idea "city government by a board of directors," and such comparisons were standard procedure in commission campaigns.[15] But manager advocates turned the analogy against the Galveston–Des Moines arrangement. In 1911 Childs wrote, "If it were really like a board of directors, the 'commission' would appoint a manager who in turn would hire the department heads, reporting regularly to the commission and submitting to it only broad matters of policy."[16] Many commentators pointed out that boards of directors, unlike city commissioners, did not actually run businesses on a day-to-day basis. The Lockport Board of Trade's pamphlet outlining the Childs-Gilbertson proposal argued that "the chief improvement in this Act over previous Commission Plans is the creation of this City Manager, thus completing the resemblance of the plan to the private business corporation with its well demonstrated capacity for efficiency."[17] A local engineer put it even more bluntly: "In short, the Lockport plan is an exact parallel of the organization of a private business corporation with the city council corresponding to the board of directors and the city manager to the general manager."[18]

Such arguments were, of course, technically correct. The city manager plan did correspond much more closely to the business ideal than did the commission arrangement. For those progressives who had the rationalization of political and administrative power as their major goal, the appeal could not help but be persuasive. As Benjamin DeWitt put it, "The city manager plan retains all the advantages of the commission form and eliminates most of its weaknesses."[19] The commission-manager structure was not plagued by a five-headed executive, nor was there the problem of placing complicated administrative duties into the hands of amateurs. Working men, Socialists, and others who had philosophical objections to the commission plan's concentration of power or to its affinity with the business community would still tend to oppose the manager variation; but the efficiency-oriented structural reformers were soon converted. Childs had merged the symbols of business efficiency with those of the New Freedom's democracy. He was, in his own words, "the minister who performed the marriage ceremony between the city manager as first thought of in Staunton, and the commission plan in Des Moines."[20] The short ballot, often in conjunction with nonpartisanship, was to bring city government close to the people, but the manager would ensure that expertise would reign in administrative matters. The plan, Childs wrote, "leaves to the commissioners simply the function of telling their city manager what the people want."[21]

The turning point for the commission-manager plan was its endorsement by the National Municipal League. The league, older and more prestigious than the Short Ballot Organization, had been friendly to the commission system but had never formally approved it. The Galveston innovation had a place on the program of every league conference for a decade after 1904. Secretary Clinton Rogers Woodruff's 1911 volume on commission government was the first in a major National Municipal League book series. His preface explained the league's stance on the commission plan. "To the extent that the commission government provides a short ballot, a concentration of authority in the hands of responsible officials, the elimination of ward lines and partisan designations in the selection of elective officials, adequate publicity in the conduct of public affairs, the merit system, and a city administration and a city administrator responsive to the deliberately formed and authoritatively expressed local public opinion of the city, it embodies principles for which the League stands. There are many other features upon which it has expressed no opinion."[22]

In 1910 the league appointed a standing committee on commission government consisting of Woodruff, Childs, Beard, Professor William B. Munro, and Ernest S. Bradford. The group reported at the November 1911 conference in Richmond. Their official determination was that commission government was "a relative success as compared with the older forms," and the report was full of praise for the results of the new governmental format. "The people who live under it are generally more content. They feel that they are more effective politically and that commission government is an asset to their town. Substantial financial improvements have generally resulted, demonstrating a striking increase in efficiency and a higher standard of municipal accomplishment, and this may fairly be credited to the better working of the new plan."[33]

The committee attributed the relative accomplishments to the so-called democratic features of the short ballot and concentrated power. Other provisions, such as nonpartisan ballots, direct democracy, civil service, and at-large elections, they found not essential but usually desirable. The only matters on which the five experts disagreed were the system's applicability to large cities and the practice of designating each commissioner to head a specific department. Although Staunton had had its manager for three years and Childs had already formulated the Lockport plan, the 1911 committee made no overt mention of the city manager idea. They concluded: "Commission government is in general to be recommended for cities of 100,000 population and under, and *possibly* also for cities of much larger size in preference to any other plan now in operation in any American city." The conference delegates immediately began to debate and argue the merits of the report. The gist of these discussions, according to an annotation in the final printed version of the report, was that the Galveston–Des Moines system, for all its advantages, was "by no means the ultimate form of American municipal government, but a transitional form."[24]

The committee remained constituted and reported again two years later when the league was meeting in Toronto. In the meantime the commission-manager system had spread rapidly. The publicity surrounding the Lockport proposal had inspired many progressie businessmen to action. Sumter, of course, adopted the plan in 1912. Seven other cities, including Dayton, Ohio, voted in 1913 to try the new plan although some of them did not put it into immediate operation. Youngstown and Elyria, Ohio, had defeated manager referenda. This time Childs led a majority of the committee to endorse the coming idea. With Bradford dissenting, they declared, "The city manager feature is a valuable addition to the commission plan, and we recommend to charter-makers serious consideration of the inclusion of this feature in new commission government charters." The majority listed a dozen reasons why the manager variation was superior to either the traditional mayor-council system or the basic commission format. All of the structural weaknesses in the commission method, they argued, would disappear, but the fundamental advantages of a small, all-powerful council would remain. Bradford argued that the city manager plan was an entirely new type of government too different to be classified as a mere refinement of the Galveston principle. Taking the executive functions away from the commissioners and making them part-time, nominally paid policy makers would, in his opinion, violate the fundamental feature of the plan. He thought that most of the problems with commission government could be solved by strengthening the mayor's position vis-à-vis the rest of the council. Although not an official member of the committee, league President William Dudley Foulke participated in the discussion that followed the report and expressed some caution about the manager concept. He thought the plan would be especially dangerous in cities where a boss might dominate the commission and hence the manager.[25]

Despite the hesitations of Bradford and Foulke, the commission government committee's report was the starting point for the league's new municipal program. The first model charter had advocated the strong-mayor form, but the new recommendation incorporated the commission-manager plan. With some revisions, it is still the basic charter that the league advocates. Childs and others, who privately called themselves "Young Turks," combined with such established academicians as Merriam, Frank J. Goodnow, and A. R. Hatton to get the manager idea made league doctrine.[26]

Thus, by 1915 the commission movement had lost its momentum (see table 7). The popular press no longer treated it as a promising novelty. John Mac-Vicar and the League of American Municipalities had lost their national influence, and the National Municipal League and the Short Ballot Organization had abandoned the Galveston–Des Moines system to boost the city manager plan. By 1920, with Childs' blessings, the NML had absorbed the short-ballot program. The press turned its attention to spectacular-appearing manager successes, and business-minded reformers began to think that the manager plan could bring increased efficiency to their cities even if they already had commission charters.

Table 7. Comparative Number of Commission and
Manager Cities by Year, 1901–1922

Year	Commission cities	Manager cities
1901	1	0
1902	0	0
1903	0	0
1904	0	0
1905	1	0
1906	0	0
1907	7	0
1908	4	1
1909	27	0
1910	52	0
1911	92	0
1912	64	3
1913	89	8
1914	46	19
1915	40	21
1916	19	14
1917	15	15
1918	10	24
1919	6	27
1920	4	32
1921	5	48
1922	5	28

Source: For commission cities the Appendix; for manager cities
The Municipal Year Book, 1934, p. 92. Other sources may give
slightly different numbers and dates.

If Staunton and/or Sumter were the Galvestons of the city manager movement, Dayton was its Des Moines. In the fall of 1912 the Chamber of Commerce began to study charter changes for the city of just over 100,000. They
investigated the straight commission plan, but decided that the manager variation promised more efficiency. With the boost of a flood-inspired emergency and under the direction of John H. Patterson, president of National Cash
Register Company, the Chamber of Commerce–based campaign committee
got the plan adopted. The early results, as in the commission pioneers, were
impressive, and the manager movement had its showcase.[27]
    From 1914 on, the manager scheme got much of the same kind of publicity
that had boosted Galveston into national prominence scarcely a decade earlier. Literary Digest wrote, "The cities with the commission form of govern-

ment doubtless have plenty of justification for boasting of their modernity, but they are a long way behind Dayton, if the editorial writers are right." *American Municipalities* picked up a Milwaukee editorial and spread it to students of municipal affairs: "Since Dayton adopted the city manager plan, a number of other American cities have begun seriously to consider this type of city government in preference to the commission plan." The article went on to make an important point about the nature of manager diffusion. "The interest in this new form on municipal government is thus seen to be nation-wide, and it is significant that as interest in it increases the objections to the original commission plan are becoming more pronounced."[28]

Academicians and reformers alike began to attack the commission plan as entirely wrongheaded. As the manager plan began to acquire a momentum of its own, it was no longer necessary to hitch it to the commission bandwagon. A good example is the evolution of attitude in Professor Munro's textbooks on municipal government. The original 1912 edition devoted twenty-five predominately favorable pages to commission government, but the version copyrighted four years later noted, "The city-manager plan was devised to remedy these two chief defects in the commission form of government, namely, the lack of concentration in administrative responsibility and the tendency to put the various departments in direct charge of men who have no expert qualifications." Ten years later his indictment of commission government was scathing. Munro even revised his opinion of Galveston's prestorm government to conform to his new impression of the island city's invention. The first edition had declared, "Prior to 1901 Galveston was one of the worst-governed urban communities in the whole country," but the fourth edition cautiously suggested, "The government of the city was no better, and perhaps no worse, than that of many other American communities of its size and type."[29]

Business sentiment paralleled that of the academicians and municipal experts. A 1914 questionnaire found that twenty-two of twenty-eight bankers and businessmen in Pennsylvania's commission-governed cities had high praise for their local governments and regarded them as successful. On the other hand, all but one of these observers believed that the manager system would produce even better results.[30] A few years later Childs boasted, "Businessmen continue to take to the commission-manager plan like ducks to water. . . . One cannot imagine the Rotary Clubs all over the country discussing a charter of any other type than this."[31]

By the spring of 1915, 45 cities had adopted the commission-manager plan by ordinance or charter. By 1918 there were about 100, and five years later there were over 250 manager towns. The greatest period of growth was from the end of the First World War through the 1920s (see table 8).[32] Some of the enthusiasm may have been a legacy of Progressive Era reform sentiments. Manager charters usually included direct democracy to please democratic reformers and always offered expert administration to please the efficiency cult. But the most likely reason for the plan's popularity in the twenties was its celebration of business virtue. It was a plan that a George Babbit could

Table 8. Growth of the Council-Manager Plan by Year, 1908–1933

Year	Number of adoptions	Cumulative total
1908	1	1
1912	3	4
1913	8	12
1914	19	31
1915	21	52
1916	14	66
1917	15	81
1918	24	105
1919	27	132
1920	32	164
1921	48	212
1922	28	240
1923	29	269
1924	12	281
1925	23	304
1926	18	322
1927	23	345
1928	16	361
1929	18	379
1930	18	397
1931	17	414
1932	18	432
1933	16	448

Source: *The Municipal Year Book, 1934*, p. 92.

identify with, yet at the same time it was one that Woodrow Wilson had enthusiastically endorsed.

The commission plan did not immediately disappear with the advent of the manager concept. Some cities continued to adopt the system well into the postwar decade. Manager doctrine did not diffuse instantaneously, and some cities faced state laws hostile to the Dayton plan. But the commission movement had lost its momentum. The manager idea even made inroads in commission strongholds. When a Dayton commissioner toured Galveston and ten other Texas cities in 1916, he found his audiences, predominately businessmen, very receptive to his praise of city manager principles.[33] In 1914 four Iowa cities had extralegal managers, and the next year the general assembly passed an act providing for managers by ordinance.[34] From 1920 into the early 1950s various organizations in New Jersey studied the commission plan. Consistently, boards of trade, junior chambers of commerce, and bureaus of research recommended that the system be abandoned.[35]

One by one the commission pioneers began to move on to the manager plan although in a few cases they went to strong-mayor charters. In the 1920s Houston, Fort Worth, and Dallas all conducted long, detailed, and successful campaigns to abandon their twenty-year-old charters.[36] Childs worked hard personally to help the League of Women Voters rid Des Moines of commission government in 1949 after several earlier attempts had failed. He wrote one of the women involved in the manager campaign that the National Municipal League had "a lively interest in the winning of Des Moines for historical reasons and because it is a fine town anyway and likely to make a fine record with the plan." Twenty-five years later tears came to his eyes as he remembered the symbolic importance of this victory for the plan he fathered.[37] By the time Galveston "repented" in 1960, it was anticlimactic. There had been no commission adoptions for nearly twenty years anyway. One commentator viciously asserted, "The Galveston tidal wave did more damage to other cities than it did to Galveston." A year earlier when the Wisconsin legislature was considering a bill to repeal its commission enabling act, no one showed up to testify in the system's behalf.[38] According to political scientist Charles R. Adrian, the few cities that retain the plan do so out of inertia and entrenched interests—not from any theoretical dedication to its principles.[39]

CONCLUSION

Whileile business elites almost invariably favored and laboring classes usually opposed the adoption of the commission form of municipal government, the story involved much more than a conflict between a single-minded business community and a unified lower-class opposition. Neither side was monolithic. In such places as Galveston, Fort Worth, and Cedar Rapids, businessmen managed to bring organized labor into coalitions that worked to change the existing forms of government. Labor did not automatically reject the drives for administrative efficiency, especially if such efforts were combined with some of the labor's own objectives, such as direct democracy. Even the Socialists were not unanimously against commission government. The businessmen also could be split as they were in Denver. Undoubtedly, the Galveston–Des Moines plan did tend to increase commercial influence in municipal government, but the system failed to revolutionize the type of politician who sat in city hall. A full understanding of the commission movement must go beyond a purely class interpretation.

It is important to place individual struggles for the commission innovation in the context of national diffusion. The Galveston idea should be seen as a reform contagion that spread from state to state and city to city in a remarkably short period of time. In that context modernization and the affirmation of corporate values, in addition to selfish interests, emerge as important motives for reform. In a scant ten years from 1907 to 1917, about five hundred cities built upon the pioneering examples of Galveston, Houston, Dallas, Fort Worth, and Des Moines. To be sure, in some cases, Galveston itself included, the commission alternative appeared at an opportune time for businessmen who were struggling to obtain or maintain dominance over city politics. But the particular innovation of government by a board of men who exercised both legislative and executive authority had to be communicated before it could spread. That communication did not rely solely on power-seeking businessmen. Municipal experts, journalists, and many stripes of Progressive Era politicians carried the commission gospel around the country.

The wide publicity that the Galveston–Des Moines plan received came at a time when the nation was actively seeking modern—or progressive—solutions to urban-industrial problems. Civic leaders wanted to be up to date. They did not want to be left out in the drive to modernize the bureaucracy of city hall just as many of them had modernized their own corporate organizations in a never-ending search for efficiency. One of the businessmen who led the commission movement in Dallas wrote in 1909, "Government by Commission means simply that the people of a progressive age have made up their minds to have the public service advance in methods, and improve in results, just as almost all lines of private business have improved."[1] The new system had made Galveston and Des Moines famous, and boosters hoped it could do the same for their hometowns. Moreover, most commercial men conceived of municipal corporations more as businesses than governments; consequently, when they learned of a charter innovation that claimed to institutionalize just such a conception, they were naturally impressed.

Many people supported the commission movement because it involved much more than just the bare basics of the Galveston plan. Many commission charters, especially after Des Moines, were in essence reform packages that appealed to diverse groups of reformers. Advocates of such measures as direct democracy, civil service, short ballots, nonpartisan elections, and at-large representation latched onto the commission movement (and later the manager plan) as a convenient vehicle for their particular programs. When most administrative reformers looked at commission government, they saw much more than a small council whose members had particular departmental responsibilities in addition to general legislative power for the whole city. They envisioned a thorough-going revision of their cities' entire governmental structure. Too often they thought that new machinery would do the job. The innovative charters seldom fully lived up to their promises of economy, efficiency, and democracy. But it had been an attractive package and a significant departure from the days when variations of the mayor-council structure had been the only alternatives.

Thus, the motives for support of the Galveston–Des Moines format are multifaceted. Some businessmen wanted procedures which would ensure that commercial interests had direct and dominant influences on municipal public policy. Others were more generally concerned with giving their cities the latest in efficient municipal innovation so that the entire city might prosper, and themselves with it. The advocates of many particular electoral or administrative reforms saw the plan as a reform package of which their pet ideas were the most important parts. The commission movement flourished because it offered to do these many things. It declined because it did not always do them and because the city manager system promised to do them better.

APPENDIX

COMMISSION CITIES, 1901–1922,

BY STATE, DATE OF OPERATION,

AND POPULATION

State	Date of operation[1]	City[2]	1920 Population
Alabama	1911	Birmingham	178,806
		Mobile	60,777
		Montgomery	43,464
		Tuscaloosa	11,996
		Huntsville*	8,018
		Talladega	6,546
		Hartselle	2,009
		Cordova	1,622
	1912	Sheffield	6,682
		Carbon Hill	2,666
		Elba	1,681
	1914	Florence	10,529
Arizona	1913	Phoenix*	29,053
	NA	Douglas	6,437
Arkansas	1913	Ft. Smith	28,870

*Indicates cities known to have abandoned the commission plan by 1923. Other cities probably dropped the plan also without the sources noting the fact.

[1]It was often a year or more between the decision to adopt a commission charter and the formal beginning of operation of the new form of government. In some cases the sources made it difficult to distinguish between the date of operation and the date of adoption.

[2]The available sources are not in agreement about which cities should be listed as having commission charters. Confusion about what essentials constitute commission government, extravagant claims made for city-boosting purposes, unclear distinction between commission and commission-manager cities, and simple misinformation account for the differences. When such discrepancies occurred it was necessary to make judgments based on wide reading of the relevant evidence. While this is the most comprehensive listing of commission cities extant, some errors no doubt remain. The most helpful sources in compiling this list included "A Summary of State General Laws and Constitutional Provisions Concerning Municipal Organization," *Equity* 18 (October 1916): 181–309; Lamar T. Beman, comp., *Selected Articles on Current Problems in Municipal Government*, pp. 518–535; Tso-Shuen Chang, *History and Analysis of the Commission and City Manager Plans*; Charles A. Beard, ed., *Loose Leaf Digest of Short Ballot Charters*; and numerous articles and notes in *Short Ballot Bulletin*, *National Municipal Review*, *City Hall*, *American City*, and other periodicals.

State	Date of operation[1]	City[2]	1920 Population
California	1906	Glendale*[3]	13,536
	1907	Riverside[3]	19,341
	1909	San Diego*	74,683
		Berkeley*	56,036
	1911	Oakland	216,261
		Stockton*	40,296
		Vallejo	21,107
		Pomona	13,505
		Santa Cruz	10,917
		Modesto	9,241
		San Mateo*	5,979
		San Luis Obispo	5,895
		Monterey	5,479
	1912	Sacramento*	65,908
		San Rafael*	5,512
	1913	Pasadena*	45,354
	1915	Long Beach*	55,593
		Alhambra	9,096
		Napa	6,757
	1916	Santa Monica	15,252
	1921	Fresno	45,086
Colorado	1909	Colorado Springs*	30,105
		Grand Junction*	8,665
	1911	Pueblo	43,050
	1913	Denver*	256,491
		Ft. Collins	8,755
	NA	Durango*	4,116
Florida	1911	Green Cove Springs	2,093
		Passagrille	NA
	1913	Pensacola	31,035
		St. Petersburg	14,237
		West Palm Beach	8,659
		Orange Park	333
	1914	Orlando	9,282
	1915	Apalachicola	3,066
	1916	Datona*	5,445
Georgia	1911	Marietta	6,190
		Cartersville	4,350
	1914	Rome	13,252
Idaho	1907	Lewiston	6,574
	1912	Boise	21,393
	1922	Twin Falls	8,324

[3]These early dates are from "A Summary of State General Laws and Constitutional Provisions Concerning Municipal Organization," pp. 186, 193. Other sources do not list them and they are not reflected in any totals or tables drawn from the Appendix.

State	Date of operation[1]	City[2]	1920 Population
Illinois	1911	Springfield	59,183
		Decatur	43,818
		Rock Island*	35,177
		Moline*	30,734
		Elgin	27,454
		Waukegan	19,226
		Kewanee	16,026
		Jacksonville*	15,713
		Pekin	12,086
		Ottawa	10,816
		Forest Park	10,768
		Dixon	8,191
		Spring Valley	6,493
		Carbondale	6,267
		Clinton	5,898
		Hillsboro	5,074
		Rochelle	3,310
		Hamilton	1,698
		Braceville	303
	1912	Naperville	3,830
		Marseilles	3,391
		Geneseo	3,375
	1913	Cairo	15,203
		Murphysboro	10,703
		Harvey	9,216
		Harrisburg	7,125
		Catlin	931
		Port Byron	510
	1914	Effingham	4,024
		Flora	3,558
	1915	Joliet	38,442
		Bloomington	28,725
		Lincoln*	11,882
		Sterling	8,182
		Paris	7,985
		Highland Park	6,167
		Princeton	4,126
		Coal City	1,744
		Palos Park	240
	1917	Champaign	15,873
		Centralia	12,491
		Mt. Carmel	7,456
		Downers Grove	3,543
		Salem	3,457
	1919	East St. Louis	66,767
		Collinsville	9,757
		Marion	9,582

State	Date of operation[1]	City[2]	1920 Population
	1921	Aurora	36,397
		Streator	14,779
		LaSalle	13,050
Iowa	1908	Des Moines	126,468
		Cedar Rapids	45,566
	1910	Sioux City	71,227
		Burlington	24,057
		Keokuk	14,423
	1911	Ft. Dodge	19,347
		Marshalltown	15,731
	1913	Ottumwa	23,003
		Mason City	20,065
		Clarinda	4,511
	NA	Bloomfield	2,064
Kansas	1908	Leavenworth	16,912
		Caldwell	2,191
	1909	Wichita*	72,217
		Hutchinson	23,298
		Independence	11,920
		Junction City	7,533
		Anthony	2,740
	1910	Kansas City	101,177
		Topeka	50,022
		Parsons	16,028
		Coffeyville	13,452
		Emporia	11,273
		Newton	9,781
		Iola	8,513
		Wellington	7,048
		Abilene	4,895
		Cherryvale	4,698
		Neodesha	3,943
		Girard	3,161
		Holton	2,703
		Eureka	2,606
		Marion	1,928
	1911	Pittsburg	18,052
		Chanute	10,286
		Pratt	5,183
		Dodge City	5,061
		Hiawatha	3,222
		Council Grove	2,857
	1912	Arkansas City	11,253
		Manhattan	7,989
		Great Bend	4,460
		Olathe	3,268
		Kingman	2,407

State	Date of operation[1]	City[2]	1920 Population
	1913	Ottawa	9,018
		Osawatomie	4,772
		Fredonia	3,954
		Garden City	3,848
		Garnett	2,329
		Sabetha	2,003
	1914	Lawrence	12,456
		Ft. Scott	10,693
		McPherson	4,595
	1915	Horton	4,009
		St. Mary's	1,321
Kentucky	1911	Newport	29,317
	1912	Lexington	41,534
	1914	Covington	57,121
	1915	Paducah*	24,735
	1916	Hopkinsville	9,696
		Cynthiana	3,857
	1918	Owensboro	17,424
	1922	Henderson*	12,169
		Winchester	8,333
	NA	Middlesboro	8,041
		Harrodsburg	3,767
Louisiana	1910	Shreveport	43,874
	1912	New Orleans	387,219
		Hammond	3,855
		Donaldsonville	3,745
		Natchitoches	3,388
	1913	Alexandria	17,510
		Lake Charles	13,088
		New Iberia	6,278
		Jennings	3,824
	1914	Baton Rouge	21,782
		Lafayette	7,855
	1919	Monroe	12,675
Maine	1912	Gardiner	5,475
Maryland	1910	Cumberland	29,837
	1914	Ellicott City	1,246
Massachusetts	1909	Haverhill	53,884
		Taunton*	37,137
		Gloucester	22,947
	1910	Lowell*	112,759
	1911	Lynn*	99,148
	1912	Lawrence	94,270
		Salem*	42,529

State	Date of operation[1]	City[2]	1920 Population
Michigan	1910	Harbor Beach	1,927
	1911	Pontiac*	34,275
		Port Huron	25,944
		Wyandotte	13,851
		East Jordan	2,428
		Fremont	2,180
	1913	Battle Creek	36,164
		Owosso	12,575
		Traverse City	10,925
	1914	Saginaw	61,903
		Marquette	12,718
		Monroe	11,575
		Grand Haven	7,205
		Eaton Rapids	2,379
	1915	Adrian	11,878
		Munising	5,037
	1916	Benton Harbor	12,233
	1917	Ludington	8,810
	1918	Highland Park	46,499
		Mt. Clemens	9,488
Minnesota	1911	Mankato	12,469
		Faribault	11,089
	1912	St. Cloud	15,873
		Tower	706
	1913	Duluth	98,917
		Eveleth	7,205
		Pipestone	3,325
	1914	St. Paul	234,698
	1915	Two Harbors	4,546
	1916	Stillwater	7,735
Mississippi	1910	Clarksdale	7,552
	1911	Hattiesburg	13,270
	1912	Jackson	22,817
		Laurel	13,037
		Gulfport	8,157
		Charleston	3,007
	1913	Meridian	23,399
		Vicksburg	18,072
	1915	Greenwood	7,793
Missouri	1914	Joplin	29,902
		Kirksville	7,213
		Monett	4,206
		West Plains	3,178
	1915	Aurora	3,575
	1916	Springfield	39,631

State	Date of operation[1]	City[2]	1920 Population
	1917	Maplewood	7,431
	1919	Webster Groves	9,474
Montana	1911	Missoula	12,668
	1912	Polson	1,132
	1915	Helena	12,037
Nebraska	1912	Omaha	191,601
		Nebraska City	6,279
	1913	Lincoln	54,948
		Beatrice	9,664
	1917	Kearney*	7,702
Nevada	1911	Las Vegas	2,304
New Jersey	1911	Trenton	119,289
		Passaic	63,841
		Ridgewood	7,580
		Hawthorne	5,137
		Ocean City	2,512
		Margate	249
	1912	Atlantic City	50,707
		Long Branch	13,521
		Nutley	9,421
		Ridgefield Park	8,575
		Wildwood	2,970
		Borough Deal	420
		Longport	100
	1913	Jersey City	298,103
		Union	20,651
		Phillipsburg	16,923
		Millville	14,691
		Vineland	6,709
		Bordentown	4,371
		Beverly	2,562
		Sea Isle City	564
	1914	Orange	33,268
		Irvington	25,480
		Belleville	15,660
		Haddonfield	5,646
	1915	Bayonne	76,754
		Hoboken	68,166
		New Brunswick	32,779
		Asbury Park	12,400
		Cape May	2,999
		Bradley Beach	2,307
	1916	Lambertville	4,660
		Allenhurst	343
	1917	Newark	414,524
		Montclair	28,810

State	Date of operation[1]	City[2]	1920 Population
		Collingswood	8,714
	1918	Rahway	11,042
New Mexico	1913	Las Vegas	4,304
New York	1913	Beacon	10,996
	1915	Saratoga Springs	13,181
		Mechanicville	8,166
	1916	Buffalo	506,775
		White Plains	21,031
	1918	Watertown	31,285
		Glen Cove	8,664
	1920	Watervliet*	16,073
North Carolina	1909	High Point*	14,302
	1911	Wilmington	33,372
		Greensboro*	19,861
	1913	Raleigh	24,418
	1915	Asheville	28,504
	1917	Charlotte	46,338
North Dakota	1907	Mandan	4,336
	1909	Minot	10,476
		Bismarck	7,122
	1913	Fargo	21,961
		Devils Lake	5,140
		Williston	4,178
		Hillsboro	1,183
	1914	Ray	563
	1915	Marmath	1,318
	1916	Washburn	558
	1920	Grand Forks	14,010
Ohio	1913	Lakewood	41,732
	1914	Middletown*	23,594
Oklahoma	1909	Tulsa	72,075
		Enid	16,576
		Ardmore*	14,181
	1910	Bartlesville	14,417
		McAlester*	12,095
		Sapulpa*	11,634
		El Reno	7,737
		Miami	6,802
		Duncan	3,463
		Wagoner	3,436
		Purcell	2,938
	1911	Oklahoma City	91,295
		Muskogee*	30,277
		Guthrie	11,757
		Lawton*	8,930

State	Date of operation[1]	City[2]	1920 Population
		Pawhuska	6,414
		Stillwater	4,701
		Holdenville	2,932
	1912	Okmulgee	17,430
	1913	Ada	8,012
		Weatherford	1,929
		Wewoka	1,520
	1916	Henryetta*	5,889
	1917	Blackwell	7,174
Oregon	1910	Baker	7,729
	1913	Porland	258,288
Pennsylvania	1912	Monongahela	8,688
		Titusville	8,432
	1913	Reading	107,784
		Erie	93,372
		Harrisburg	75,917
		Wilkes-Barre	73,833
		Allentown	73,502
		Johnstown	67,327
		Altoona	60,331
		Chester	58,030
		McKeesport	46,781
		New Castle	44,938
		Williamsport	36,198
		Hazleton	32,277
		Lebanon	24,634
		Oil City	21,274
		Carbondale	18,640
		Meadville	14,568
		Lockhaven	8,557
		Corry	7,228
	1914	Easton	33,813
		Pittston	18,497
		Bradford	15,525
		Beaver Falls*	12,802
		Franklin	9,970
	1916	Uniontown	15,692
		DuBois	13,681
	1917	Coatesville	14,515
	1918	Bethlehem	50,358
		Butler	23,778
	1920	Sharon	21,747
	1922	Monessen	18,179
		Sunbury	15,721
	NA	Lancaster	53,150
		Pottsville	21,876
		Connellsville	13,804

State	Date of operation[1]	City[2]	1920 Population
		South Bethlehem	485
South Carolina	1910	Columbia	37,524
	1913	Florence*	10,968
		Orangeburg	7,290
	1916	Spartanburg	22,638
		Rock Hill	8,809
South Dakota	1909	Sioux Falls	25,202
	1910	Huron	8,302
		Rapid City*	5,777
		Yankton	5,024
		Pierre	3,209
		Vermillion*	2,590
		Canton	2,225
		Dell Rapids	1,677
		Chamberlain	1,303
	1911	Aberdeen	14,537
	1912	Watertown	9,400
		Lead	5,013
		Madison	4,144
		Belle Fourche	1,616
	1914	Springfield	719
Tennessee	1909	Etowah	2,516
	1910	Memphis	162,351
	1911	Chattanooga	57,895
		Lebanon	4,084
		St. Elmo	3,890
	1912	Knoxville*	77,818
	1913	Nashville*	118,342
		Bristol	8,047
		Springfield	3,860
	1914	Murfreesboro*	5,367
		LaFollette	3,056
	1915	Jackson	18,860
		Lawrenceburg	2,461
Texas	1901	Galveston	44,255
	1905	Houston	138,276
	1907	Dallas	158,976
		Ft. Worth	106,482
		El Paso	77,560
		Denison	17,065
		Greenville	12,384
	1909	Waco	38,500
		Austin	34,876
		Marshall	14,271
		Palestine	11,039

State	Date of operation[1]	City[2]	1920 Population
		Corpus Christi	10,522
	1910	Amarillo*	15,494
		Sherman	15,031
		Kenedy	2,015
		Aransas Pass	1,569
		Port Lavaca	1,213
		Robstown	948
		Marble Falls	639
		Lyford	NA
	1911	Port Arthur	22,251
		Abilene	10,274
		McAllen	5,331
		San Benito	5,070
		Spur	1,100
	1912	Hereford	1,696
		Franklin	1,131
		Nixon	1,124
		Frankston	818
		Bishop	NA
	1913	Ennis	7,224
		McKinney	6,677
		Sweetwater	4,307
		Somerville	1,879
		Jacksboro	1,373
	1914	Orange	9,212
		Mineral Wells	7,890
		Denton	7,626
		Coleman	2,868
		Honey Grove	2,642
		Groesbeck	1,522
		Mertens	342
	1915	San Antonio	161,379
		Cleburne	12,820
		Calvert	2,099
		Luling	1,502
		Alice	1,180
	1916	Vernon	5,142
	1917	Corsicana	11,356
	1918	Weatherford	6,203
		Eagle Pass	5,765
	1919	Cisco	7,422
	NA[4]	Texarkana	11,480
		Mineral Wells	7,890

[4]This long list of Texas cities for which dates of operation are not available is from ibid., p. 295.

State	Date of operation[1]	City[2]	1920 Population
		Ennis	7,244
		Hillsboro	6,952
		Eagle Pass	5,765
		Sulphur Springs	5,558
		Commerce	3,842
		Mexia	3,482
		Mart	3,105
		Beeville	3,063
		Mineola	2,299
		Canadian	2,187
		McGregor	2,081
		Hico	1,635
		West	1,629
		Van Alstyne	1,588
		Anson	1,425
		Nocona	1,422
		Richmond	1,273
		Goldthwaite	1,214
		Devine	995
		Robstown	948
		Arlington	NA
Utah	1912	Salt Lake City	118,110
		Ogden	32,804
		Provo	10,303
		Logan	9,439
		Murray	4,584
Washington	1910	Tacoma	96,965
	1911	Spokane	104,437
		Walla Walla	15,503
		Hoquiam	10,058
	1912	Everett	27,644
		Centralia	17,549
		Chehalis	4,558
	1921	Port Angeles	5,351
	NA	North Yakima	NA
West Virginia	1909	Huntington	50,177
		Bluefield*	15,282
	1911	Parkersburg	20,050
	1914	Fairmont	17,851
		Grafton	8,517
Wisconsin	1910	Eau Claire	20,906
	1911	Appleton*	19,561
	1912	Superior	39,671
		Oshkosh	33,162
		Janesville*	18,293
		Portage*	5,582

State	Date of operation[1]	City[2]	1920 Population
		Menomonie	5,104
	1913	Ashland*	11,334
		Rice Lake	4,457
		Ladysmith	3,581
	1914	Antigo	8,451
	1915	Fond du Lac	23,427
	1916	Green Bay	31,017
	1920	Chippewa Falls	9,130
Wyoming	1911	Cheyenne	13,829
		Sheridan	9,175

NOTES

Abbreviations Used

BLAM   *Bulletin of the League of American Municipalities*

NML   National Municipal League

NMR   *National Municipal Review*

The Annals *The Annals of the American Academy of Political and Social Science*

SBB   *Short Ballot Bulletin*

Introduction

1. Neal Jones, "The Des Moines Plan of Municipal Government," *City Hall* 10 (July 1908): 18.
2. "Two Views of Commission Government," *American Municipalities* 26 (March 1914): 201 (quoting the *Kansas City Journal*).
3. See, for example, Robert L. Lineberry and Edmund P. Fowler, "Reformism and Public Policies in American Cities," *American Political Science Review* 62 (September 1968): 796–813.
4. Ernest S. Griffith, *A History of American City Government: The Conspicuous Failure, 1870–1900.*
5. Melvin G. Holli, *Reform in Detroit*, pp. 157–181.
6. Frank Mann Stewart, *A Half-Century of Municipal Reform*, pp. 1–49.
7. William L. Riorden, *Plunkitt of Tammany Hall*, pp. 17–20.
8. Benjamin P. DeWitt, *The Progressive Movement*, p. 302.
9. *Galveston Daily News*, May 22, 1911 (quoting Wilson); *Municipal Year Book, 1976* (see table 3).
10. Ernest S. Griffith, *A History of American City Government: The Progressive Years and Their Aftermath, 1900–1920*, p. 58.
11. Tso-Shuen Chang, *History and Analysis of the Commission and City Manager Plans.*
12. Convenient summaries of this controversy include David P. Thelen, "Social Tensions and the Origins of Progressivism," *Journal of American History* 56 (September 1969): 323–341; and John D. Buenker, *Urban Liberalism and Progressive Reform.*
13. Peter Filene, "An Obituary for the 'Progressive Movement,'" *American Quarterly* 22 (Spring 1970): 33; Buenker, *Urban Liberalism*, p. viii; William L. O'Neill, *The Progressive Years*, p. 156.
14. DeWitt, *The Progressive Movement*, pp. 299–318; see chapters 4 and 5 on Wilson and Roosevelt.
15. Samuel P. Hays, "The Politics of Reform in Municipal Government in the Progressive Era," *Pacific Northwest Quarterly* 55 (October 1964): 157–169; James Weinstein, "Organized Business and the City Commissioner and Management Movements," *Journal of Southern History* 28 (May 1962): 166–182. Chapter 4 of Weinstein, *The Corporate Ideal in the Liberal State, 1900–1918*, is essentially the same.
16. Ibid.

17. Thomas M. Scott, "The Diffusion of Urban Governmental Forms as a Case of Social Learning," *Journal of Politics* 30 (November 1968): 1091–1108.
18. Ibid., p. 1093.
19. Ibid., pp. 1093–1094.
20. Ibid.; Richard S. Childs, *The Story of the Short Ballot Cities*, p. 7.
21. Scott, "The Diffusion," p. 1094.
22. John Judson Hamilton, *The Dethronement of the City Boss*, p. 19; Henry Bruere, *The New City Government*, p. 40.
23. *Municipal Year Book, 1976*, p. viii.

1. The Galveston Plan

1. Frank T. Harrowing, "The Galveston Storm of 1900" (M.A. thesis), p. i. See Bradley R. Rice, "The Galveston Plan of City Government by Commission: The Birth of a Progressive Idea," *Southwestern Historical Quarterly* 73 (April 1975): 365–408.
2. Harrowing, "The Galveston Storm," p. 56. See Herbert Malloy Mason, Jr., *Death from the Sea*, and John Edwards Weems, *A Weekend in September*.
3. City of Galveston, *Record of Proceedings of the City Council*, September 24, 1900; *Galveston Tribune*, September 25, 28, 1900; Walter Gresham, "Galveston's Charter Government," *BLAM* 4 (December 1905): 183–184.
4. William Bennett Munro, *The Government of American Cities* (1912), p. 295.
5. H. S. Cooper, "Something New in Government," *Success Magazine* 11 (February 1908): 83.
6. Annette Austin, "Galveston City Commission," *Smith's Magazine*, October 1906, pp. 43–44.
7. Charles A. Beard, *American City Government*, p. 93; James A. Tinsley, "The Progressive Movement in Texas" (Ph.D. diss.), pp. 207–211.
8. *Galveston Daily News*, May 1, 1895.
9. Ibid., March–June 1895; Ernest S. Bradford, *Commission Government in American Cities*, p. 4n.; George Kibbe Turner, "Galveston: A Business Corporation," *McClure's Magazine* 27 (October 1906): 611.
10. *Galveston Daily News*, June 5–9, 1897.
11. Ibid., June 4, 1899; campaign flyer 1899, Galveston Commission Campaign Folder.
12. *Galveston Daily News*, June 6–7, 1899.
13. *Galveston Tribune*, June 16, 1900.
14. Galveston, *Record of Proceedings*, October 2, 1899.
15. Ibid., February 5, 1900.
16. D. B. Henderson to Messrs. McKim & Co., January 17, 1902, Henry White Papers.
17. *Galveston Tribune*, January 3, 1901.
18. *Galveston Daily News*, February 10, 1901.
19. Turner, "Galveston: A Business," p. 610.
20. *Galveston Daily News*, February 16, 1901.
21. The Deep Water Committee members were Bertrand Adoue, Leon Blum, Charles Fowler, Walter Gresham, W. F. Ladd, Morris Lasker, R. G. Lowe (of the *Galveston Daily News*), W. L. Moody, Clarence Ousley (of the *Galveston Tribune*), Julius Runge, George Sealy, J. D. Skinner, R. Waverly Smith, A. J. Walker, and C. L. Wallis. In addition, I. H. Kempner, Farrell D. Minor, and John Sealy served on subcommittees but were not listed as full members. Biographical information regarding the personal and business connections of the men came from the newspapers and the following: *General Directory of the City of Galveston, 1901–*

1902; S. C. Griffin, *History of Galveston, Texas*; and the Biographical Clipping File, Barker Texas History Center.
22. Ibid.
23. Ibid.; *Galveston Daily News*, August 7, 1901.
24. *Galveston Daily News*, November 24, 1900.
25. Ibid., November 14, 1900; Weinstein, "Organized Business," p. 167.
26. Galveston, *Record of Proceedings*, October 15, 1900; Galveston Wharf Company, *Minute Book*, December 1, 1900; Marilyn McAdams Sibley, *The Port of Houston*, p. 125.
27. Gresham, "Galveston's Charter," pp. 183–184; *Galveston Daily News*, February 10, 1901; *Galveston Tribune*, January 3, 1901; Edmund R. Cheesborough, *Galveston's Commission Form of City Government*, [p. 2].
28. Charles A. Beard, ed., *Loose Leaf Digest of Short Ballot Charters*, p. 21101; William O. Scroggs, "Commission Government in the South," *The Annals* 38 (November 1911): 16.
29. *Galveston Tribune*, September 25, 1900, January 3, 1901; I. H. Kempner, "The Drama of the Commission Plan in Galveston," *NMR* 26 (August 1937): 409–412.
30. Ford Herbert MacGregor, *City Government by Commission*, pp. 36–37.
31. *Galveston Tribune*, May 7, 1901.
32. Turner, "Galveston: A Business," p. 612.
33. *Galveston Daily News*, October 19, 1900.
34. *Galveston Tribune*, September 27, 1900.
35. *Galveston Daily News*, January 15, February 16, 1901.
36. Ibid., December 2, 1900.
37. 27th Texas Legislature, *Journal of the House of Representatives* (Austin, 1901), pp. 261, 373–374; Galveston, *Record of Proceedings*, December 17, 1900, January 3, 7, 1901.
38. *Galveston Tribune*, January 26–February 22, 1901.
39. Weinstein, "Organized Business," pp. 175–182; Hays, "The Politics of Reform."
40. *Galveston Tribune*, February 7, 1901 (quoting the *Austin Statesman*); *Galveston Daily News*, March 13–24, 1901.
41. *Galveston Tribune*, January 9, 1901.
42. *Galveston Daily News*, January 15, 1901.
43. *Austin Statesman*, March 15, 1901; *Galveston Daily News*, March 13–15, 1901; 27th Texas Legislature, *Journal of the House*, p. 836.
44. *Austin Statesman*, February 6, 1901; *Galveston Tribune* and *Galveston Daily News*, February 3–19, 1901.
45. *Galveston Tribune*, January 21, 1901; *Galveston Daily News*, February 3, March 13, 1901; *Galveston City Times*, October 27, 1900.
46. *Galveston Daily News*, March 24, 1901.
47. Ibid., March 12, 1901.
48. Ibid., March 13, February 10, 1901.
49. Ibid., February 16, 1901.
50. Ibid.
51. Galveston, *Record of Proceedings*, February 4, 1901.
52. *Galveston Daily News*, March 24, 1901.
53. 27th Texas Legislature, *Journal of the House*, p. 837.
54. Ibid., p. 1240; 27th Texas Legislature, *Journal of the Senate* (Austin, 1901), p. 866; *Galveston Daily News*, March 2–24, 1901.
55. *Galveston Daily News* and *Galveston Tribune*, April–May 1901.
56. *Galveston Daily News*, June 30, 1901.
57. Ibid., September 11, 1901.

58. *Galveston Tribune*, September 14, 1901.
59. *Galveston Daily News*, February 11, 1902.
60. *Ex Parte* Lewis, 75 *Southwest Reporter* 811 (1903); *A. A. Brown et al* v. *City of Galveston*, 97 *Texas Reports* 1 (1903).
61. H. A. Landis [Landes], "Galveston's Civic Management," *BLAM* 7 (February 1907): 51; Austin, "Galveston City Commission," p. 45; 28th Texas Legislature, *Journal of the House of Representatives* (Austin, 1903), pp. 1032–1044, 1090–1091; *Galveston Daily News*, March 26, 28, April 29, 1903.
62. *Galveston Daily News*, April 28–29, 1903.
63. E. R. Cheesborough to Clara Homes, May 30, 1910, and an unidentified clipping ca. 1908 enclosed with letter, John Cheesborough Papers; *Des Moines Register and Leader*, January 16, 1906.
64. A. P. Norman to editor of *Galveston Tribune*, ca. 1915–1916, Galveston Commission Campaign Folder; *Galveston Daily News*, May 2–10, 1911; *Des Moines Register and Leader*, June 1, 1909.
65. Marsene Johnson, "An Address to the Voters of Galveston County," ca. 1910, Galveston Election Propaganda Folder, 1908–1921.
66. Clarence Ousley, "The New Galveston," *Harper's Weekly*, November 16, 1901, p. 1152; W. B. Slosson, "The New Galveston," *Independent*, June 16, 1904, p. 1386; C. Arthur Williams, "Government of Municipalities by Boards of Commissioners," *Gunton's Magazine* 27 (December 1904): 562; "A Municipal Experiment," *Outlook*, January 6, 1905, p. 5; "Municipal Government by Commission," *Nation*, October 18, 1906, p. 322; W. Watson Davis, "How Galveston Secured Protection against the Sea," *Review of Reviews* 33 (February 1906): 200–205; Ethel Hutson, "Galveston: An Achievement Story," *Reader* 8 (October 1906): 545–556; C. Arthur Williams, "Governing Cities by Commission," *World To-Day* 11 (September 1906): 945; "Galveston's Government," *Tradesman*, June 15, 1906, p. 50; *Galveston Daily News*, September 27, 1906.
67. Stewart, *Half-Century of Municipal Reform*, p. 73; E. R. Cheesborough, "The Success of the Galveston Experiment," in *Proceedings of the Atlantic City Conference for Good City Government and the Twelfth Annual Meeting of the National Municipal League* ([Philadelphia], 1906), pp. 181–193; William Bennett Munro, "The Galveston Plan of City Government," in *Proceedings of the Providence Conference for Good City Government and the Thirteenth Annual Meeting of the National Municipal League* ([Philadelphia], 1907), pp. 142–155, iii (quoting Woodruff); "Municipal and Civic Reform," *Outlook*, December 7, 1907, p. 757.
68. Gresham, "Galveston's Charter"; "Municipal Government by the People," *Midland Municipalities* 9 (July 1905): 149–150; "The Galveston Plan of City Government," *Municipal Engineering* 32 (April 1907): 255–258.
69. Turner, "Galveston: A Business"; Peter Lyon, *Success Story*, plate 6 following p. 308; Harold S. Wilson, *McClure's Magazine and the Muckrakers*, pp. 246–247; Cheesborough, *Galveston's Commission Form*, p. 1; George Kibbe Turner, "The City of Chicago: A Study of the Great Immoralities," *McClure's Magazine* 28 (April 1907): 575–592; "Chicago and Galveston," *McClure's Magazine* 28 (April 1907): 685–686; "The Way to Decent City Government," *Independent*, April 4, 1907, p. 806.

2. The Texas Idea

1. Scott, "The Diffusion," p. 1093.
2. Sibley, *The Port of Houston*, pp. 125–126, 167–168.

3. *Houston Post*, November 5, 1902, March 6, 12, 1904.

4. Ibid., February 18, 1905.

5. City of Houston, *Minutes*, October–November 1904; *Houston Chronicle* and *Houston Post*, October–November 1904.

6. *Houston Chronicle*, November 2, 1904.

7. *Houston Post*, December 9, 1904.

8. *Houston Chronicle*, October 26, 1904; Harold Lawrence Platt, "Urban Public Services and Private Enterprise" (Ph.D. diss.), pp. 183–197.

9. *Houston Post*, September 7, November 1, 1904; *Houston Chronicle*, November 6, 1904.

10. *Houston Chronicle*, January 12, 1905.

11. *Houston Post*, November 10, 1904.

12. George W. James, "Houston and Its City Commission," *Arena* 38 (August 1907): 146; *Houston Post*, October 31–November 20, 1904; *Houston Chronicle*, November 13, 26, December 1, 1904.

13. Houston, *Minutes*, December 12, 1904; *Houston Chronicle*, December 1, 1904; *Houston Post*, December 11, 1904; Platt, "Urban Public Services," pp. 183, 194.

14. *Houston Post*, December 13 (quoting Jones), 21, 1904; *Houston Chronicle*, December 18, 21, 1904; Houston, *Minutes*, January 9, 1905.

15. Houston, *Minutes*, January–February 1905; *Houston Post*, January 8–February 20, 1905; *Houston Chronicle*, February 17, 1905; Platt, "Urban Public Services," p. 194.

16. *Houston Post*, February 18–21, 1905; Houston, *Minutes*, February 20, 1905.

17. *Houston Post*, February 22, 1905.

18. Ibid., February 23, 1905.

19. Ibid.

20. Ibid., March 1–11, April 8–May 7, 1905; 29th Texas Legislature, *Journal of the House of Representatives* (Austin, 1905), pp. 439–1103; 29th Texas Legislature, *Journal of the Senate* (Austin, 1905), pp. 381–883.

21. *Houston Post*, May 16, 1905; *Houston Chronicle*, May 27, 1905.

22. *Houston Post* and *Houston Chronicle*, May 1905.

23. *Houston Chronicle*, May 27, 1905; *Houston Post*, May 30–31, June 28, 1905; Houston, *Minutes*, May 15, June 19, July 5, 1905.

24. City of Houston, *Mayor's Annual Message and Department Reports* (Houston, 1906), p. 11.

25. Houston Business League, *Houston: The Commercial Capital of Texas* (Houston, 1906), [p. 25]; *Dallas Morning News*, March 25, 1906 (quoting editor of *Houston Chronicle*).

26. *Dallas Morning News*, March 25, 1906 (quoting Ball); W. B. Slosson, "Government by Commission in Texas," *Independent*, July 25, 1907, p. 199.

27. Houston Business League, *Houston*, p. 25; *Houston Chronicle*, May 23, 25, 1905; *Dallas Morning News*, March 7, 1906.

28. H. J. Haskell, "The Texas Idea: City Government by a Board of Directors," *Outlook*, April 13, 1907, p. 839–843; "The Texas Idea," ibid., pp. 834–835.

29. *Fort Worth Record*, April 2, 1907.

30. City of Dallas, *Minute Book*, January 23, 1906; City of Fort Worth, *Minutes of the City Council*, February 19, 1906.

31. *Denison Herald*, December 4, 1906; Haskell, "Texas Idea," p. 843; Houston Business League, *Houston*, p. 25.

32. *Dallas Morning News*, January 7, April 4–18, 1906; Dallas, *Minute Book*, January 23, April 17, 1906.

33. Fort Worth, *Minutes*, February 19, 1906; *Fort Worth Record*, July 26, 1906, March 28, April 3, 1907; *Dallas Morning News*, March 31, 1906.

34. *El Paso Herald*, January 19, April 13, 1907; *El Paso Evening News*, November 17, 1906–April 13, 1907; 30th Texas Legislature, *Journal of the House of Representatives* (Austin, 1907), pp. 951–1063; 30th Texas Legislature, *Journal of the Senate* (Austin, 1907), pp. 295, 338.

35. *Dallas Morning News*, February 2, March 30, 1906; *Denison Herald*, December 3–20, 1906, January 1–5, March 1–8, 1907; *Denison Sunday Gazetteer*, December 23, 1906, February 3, 1907; 30th Texas Legislature, *Journal of the House*, pp. 951–1063; 30th Texas Legislature, *Journal of the Senate*, pp. 504–598.

36. 30th Texas Legislature, *Journal of the House*, pp. 711–956; 30th Texas Legislature, *Journal of the Senate*, 504–598.

37. *Houston Chronicle*, January 6, 1905.

38. *Austin Daily Statesman*, September 5, 1908.

39. Ruth Ann Overbeck, *Alexander Penn Wooldridge*, pp. 44–46; Stuart A. MacCorkle, *Austin's Three Forms of Government*, pp. 27–43; Harold A. Stone et al., *City Manager Government in Austin (Texas)*, pp. 3–7.

40. *Denison Herald*, April 4–17, 1907; *Denison Sunday Gazetteer*, February 3, 1907.

41. Paul E. Isaacs, "Municipal Reform in Beaumont, Texas, 1902–1909," *Southwestern Historical Quarterly* 78 (April 1975): 409–430.

42. *Fort Worth Record*, March 29, 1907.

43. Lu Stephens to S. J. Dillon, May 9, 1907, quoted in *Des Moines Register and Leader*, June 3, 1907; Edwin Clyde Robbins, comp., *Selected Articles on the Commission Plan of Municipal Government*, pp. 154–156; Richard G. Miller, "Fort Worth and the Progressive Era: The Movement for Charter Revision, 1899–1907," in *Essays on Urban America*, ed. Margaret F. Morris and Elliott West, pp. 89–126.

44. Houston, *Minutes*, December 12, 1904; *Houston Post*, November 5, December 11, 1904.

45. *Dallas Morning News*, March 18, 1906; Dallas, *Minute Book*, April 17, 1907.

46. Philip Lindsley, *A History of Greater Dallas and Vicinity*, p. 311.

47. Citizens' Association, *Charter of the City of Dallas* (Dallas, 1907), [pp. i, iii]; *Dallas Morning News*, January 1, March 1–22, 1907.

48. *Denison Herald*, January 14, 17, 1907.

49. *El Paso Evening News*, January 25, 1907.

50. *Denison Herald*, April 9, 1907; *Denison Sunday Gazetteer*, February 3, 1907.

51. See Richard M. Bernard and Bradley R. Rice, "Political Environment and the Adoption of Progressive Municipal Reform," *Journal of Urban History* 1 (February 1975): 149–174.

52. Bradford, *Commission Government*; Chang, *History and Analysis*.

53. *Dallas Morning News*, March 13, 1907.

54. "Paper by Mr. Powell," *City Hall* 12 (September 1910): 101.

55. City of Dallas, *Annual Reports, 1906–1907* (Dallas, 1907), p. 16.

56. *Dallas Morning News*, October 1, 1910.

57. "Paper by Mr. Powell," p. 102.

58. Clinton Rogers Woodruff, ed., *City Government by Commission*, p. 225.

59. "City Government by Commission," *City Hall* 10 (March 1909): 318.

60. Albert Bushnell Hart, "Observations on Texas Cities," in *City Government by Commission*, ed. Woodruff, pp. 227–241.

61. Illinois General Assembly, Senate Committee on Municipalities, *Report Made to Senate, April 15, 1909 by Special Subcommittee (to investigate the operation of the commission form of City Government in the Cities of Galveston, Houston, and Dallas)*, pp. 10–11.

62. *Galveston Daily News*, September 27, 1906; *Dallas Morning News*, March 13, 27, 1907.

63. James Bryce to Sir Edward Grey, July 8, 1909, British Embassy Papers, vol. 28, Bryce Papers; Bryce to Grey, July 22, 1907, British Foreign Office 371/357; Houston Business League, *Houston*, p. 25.
64. H. D. Slater, "El Paso Today," in *The 1911 Report of the El Paso Chamber of Commerce* (El Paso, 1911), p. 8.
65. *Denison Herald*, April 4, 1907.
66. "Spread of the Galveston Plan," *Literary Digest*, July 13, 1907, p. 42 (quoting the *Houston Post*); "Explanatory," *Progressive Houston*, May 1909, p. 3.
67. *Galveston Daily News*, April 18, 1909; Chang, *History and Analysis*, p. 105.
68. Citizens' Association, *Charter of the City of Dallas*, p. iii.
69. *Dallas Morning News*, October 1, 1910.
70. Ibid.

3. The Des Moines Plan

1. U.S. Bureau of the Census, 13th Census, 1910, *Reports by States, Iowa* (Washington, D.C.: Government Printing Office, 1913), pp. 636–641; Hamilton, *The Dethronement*, p. 26.
2. Ibid.; P. H. Ryan, *Foxy Government*, p. 15.
3. "The American City, the Storm Center in the Battle for Good Government," *Arena* 38 (October 1907): 433–434; Hamilton, *The Dethronement*, pp. 86–88.
4. James G. Berryhill, "The Des Moines Plan of Municipal Government," typescript, July 9, 1908, in Library, Iowa State Department of History and Archives.
5. *Des Moines Register and Leader*, November 9, 1905, March 13–29, April 2, 1906; Hamilton, *The Dethronement*, pp. 93–94.
6. Johnson Brigham, *Des Moines*, 1:397n., 2:236; Berryhill, "The Des Moines Plan"; James G. Berryhill, "City Government by Commission," *City Hall* 11 (June 1910): 368; *Des Moines Register and Leader*, April 10, 1906.
7. *Des Moines Register and Leader*, November 18, 1905.
8. Ibid., November 29, 1905–January 29, 1906; Hamilton, *The Dethronement*, pp. 105–106.
9. *Des Moines Register and Leader*, March 18, 1906.
10. Benjamin F. Shambaugh, "Commission Government in Iowa: The Des Moines Plan" *The Annals* 38 (November 1911): 31.
11. Berryhill, "The Des Moines Plan," p. 4; *Des Moines Register and Leader*, December 17, 1905, January 21–29, March 18, 1906.
12. *Des Moines Register and Leader*, September 13, 1906.
13. Ibid., April 8, 1906.
14. Ibid., November 30, December 14–26, 1906, January 9, 15, 1907.
15. Ibid., January 10, 1907.
16. Ibid., January 13, 1907; Hamilton, *The Dethronement*, p. 109.
17. *Des Moines Register and Leader*, January 7, 1907.
18. [William H. Baily], "Forms of City Government," *BLAM* 7 (March 1907): 75; Berryhill, "The Des Moines Plan," pp. 4–5; Hamilton, *The Dethronement*, pp. 109–110; *Des Moines Register and Leader*, January–February 1, 1907.
19. *Des Moines Capital*, May 23, 1907, clipping in Frank Irving Herriott Scrapbooks; *Des Moines Register and Leader*, February 11, 1907 (quoting the *Des Moines News*).
20. *Des Moines Register and Leader*, February 7, 14, 18, March 5, June 7, 1907; Hamilton, *The Dethronement*, pp. 156–158.
21. "Comment," *Midland Municipalities* 11 (April 1906): 38.

22. "Comment," *Midland Municipalities* 10 (February 1906): 166.
23. Albert B. Cummins to John C. Hartman, March 29, 1907, Cummins Papers; *Des Moines Register and Leader*, March 9, 12, 1907.
24. Chang, *History and Analysis*, pp. 81–83; Berryhill, "The Des Moines Plan," p. 5; *Des Moines Register and Leader*, March 13–30, 1907.
25. *Des Moines Register and Leader*, March 30–April 23, May 5, 12, 1907.
26. Sidney J. Dillon to Harold Young, June 10, 1907, William Howard Taft Papers (microfilm); *Des Moines Register and Leader*, May–June 1907.
27. *Des Moines Register and Leader*, February 14, 1907.
28. George Kibbe Turner, "The New American City Government: The Des Moines Plan—A Triumph of Democracy. Its Spread across the United States," *McClure's Magazine* 35 (May 1910): 98; W. N. Jordan, "Some Facts and Figures," *Plain Talk* (Des Moines), January 16, 1907, reprinted in *Selected Articles*, comp. Robbins, pp. 160–169; *Des Moines News*, January 16, 1907, clipping in Herriott Scrapbooks.
29. *Des Moines Register and Leader*, March 11, 1907.
30. Ibid., June 16, 1907.
31. *Des Moines News*, undated clipping ca. May 1907, in Herriott Scrapbooks.
32. *Des Moines Register and Leader*, June 6, 1907 (quoting the *Cedar Rapids Gazette*).
33. Ibid., June 4, 1907.
34. J. S. Clark et al. to J. A. T. Hull, June 16, 1907, J. A. T. Hull Papers.
35. *Des Moines Tribune*, various clippings in Herriott Scrapbooks.
36. F. I. Herriott and Harvey Ingham, "Should Iowa Adopt the Commission System of City Government?" typescript of a debate, January 12, 1907, Library, Iowa State Department of History and Archives.
37. *Des Moines Register and Leader*, May 1, 31, June 9, 14, 17, 20, 1907.
38. Seth Low to W. H. Wiseman, June 11, 1907, Low Papers.
39. *Des Moines Register and Leader*, May 1, 31, June 14, 20, 1907.
40. "Organized Labor Opposed to Commission Plan," *Iowa Unionist*, April 12, 1907, reprinted in *Selected Articles*, comp. Robbins, p. 156; "The American City, the Storm Center," p. 434; *Des Moines Register and Leader*, March 18, June 8, 14, 1907.
41. Citizens' Committee, *The Proposed Galveston–Des Moines Plan for City Government* (Des Moines, [1907]), [p. 1].
42. *Plain Talk* (Des Moines), June 1, 1907, in Herriott Scrapbooks; *Des Moines Register and Leader*, November 29, 1905, March 6, April 5–May 31, June 8, 1907.
43. *Des Moines Tribune*, undated clipping ca. May 1907, in Herriott Scrapbooks.
44. *Des Moines Register and Leader*, May 9, 1907.
45. Charles O. Holly, *Comments on the "Proposed Galveston–Des Moines Plan of Government,"* (Des Moines: Citizens' Committee, [1907]); Citizens' Committee, *The Proposed Galveston–Des Moines Plan*, "The American City, the Storm Center," p. 434; *Des Moines Register and Leader*, March–June 1907.
46. Sidney J. Dillon, "The Des Moines Plan," *City Club Bulletin* (Chicago), December 18, 1907, pp. 291–292.
47. John MacVicar to John B. Lucas, October 25, 1907, MacVicar Papers in Sheets Collection. See also MacVicar to Walt Butler, October 25, 1907, and John J. Hamilton to MacVicar, October 18, 1907, MacVicar Papers.
48. Ibid.
49. Citizens' Committee, *The Proposed Galveston–Des Moines Plan*, p. 7; various clippings in Herriott Scrapbooks, February–May 1907.
50. Holly, *Comments*, p. 3.
51. *Des Moines Register and Leader*, May 21, 27–28, June 2, 5, 1907.
52. Citizens' Committee, *The Proposed Galveston–Des Moines Plan*, p. 4.

53. Holly, *Comments*, p. 2.

54. "Dominant Mayor Essential in Good City Government," *Plain Talk* (Des Moines), February 2, 1907, reprinted in *Selected Articles*, comp. Robbins, p. 173.

55. Jordan, "Some Facts and Figures," p. 167.

56. *Des Moines Tribune*, May 23, 1907, in Herriott Scrapbooks; *Des Moines Register and Leader*, January 28, February 28, March 6, April 25, May 6, 1907.

57. Dillon to Young, June 10, 1907, Taft Papers; *Des Moines Capital*, May 21, 1907, in Herriott Scrapbooks; *Des Moines Register and Leader*, April 25, May 6, 30, June 9, 1907.

58. Greater Des Moines Committee Records, vol. 1, March 27, 1907.

59. Citizens' Club, *Proposed Galveston–Des Moines Plan*; Holly, *Comments*; Dillon, "The Des Moines Plan," p. 293; Dillon to Young, June 10, 1907, Taft Papers; various clippings in Robbins, comp., *Selected Articles*, and Herriott Scrapbooks.

60. *Des Moines Tribune*, undated clipping ca. May 1907, in Herriott Scrapbooks.

61. *Des Moines Register and Leader*, February 28, 1907.

62. Ibid., January 9, 1907.

63. Des Moines Handbill Collection.

64. John MacVicar to Walt Butler, October 25, 1907, Butler to MacVicar, November 9, 1907, MacVicar to Butler, November 7, 1907, MacVicar Papers; *Des Moines Tribune*, June 14, 19, 1907, clippings in Herriott Scrapbooks; June 15, 1907, clipping in MacVicar Papers in Sheets Collection.

65. *Des Moines Register and Leader*, June 21, 1907.

66. *S. A. Eckerson, et al. v. City of Des Moines et al.*, Brief and Argument of Appellees, Library, Iowa State Department of History and Archives; Dillon, "The Des Moines Plan," p. 293; Shambaugh, "Commission Government in Iowa," pp. 45–46; Chang, *History and Analysis*, pp. 94–95.

67. Brigham, *Des Moines*, 1:402–403; Hamilton, *The Dethronement*, pp. 158–164.

68. Hamilton, *The Dethronement*, p. 161

69. John J. Hamilton to John MacVicar, November 15, 20, 23, 1907, MacVicar Papers; *Des Moines News*, January 22, March 11, 1908, clippings in MacVicar Papers in Sheets Collection; Brigham, *Des Moines*, 1:402–403; Turner, "The New American City Government," p. 100.

70. Turner, "The New American City Government," p. 100.

71. MacVicar to Frank E. Lyman, October 22, 1907, MacVicar Papers.

72. Hays, "The Politics of Reform," p. 160.

73. Greater Des Moines Committee Records, vol. 3, April 27, 1908.

74. Greater Des Moines Committee, *Des Moines Means Opportunity* (Des Moines, 1907), p. 51.

75. Des Moines Commercial Club, *Des Moines Plan of City Government* (Des Moines, [1907]), p. 3.

76. "The Des Moines Plan of City Government," *BLAM* 8 (July 1907): 17; *Des Moines Register and Leader*, December 25, 1905.

4. The Diffusion of a Progressive Idea

1. William Bennett Munro, "Ten Years of Commission Government," *NMR* 1 (October 1912): 563. See Scott, "The Diffusion."

2. "Kansas Adopts Commision Bill," *BLAM* 7 (March 1907): 85; Frank G. Bates, "Commission Government in Kansas," *The Annals* 38 (November 1911): 49–55.

3. The information on charter laws for chapter 4 and tables 4 and 5 comes mainly from

Chang, *History and Analysis*; Beard, ed., *Loose Leaf Digest*; "A Summary of State General Laws and Constitutional Provisions Concerning Municipal Organization," *Equity* 18 (October 1916): 181–309; and various notes and articles in *Short Ballot Bulletin, National Municipal Review, City Hall, American City, American Political Science Review*, and other periodicals. See Bradley R. Rice, "The Rise and Fall of the Galveston–Des Moines Plan" (Ph.D. diss.).

4. Commonwealth of Massachusetts, *Commission Government in American Cities*, bulletin no. 12 of the Constitutional Convention of 1917, pp. 17–21; De Mont Goodyear, "Example of Haverhill," *Independent*, January 28, 1909, pp. 194–195.

5. Illinois General Assembly, Senate Committee on Municipalities, *Report Made to Senate, April 15, 1909 by Special Subcommittee*; John A. Fairlie, "Commission Government in Illinois Cities," *The Annals* 38 (November 1911): 78–86.

6. Oswald Ryan, *Municipal Freedom*, pp. 36–47.

7. Bruere, *The New City Government*, p. 17.

8. Woodruff, ed., *City Government by Commission*, p. 1.

9. A. M. Fuller, "Commission Government for All Third Class Cities of Pennsylvania," *American City* 9 (August 1913): 123–124.

10. Munro, "Ten Years," pp. 562–563.

11. Jones, "The Des Moines Plan of Municipal Government," p. 15.

12. "Spread of the Galveston Plan," p. 42.

13. Library of Congress, *Select List of References on Commission Government for Cities, 1913*, supplements, October 8, 1917, and February 21, 1920; New York State Library, "Commission Government for Cities," April 22, 1909, NML Files— Commission Government; MacGregor, *City Government by Commission*; *Commission Plan of City Government*, bulletin of University of Wisconsin, serial no. 259: general series no. 141, November 1908.

14. James Bryce to Sir Edward Grey, July 8, 1909, British Embassy Papers, vol. 28, Bryce Papers.

15. "Roosevelt Goes to Work for Us," *SBB* 1 (April 1911): 3.

16. William Codman, "Commission Government for Cities," in Minnesota Academy of Social Science, *Papers and Proceedings of the Fifth Annual Meeting* (Minneapolis, 1912), p. 86.

17. "Paper by Mr. Powell," p. 101.

18. Griffith, *A History: The Progressive Years*, p. 159.

19. Herbert Croly, *Progressive Democracy*, p. 287.

20. Martin J. Schiesl, "The Politics of Efficiency" (Ph.D. diss.).

21. "City Government by Commission, Statement of the Allied Civic Bodies of Pennsylvania," *City Hall* 12 (November 1910): 193.

22. Asa Briggs, *Victorian Cities*, pp. 204–205.

23. Denver Chamber of Commerce, *Reports of the Special Committee on Commission Form of Government*, September 30, 1911, p. 6.

24. MacGregor, *City Government by Commission*, p. 17.

25. Carl Dehoney, "Commission Government and Democracy," *American City* 2 (February 1910): 76.

26. "The Fight for Better Government in Kansas City," *City Hall* 11 (July 1909): 9–10.

27. Melvin P. Porter, "The Buffalo Charter," *NMR* 6 (January 1917): 79–84; Christie Benet, "A Campaign for a Commission Form of Government," *American City* 3 (December 1910): 276–278; Garin Burbank, "Socialism in an Oklahoma Boomtown: 'Milwaukeeizing' Oklahoma City," in *Socialism and the Cities*, ed. Bruce M. Stave, pp. 99–115; Bates, "Commission Government in Kansas."

28. "Spreading the Commission Idea," *Literary Digest*, April 26, 1913, pp. 934–935 (quoting Wilson); "Trenton Adopts Commission Government," *American City* 5 (July 1911): 35; Michael H. Ebner, "Socialism and Progressive Political Reform: The 1911 Change-of-Government in Passaic, New Jersey," in *Socialism and the Cities*, ed. Stave, pp. 116–140; Richard J. Conners, "Politics and Economics in Frank Hague's Jersey City," in *New Jersey since 1860*, ed. William Wright, p. 79; James Kerney, *The Political Education of Woodrow Wilson*, p. 112.

29. "Progress of Commission Government in New Jersey," *American City* 12 (October 1913): 361.

30. P. A. Randall to William Allen White, May 2, 1910, White Papers; William L. Bowers, "Davenport, Iowa, 1906–1907: A Glimpse into a City's Past," *Annals of Iowa* 38 (Summer 1966): 363–387; Commercial Club of Peoria, Illinois, *Proceedings of the Annual Meeting January 1909* (Peoria, 1909); [Walter M. Walker], "A Returned Visitor's View of Des Moines," *City Hall* 12 (July 1910): 26–27; A. M. Fuller, "Speech to Pittsburgh Chamber of Commerce," January 14, 1909, in MacVicar Papers; M. L. Blumenthal, "How Pittsburgh Got Half a Loaf," *Saturday Evening Post*, January 27, 1912, pp. 3–5; Chang, *History and Analysis*, p. 149; Tom M. Deaton, "The Chamber of Commerce in the Economic and Political Development of Atlanta from 1900 to 1916," *Atlanta Historical Bulletin* 19 (1975): 26–32; Martin J. Schiesl, "Progressive Reform in Los Angeles under Mayor Alexander: 1909–1913," *California Historical Quarterly* 54 (Spring 1975): 49.

31. J. Paul Mitchel, "Boss Speer and the City Functional: Boosters and Businessmen vs. Commission Government in Denver," *Pacific Northwest Quarterly* 63 (October 1972): 155–164; R. D. Leigh, "Commission Government Ratified in Portland, Oregon," *NMR* 7 (January 1918): 90–91; "Sacramento Sustains Commission Government," *NMR* 6 (May 1917): 418–419.

32. Clarence Kendall, "The City Government of Galveston," *University of Texas Record*, March 15, 1907, pp. 186–191; H. D. W. English, *The Functions of Business Bodies in Improving Civic Conditions* (Philadelphia: National Municipal League, 1909), p. 4.

33. Lyle W. Dorsett, "The City Boss and the Reformer: A Reappraisal," *Pacific Northwest Quarterly* 63 (October 1972): 150–154.

34. Williams, "Governing Cities by Commission," pp. 943–946.

35. Ryan, *Municipal Freedom*, p. 83.

36. "City Government by Commission, Statement of the Allied Civic Bodies," p. 193.

37. William Allen White to Richard S. Childs, September 24, 1910, White Papers.

38. *Fort Worth Record*, March 31, April 2, 1907.

39. Haskell, "The Texas Idea," p. 839.

40. "Two Views of Commission Government."

41. Jones, "The Des Moines Plan."

42. J. R. Hornaday, "Amazing Growth of a New Idea," *Uncle Remus's Home Magazine* 28 (March 1911): 9.

43. Oswald Ryan, "Commission Government Described," in *City Government by Commission*, ed. Woodruff, pp. 75–76.

44. Woodruff, ed., *City Government by Commission*, p. 41.

45. Bruere, *The New City Government*, pp. 88–90; Munro, "Ten Years," p. 564.

46. Munro, "Ten Years," p. 564.

47. Ibid.; Ryan, *Municipal Freedom*, p. 75; Ernest S. Bradford, "Commission Government and City Planning," *American City* 7 (August 1912): 114.

48. Bruere, *The New City Government*, pp. 380–381.

49. Ibid.

50. Ibid., p. 379.

51. Benet, "A Campaign," 276.

52. Beard, ed., *Loose Leaf Digest*, p. 74505.

53. Denver Chamber of Commerce, *Reports of the Special Committee*, p. 10.

54. Hamilton, *The Dethronement*, p. 23.

55. Martin A. Gemunder, "Commission Government: Its Strength and Its Weakness," *NMR* 1 (August 1912): 192.

56. "The Relation of Charter Forms to Municipal Improvements," *American City* 6 (April 1912): 647–650.

57. Beard, ed., *Loose Leaf Digest*, p. 74508.

58. *Quincy (Illinois) Optic*, August 20, 1910, in MacVicar Papers Scrapbooks.

59. Bruere, *The New City Government*, p. 70.

60. MacGregor, *City Government by Commission*, pp. 96–97.

61. Ernest S. Bradford, "Financial Results under the Commission Form of City Government," *NMR* 1 (July 1912): 372–377.

62. Ibid., p. 374.

63. "Big Commission Government Gains," *SBB* 2 (June 1913): 3.

64. A. P. Wooldridge, "The Commission as It Operates in Austin, Texas," *The Annals* 38 (November 1911): 237.

65. Carlos C. Alden, quoted in Lamar T. Beman, comp., *Selected Articles on Current Problems in Municipal Government*, pp. 328–329.

66. Beard, ed., *Loose Leaf Digest*, p. 76022.

67. John MacVicar to Gifford Pinchot, May 28, 1910, Pinchot Papers; MacVicar to Charles J. Bonaparte, May 2, 1910, Bonaparte Papers.

68. Bureau of the Census, *Comparative Financial Statistics of Cities under Council and Commission Government*. See "Commission Government Efficiency," *NMR* 3 (October 1914): 767; Kenneth Paul Fox, "The Census Bureau and the Cities" (Ph.D. diss.). On city size as the dominant variable explaining municipal expenditures, see Melvin G. Holli, "Urban Reform in the Progressive Era," in *The Progressive Era*, ed. Lewis L. Gould; and J. Rogers and Ellen J. Hollingsworth, "Expenditures in American Cities," in *The Dimensions of Quantitative Research in History*, ed. William O. Aydelotte et al.

69. P. J. Seberger, "Municipal Improvements and Lower Taxes under the Commission Form," *American City* 12 (February 1915): 106–110.

5. Direct Democracy, At-Large Election, and the Short Ballot

1. Clipping, dateline Galesburg, Ill., May 24, 1909, in MacVicar Papers Scrapbooks.

2. Charles F. Taylor, "The March of Democracy in Municipalities," *NMR* 2 (April 1913): 196.

3. Ryan, *Municipal Freedom*, p. 24.

4. Munro, "Ten Years," p. 563; Bruere, *The New City Government*, p. 41.

5. William Allen White to V. E. Sayre, April 11, 1911, White Papers; John J. Hannan to Frank Butler, January 27, 1911, Robert M. LaFollette Papers; "Address by Brand Whitlock on the Commission Form of City Government," ca. 1910, Whitlock Papers; "The American City, the Storm Center," pp. 429–436.

6. "Robert Treat Paine, Jr., "On the Progress of Direct Legislation in American Munici-

pal Government," *Arena* 41 (January 1909): 109; Taylor, "The March of Democracy," p. 194.

7. Berryhill, "City Government by Commission," p. 370; *Fort Worth Record*, April 2, 1907; *Dallas Morning News*, March 3, 21, 1907, October 1, 1910; Miller, "Fort Worth and the Progressive Era," pp. 89–126; Burbank, "Socialism in an Oklahoma Boom-town," pp. 99–115; "Experiments in Municipal Government," *Outlook*, July 4, 1908, pp. 496–497.

8. "City Government by Commission," *City Hall* 12 (November 1910): 194.

9. Denver Chamber of Commerce, *Reports of the Special Committee*, p. 14; [Baily], "Forms of City Government," pp. 71–76; Ryan, *Municipal Freedom*, p. 13.

10. "A Summary of State General Laws."

11. "Paper by Mr. Powell," p. 101; Citizens' Committee of Des Moines, *The Proposed Galveston–Des Moines Plan for City Government* (Des Moines, 1907), p. 7.

12. Ryan, *Foxy Government*, pp. 79–80.

13. Kempner, "The Drama of the Commission Plan," p. 412; *An Address of H. B. Rice on the Commission Form of Government, November 18, 1908* (Houston, 1908); E. R. Cheesborough, "Galveston's Commission Plan of City Government," *The Annals* 38 (November 1911): 228; "Papers and Discussions on Municipal Government by Board (or Commission) vs. Mayor and Council," *BLAM* 8 (October 1907): 112.

14. Lewis L. Gould, *Progressives and Prohibitionists*, pp. 78, 87; Chang, *History and Analysis*, p. 126.

15. Dillon, "The Des Moines Plan." See Edwin M. Bacon and Morrill Wyman, *Direct Elections and Law-Making by Popular Vote*; and William B. Munro, ed., *The Initiative, Referendum, and Recall*.

16. National Municipal League, *Commission Plan and Commission-Manager Plan of Municipal Government*, pp. 7–8; Bruere, *The New City Government*, p. 72.

17. S. J. Dillon to Harold Young, June 10, 1907, William Howard Taft Papers (microfilm); "City Government by Commission," *City Hall* 11 (March 1910): 288; H. S. Gilbertson, "The Practice of Recall," in *Loose Leaf Digest*, ed. Beard, pp. 21801–21804; William Allen White to Richard S. Childs, September 24, 1910, White Papers.

18. "City Government by Commission," *City Hall* 10 (March 1909): 317; *Dallas Morning News*, October 1, 1910; A. J. Mathis, "Eighteen Months Trial of the Des Moines Plan," *City Hall* 11 (November 1909): 166–173.

19. Cheesborough, "Galveston's Commission Plan," p. 220.

20. Clinton Rogers Woodruff, "The Socialists and the Commission Form of Government," *NMR* 2 (January 1913): 133; "How the Short Ballot Helps Real Parties," *SBB* 1 (August 1911): 4.

21. "City Government by Commission," *City Hall*, 10 (March 1909): 317; Denver Chamber of Commerce, *Reports of the Special Committee*, p. 5; Mathis, "Eighteen Months Trial," p. 168; Hamilton, *The Dethronement*, p. 41.

22. *An Address of H. B. Rice*, p. 2; Hamilton, *The Dethronement*, p. 45.

23. Charles D. Huston, "Municipal Government by Commission," *City Hall* 10 (January 1909): 255.

24. "Commission Plan of City Government," *City Hall* 10 (February 1909): 285.

25. Oswald Ryan, "Revolutionary Movement in City Government," *New England Magazine* n.s. 45 (November 1911): 253–257.

26. Denver Chamber of Commerce, *Reports of the Special Committee*, p. 5; Shambaugh, "Commission Government in Iowa," pp. 9–10.

27. *Passaic Issue*, October 1911, quoted in Ebner, "Socialism and Progressive Political Reform"; Hamilton, *The Dethronement*, pp. 111–124; Robbins, comp., *Selected Articles*, pp. 46–57; Beard, *American City Government*, p. 96. See Robert R. Alford and Eugene C. Lee, "Voting Turnout in American Cities," *American Political Science Review* 62 (September 1968): 796–813; Robert Salisbury and Gordon Black, "Class and Party in Partisan and Nonpartisan Elections: The Case of Des Moines," *American Political Science Review* 57 (September 1963): 584–592.
28. Ryan, *Foxy Government*, p. 21.
29. *Omaha Bee*, October 2, 1908, in MacVicar Papers Scrapbooks.
30. Seth Low to Thomas P. White, March 10, 1910, Low to George S. Bixby, November 25, 1910, Low Papers; Chang, *History and Analysis*, pp. 13–14.
31. *Dallas Morning News*, March 25, 1906; Denver Chamber of Commerce, *Reports of the Special Committee*, p. 6.
32. Richard S. Childs, *The Short Ballot* [1908]. See John Porter East, *Council-Manager Government*.
33. Childs, *The Short Ballot*, p. 14.
34. Ibid., p. 30.
35. Notebook of letters reacting to *The Short Ballot*, Childs Personal Papers.
36. Ibid.
37. "First Meeting [of the Short Ballot Organization], April 22, 1909," typed minutes, and "Chronology of the Short Ballot Movement," Childs Personal Papers; Childs Interviews. Childs to Woodrow Wilson, July 10, September 25, October 14, 25, December 4, 9, 13, 27, 30, 31, 1909; "To Advocates of the Short Ballot," October 1909; Childs to Advisory Board of the Short Ballot Organization, December 4, 1909, Woodrow Wilson Papers, series two (microfilm). Childs to William Allen White, December 4, 1909, January 24, February 3, 1910, and "Brief Statement Explaining the Proposed Short Ballot Organization," n.d., ca. 1909, White Papers.
38. Childs, *The Short Ballot*, p. 3; Short Ballot Organization, *Progress Report #2*, November 5, 1909, Childs Personal Papers.
39. Childs to Short Ballot Organization Advisory Board, November 15, 1909; Childs to Wilson, January 5, 1910, Wilson Papers, series two (microfilm); Richard S. Childs, "A Legacy from Woodrow Wilson," typescript, Childs Personal Papers; Richard S. Childs, "Woodrow Wilson Legacy," *NMR* 47 (January 1957): 14–19; Arthur S. Link, *Wilson: The Road to the White House*, pp. 123–126. Link argues that Wilson soon forgot the short ballot, but Childs disagrees, pointing to Childs-Wilson correspondence that continued to 1923.
40. Childs to Advisory Board, July 13, August 4, 16, 1910, Wilson Papers, series two (microfilm).
41. "Getting Commission Government in Your Town," *SBB* 1 (February 1911): 9.
42. Beard, ed., *Loose Leaf Digest*, p. 10201; "A Six Years' Review," *SBB* 3 (February 1916): 5.
43. "Roosevelt Goes to Work for Us," p. 3.
44. See *Short Ballot Bulletin*, 1911–1920.
45. Richard S. Childs, "The Ballot Is Still Too Long!" *NMR* 35 (February 1946): 67–70; Childs Interviews; see the selected list of Childs' publication in the bibliography.

6. Structural Weaknesses and Unmet Goals

1. "Municipal Government by Commission," *BLAM* 9 (February 1908): 37; Joseph A. Dear, "Adoptions and Rejections under the Commission Statute of New Jersey," *The Annals* 38 (November 1911): 108–110; James W. S. Peters, "The Commission Movement in Missouri," *The Annals* 38 (November 1911): 177; Charles M. Fassett, "The Weaknesses of Commission Government," *NMR* 9 (October 1920): 642–643.

2. Holli, *Reform in Detroit*, pp. 157–181; Buenker, *Urban Liberalism*.

3. Bruere, *The New City Government*, p. 87.

4. "Papers and Discussions on Municipal Government," *BLAM* 8 (October 1907): 113.

5. Vincent Starzinger, "City Not a Business Corporation," in *Selected Articles*, comp. Robbins, p. 120.

6. Agnes Thurnau, "Criticizes Des Moines Plan," *City Hall* 11 (February 1910): 251–252.

7. Minnesota Academy of Social Sciences, *Papers and Proceedings of the Fifth Annual Meeting* (Minneapolis, 1912), p. 112.

8. Holli, *Reform in Detroit*, pp. 169–170.

9. Haskell, "The Texas Idea," p. 840; H. C. Trousdale, "Municipal Ownership under the Commission Plan," *City Hall* 11 (August 1909): 38–39.

10. "The Re-election of the Mayor of Austin, Texas," *NMR* 4 (July 1915): 491.

11. Ernest S. Bradford, "Financial Results under the Commission Form"; William D. Miller, *Mr. Crump of Memphis*, pp. 60–103; Frederick W. Donnelly, "Securing Efficient Administration under the Commission Plan," *The Annals* 41 (May 1912): 218–232.

12. Bruere, *The New City Government*, p. 87.

13. "Socialists Oppose Commission Plan" *American Municipalities* 26 (February 1914): 151; Weinstein, *The Corporate Ideal*, pp. 107–108. See Stave, ed. *Socialism and the Cities*.

14. Woodruff, "The Socialists and the Commission Form," pp. 132–134.

15. *Des Moines Register and Leader*, February 4, 1907.

16. "Labor Leader Favors Commission Plan," *SBB* 3 (April 1915): 2; "What Labor Secretaries Say: Commission Government not 'Capitalistic,'" *SBB* 1 (October 1912): 3; Miller, "Fort Worth and the Progressive Era," pp. 89–126; Burbank, "Socialism in an Oklahoma Boom-town," pp. 99–115; Peoria, Illinois, Friends of Commission Government, *Commission Form of Municipal Government: Campaign Handbook* (Peoria [1911]), [pp. 20–21].

17. *Iowa Unionist*, December 23, 1910, in MacVicar Papers Scrapbooks.

18. *Denison Daily Herald*, January 17, 1907.

19. Samuel Peterson, "Some Fundamental Policy Principles Applied to Municipal Government," *Bulletin of the University of Texas*, June 1, 1905, no. 61, Humanistic Series, no. 4, p. 8.

20. "Municipal Government by Commission," *City Hall* 10 (January 1909): 258.

21. See Bernard and Rice, "Political Environment," pp. 149–174.

22. Childs, *The Story of the Short Ballot Cities*, (1914), p. 7; Beman, comp., *Selected Articles*, p. 330.

23. Walter G. Cooper, "Objections to Commission Government," *The Annals* 38 (November 1911): 188.

24. Herriott and Ingham, "Should Iowa Adopt the Commission System"; Ryan, *Municipal Freedom*, p. 86.

25. Clinton Rogers Woodruff, "Simplicity, Publicity, and Efficiency in Municipal Affairs," *NMR* 2 (January 1913): 1–10.

26. Gemunder, "Commission Government," p. 179.
27. "City Government by Commission," *City Hall* 12 (September 1910): 107.
28. "Dominant Mayor Essential in Good City Government," p. 172.
29. "Report of Norfolk Chamber of Commerce," *Municipal Engineering* 49 (August 1915): 52 (quoting Hanna); "Where the Commission Plan Fails," *SBB* 5 (February 1920): 8.
30. Mitchel, "Boss Speer and the City Functional"; H. S. Gilbertson, "Denver Goes Back," *American City* 14 (June 1916): 577–578 (quoting the *Denver Times*); E. C. MacMechen, "The Denver Reversion," *American City* 15 (August 1916): 133.
31. H. S. Gilbertson, "Some Serious Weaknesses of the Commission Plan," *American City* 9 (September 1913): 237.
32. Beard, ed., *Loose Leaf Digest*, p. 76014.
33. Oswald Ryan, "The Real Problem of Commission Government," *Popular Science Monthly*, September 1912, p. 282.
34. Lewis J. Johnson, "Commission Government for Cities: Election to Specific Office vs. Election at Random," *NMR* 2 (October 1913): 661.
35. Ibid., p. 663; "Municipal Election at Dallas, Texas," *NMR* 4 (July 1915): 490.
36. "Commission Government and Efficiency," typescript ca. 1915, NML Files—Commission Government.
37. Dunbar F. Carpenter, "Some Defects of Commission Government," *The Annals* 38 (November 1911): 199.
38. Arthur Harris, *City Manager Government in Berkeley (California)*, pp. 6–7; George A. Miller, *City Manager Government in Long Beach (California)*, p. 5; Chang, *History and Analysis*, p. 18.
39. "Municipal Election at Dallas," p. 490; Munro, "Ten Years," pp. 565–566.
40. Richard Spencer Childs, *Short Ballot Principles*, p. 71; Gilbertson, "Some Serious Weaknesses," p. 237.
41. "Commission Government and Efficiency"; Gilbertson, "Some Serious Weaknesses," p. 236.
42. Gemunder, "Commission Government," p. 174.
43. Denver Chamber of Commerce, *Reports of the Special Committee*, p. 15.
44. Bruere, *The New City Government*, pp. 93–97.
45. Richard S. Childs, "Will Commission Government Succeed in Large Cities?" in *Loose Leaf Digest*, ed. Beard, p. 21401; Seth Low to George S. Bixby, November 25, 1910, Low Papers; Gemunder, "Commission Government," p. 172.
46. "Mayo Fesler Opposed to Commission Government," *American Municipalities* 26 (March 1914): 211.
47. Childs, "Will Commission Government Succeed in Large Cities?" p. 21401; Childs to Woodrow Wilson, January 5, 1910, Childs to Short Ballot Organization Advisory Board, July 13, 1910, Woodrow Wilson Papers, series two (microfilm); John MacVicar, "Will Commission Government Succeed in Large Cities?— Yes," in *Loose Leaf Digest*, ed. Beard, pp. 21403–21404; S. S. McClure, "The Tammanyizing of Civilization," *McClure's Magazine* 34 (November 1909): 117–128.
48. James B. Crooks, *Politics and Progress*, pp. 104–107; "Boston Considers the Des Moines Plan," *BLAM* 9 (January 1908): 26.
49. L. G. Powers, "Budget Provisions in Commission-Governed Cities," *The Annals* 38 (November 1911): 128–137; Elliot H. Goodwin, "Civil Service Provisions in Commission Charters," *The Annals* 38 (November 1911): 138–145; Bradford, "Commission Government in City Planning," pp. 113–116; Delos F. Wilcox, "Franchise Provisions in Commission Charters and Statutes," *The Annals* 38

(November 1911): 113–127; "Commission Government for the Public Health," *World's Work* 27 (March 1914): 495–496.

50. Bruere, *The New City Government*, pp. vi, xi–xii, 103, 129, 232; see Jane S. Dahlberg, *The New York Bureau of Municipal Research*, p. 77.
51. "Commission Plan Proves a Failure," *Tax Association Bulletin* (Oakland, California), September 1913, p. 3; "Condemns Commission Plan," *American Municipalities* 26 (December 1913): 93; H. S. Gilbertson, "Commission Government," *NMR* 2 (October 1913): 680; Gilbertson, "Some Serious Weaknesses."
52. Gemunder, "Commission Government," pp. 177–179.
53. "Experts Discuss the Des Moines Plan," *City Hall* 10 (June 1909): 413.
54. Herman G. James, "The Recent Overturn in Houston," *NMR* 2 (August 1913): 491; "The Man Not the Plan," *American Municipalities* 26 (January 1914): 111–112.
55. Fassett, "The Weakness of Commission of Government," pp. 642–647.
56. *Galveston Tribune*, April 2, 1901.
57. Cooper, "Objections to Commission Government," p. 185.
58. *Fort Worth Record*, March 18, 1907.
59. See chapter 4.
60. Ryan, *Foxy Government*, p. 3.
61. Dorsett, "The City Boss and the Reformer."
62. "Bossing the Boss in Trenton," Short Ballot Organization Press Release, November 27, 1911, copy found in University of Colorado Library's copy of Beard, ed., *Loose Leaf Digest*; Mitchel, "Boss Speer and the City Functional."
63. Ethel Hutson, "New Orleans' Experience under Commission Government," *NMR* 6 (January 1917): 73–79; George M. Reynolds, *Machine Politics in New Orleans, 1897–1926*, pp. 104–106, 225; Beman, ed., *Selected Articles*, p. 367.
64. Mark Foster, "Frank Hague of Jersey City: The Boss as Reformer," *New Jersey History* 86 (Summer 1968): 106–117; Richard J. Conners, "The Local Political Career of Mayor Frank Hague" (Ph.D. diss.), pp. 21–22, 39–46, 290–292; Dayton D. McKean, *The Boss*, p. 37; Dayton D. McKean, "Hague's Domain Revisited," *NMR* 40 (March 1951): 135–140.
65. Miller, *Mr. Crump*, pp. 54–100.
66. John E. Bebout to Mrs. Robert Meals, January 25, 1950, NML Files—Commission Government.

7. A Transition Role

1. Richard Spencer Childs, *Civic Victories*, p. 140.
2. *The Municipal Year Book, 1976*, table 3. There are 3,868 cities over 5,000 of which 1,801 are mayor-council, 1,690 are council-manager, 163 are commission, and 214 are various town-meeting types.
3. "Twilight of Commission Government," *NMR* 38 (September 1949): 376.
4. Richard J. Stillman II, *The Rise of the City Manager*, p. 14; Griffith, *A History: The Progressive Years*, pp. 164–165; Herriott and Ingham, "Should Iowa Adopt the Commission System"; Chang, *History and Analysis*, pp. 161–162; Ford H. MacGregor, "Commision Government in the West," *The Annals* 38 (November 1911): 73.
5. Stone et al., *City Manager Government*, pp. 8–9.
6. John Crosby, "Municipal Government Administered by a General Manager—The Staunton Plan," *The Annals* 38 (November 1911): 207–213; "A Municipal Man-

ager in Staunton, Virginia," *City Hall* 10 (August 1909): 348–349; John Crosby, "Staunton's General Manager," *Municipal Journal and Engineer*, December 29, 1909, pp. 954–956; Ernest S. Bradford, "A Municipal Business Manager in Staunton, Virginia," *Municipal Engineering* 36 (May 1909): 279–280; Robert G. Hiden, "Running a Town as a Business: A General Manager in Staunton, Virginia," *Harper's Weekly*, May 21, 1910, pp. 13–14.

7. Stone et al., *City Manager Government*, p. 10; Childs, *Civic Victories*, pp. 144–145; East, *Council-Manager Government*, pp. 70, 76.

8. F. D. Silvernail, "The Lockport Proposal," *The Annals* 38 (November 1911): 214; Stillman, *The Rise of the City Manager*, p. 16; "The Lockport Plan," *SBB* 1 (February 1911): 6–7; Richard S. Childs, "The Lockport Proposal: A City That Wants to Improve the 'Commission Plan,'" *American City* 4 (June 1911): 285–287.

9. Ibid.; Beard, ed., *Loose Leaf Digest*.

10. Stone et al., *City Manager Government*, pp. 11–12; Denver Chamber of Commerce, *Reports of the Special Committee*, p. 1; "Newspapers Get Ahead of the Facts: 'Lockport Plan' Grows Marvelously," *SBB* 1 (June 1911): 7.

11. "Governor Wilson's Big Class: Teaching Short Ballot to the Westerners," *SBB* 1 (June 1911): 4; Childs, *Civic Victories*, p. 145; Richard S. Childs Interviews.

12. East, *Council-Manager Government*, p. 77n.; Stone et al., *City Manager Government*, p. 12; Childs, *Civic Victories*, p. 145.

13. "Advertising for City Manager: Sumter Takes Step under the New Plan of Government," *SBB* 1 (October 1912): 2.

14. Ibid., p. 3.

15. Turner, "Galveston: A Business," pp. 610–620; Haskell, "The Texas Idea," pp. 839–843.

16. Childs, *Short-Ballot Principles*, p. 5.

17. "The Lockport Plan," p. 2.

18. Silvernail, "The Lockport Proposal," p. 215.

19. Dewitt, *The Progressive Movement*, p. 309.

20. Richard S. Childs, Henry M. Waite, et al., "Professional Standards and Professional Ethics in the New Profession of City Manager: A Discussion," *NMR* 5 (April 1916): 195–210; D. K. Price, "The Promotion of the City Manager Plan," *Public Opinion Quarterly* 5 (Winter 1941): 563–578.

21. Childs, "The Lockport Proposal," p. 286. Many of the professional managers envisioned a more active role for themselves; see Childs and Waite, "Professional Standards," and Stillman, *The Rise of the City Manager*, pp. 28–52.

22. Woodruff, ed., *City Government by Commission*, p. viii.

23. NML, *The Commission Plan and Commission-Manager Plan of Municipal Government*, p. 6.

24. Ibid., pp. 8–9.

25. Ibid., pp. 16–21.

26. Alfred Willoughby, *The Involved Citizen*, pp. 20–21. See Stewart, *A Half-Century of Municipal Reform*, pp. 50–53.

27. Lent Dayton Upson, *A Charter Primer* (Dayton: Bureau of Municipal Research, [1914]); Harry Aubrey Toumlin, Jr., *The City Manager*, pp. 1–6.

28. "Driving Politics out of Dayton," *Literary Digest*, January 24, 1914, p. 147; "Charter Progress," *American Municipalities* 26 (February 1914): 177; "Dayton Outstrips Des Moines," *American Municipalities* 26 (February 1914): 17.

29. Munro, *The Government of America Cities*, pp. 294–319 in 1912 edition, p. 388 in revised 1916 edition, and p. 303 in 1926 edition.

30. "Commission Government in Pennsylvania," *American City* 11 (October 1914): 337.

31. Richard S. Childs, "How the Commission-Manager Plan Is Getting Along, No. 2" *NMR* 6 (January 1917): 71. See "Rotary Clubs in Line," *SBB* 3 (April 1916): 6.

32. "The City Manager Plan in Forty-Five Cities: Editor's Note," *American City* 12 (June 1915): 499; Stone et al., *City Manager Government*, p. 30.

33. "From Commission to Commission Manager?" *SBB* 3 (October 1916): 3–4.

34. John M. Pfiffner, "The City Manager Plan in Iowa," *Iowa Journal of History and Politics* 26 (October 1928): 520–521.

35. "Where the Commission Plan Fails," p. 154; Newark Bureau of Municipal Research, "Weaknesses in Newark's Commission Form of Government," June 1953, NML Files—Commission Government.

36. *Fort Worth Star Telegram*, January 31, 1926; City of Houston, *Report of the Special Committee to Assemble Data on the City Manager Form of Government*, December 18, 1929; Stone et al., *City Manager Government*, pp. 38–40.

37. Richard S. Childs to Mrs. Theodore A. Stroud, January 11, 1949, and Des Moines Tax Association, Press Release, November 15, 1949, NML Files—Commission Government; Richard S. Childs Interviews.

38. "Galveston Repents at Last," *National Civic Review* 49 (May 1960): 228.

39. Charles R. Adrian, *Governing Urban America*, p. 195.

Conclusion

1. Lindsley, *A History of Greater Dallas*, p. 315.

SELECTED BIBLIOGRAPHY

A NOTE ON SOURCES

The following is a selected list of sources. It includes all books, dissertations, and archival collections actually cited in the notes; but it is highly selective in the listing of articles, governmental records, and all other sources. In general, works pertaining to a particular city or state have been excluded unless they are of special importance. The first three chapters rely heavily on the newspapers of Galveston, Houston, Dallas, Fort Worth, and Des Moines, most of which are in the library of the University of Texas at Austin. Very important were the numerous periodicals concerned with municipal affairs in the Progressive Era. The following were searched for all or part of the period 1901–1920; *Annals of the American Academy of Political and Social Science* (especially the special issue on commission government in vol. 38, November 1911, and the revised edition of the same in 1914), *American City, American Municipalities, American Political Science Review, Bulletin of the League of American Municipalities* and its successor *City Hall* (virtually every issue from 1906 to 1910 includes material on the commission plan), *Municipal Engineering, Municipal Journal and Engineer, National Municipal Review, Outlook*, and *Short Ballot Bulletin* (especially useful from 1911 to 1920). Only the works of more general interest and usefulness are listed separately. For exhaustive bibliographies, see Bradley R. Rice, "The Rise and Fall of the Galveston–Des Moines Plan: Commission Government in American Cities, 1901–1920" (Ph.D. dissertation, University of Texas at Austin, 1976), and Library of Congress, *Select List of References on Commission Government for Cities, 1913* (supplements October 8, 1917, and February 21, 1920).

ARCHIVAL COLLECTIONS

Berryhill, James G. "The Des Moines Plan of Municipal Government," July 9, 1908, Typescript, Library, Iowa State Department of History and Archives, Des Moines.
Biographical Clipping File. Eugene C. Barker Texas History Center, University of Texas Library, Austin.
Bonaparte, Charles Joseph. Papers, Manuscript Division, Library of Congress, Washington, D.C.
British Foreign Office. Records, Public Record Office, London.
Bryce, James. Papers, Bodleian Library, Oxford, U.K.
Cheesborough, John. Papers, Duke University Library, Durham, N.C.
Childs, Richard Spencer. Personal Papers, Brooklyn, N.Y.
Cummins, Albert Baird. Papers, Archives, Iowa State Department of History and Archives, Des Moines.
Des Moines City Manager Campaign Collection. Archives, Iowa State Department of History and Archives, Des Moines.
Des Moines Handbill Collection. Archives, Iowa State Department of History and Archives, Des Moines.
Galveston Commission Campaign Folder. Archives, Rosenberg Library, Galveston, Texas.

Galveston Election Propaganda File, 1908–1921. Archives, Rosenberg Library, Galveston, Texas.
Galveston Wharf Company. Minute Book, 1893–1910, Port of Galveston Building, Galveston, Texas.
Greater Des Moines Committee. Records, 1907–1951, University of Iowa Library, Iowa City.
Herriott, F. I., and Harvey Ingham. "Should Iowa Adopt the Commission System of City Government?" January 12, 1907, Typescript, Library, Iowa State Department of History and Archives, Des Moines.
Herriott, Frank Irving. Collection, includes scrapbooks, Archives, Iowa State Department of History and Archives, Des Moines.
Hull, J. A. T. Papers, Archives, Iowa State Department of History and Archives, Des Moines.
LaFollette, Robert M. Papers, Manuscripts Divisions, Library of Congress, Washington, D.C.
Low, Seth. Papers, Columbia University Library, New York.
MacVicar, John. Papers, includes scrapbooks, Archives, Iowa State Department of History and Archives, Des Moines.
MacVicar Papers. George M. Sheets Collection, University of Iowa Library, Iowa City.
Pinchot, Gifford. Papers, Manuscripts Division, Library of Congress, Washington, D.C.
Taft, William Howard. Papers (microfilm), Manuscripts Division, Library of Congress, Washington, D.C.
White, Henry. Papers, Manuscripts Division, Library of Congress, Washington, D.C.
White, William Allen. Papers, Manuscripts Division, Library of Congress, Washinton, D.C.
Whitlock, Brand. Papers, Manuscripts Division, Library of Congress, Washington, D.C.
Wilson, Woodrow. Papers (microfilm), Manuscripts Division, Library of Congress, Washington, D.C.

THESES AND DISSERTATIONS

Blasi, Edward Joseph. "The Rise and Fall of Commission Government in Galveston." M.A. thesis, St. Mary's University (San Antonio), 1965.
Connors, Richard John. "The Local Political Career of Mayor Frank Hague." Ph.D. dissertation, Columbia University, 1966.
Fox, Kenneth Paul. "The Census Bureau and the Cities: National Development of Urban Government in the Industrial Age, 1870–1930." Ph.D. dissertation, University of Pennsylvania, 1972.
Harrowing, Frank Thomas. "The Galveston Storm of 1900." M.A. thesis, University of Houston, 1950.
Platt, Harold Lawrence. "Urban Public Services and Private Enterprise: Aspects of the Legal and Economic History of Houston, Texas, 1865–1905." Ph.D. dissertation, Rice University, 1974.
Schiesl, Martin J. "The Politics of Efficiency: Municipal Reform in the Progressive Era, 1880–1920." Ph.D. dissertation, State University of New York, Buffalo, 1972.
Tinsley, James A. "The Progressive Movement in Texas." Ph.D. dissertation, University of Wisconsin, 1953.

INTERVIEWS

Childs, Richard S. Dallas, Texas, November 1973 at the National Council on Government, and New York City, January 2–4. 1974, in Childs' office at National Municipal League headquarters and in his home in Brooklyn Heights.

BOOKS

Before 1920

American Academy of Political and Social Science. *Commission Government in American Cities*. Revised edition of vol. 38 (November 1911) issue of *Annals of the American Academy of Political and Social Science*. 1914.
Bacon, Edwin M., and Morrill Wyman. *Direct Elections and Law-Making by Popular Vote: The Initiative, the Referendum—the Recall, Commission Government for Cities, Preferential Voting*. Boston: Houghton Mifflin Co., 1912.
Beard, Charles A. *American City Government: A Survey of Newer Tendencies*. New York: Century Co., 1912.
———, ed. *Loose Leaf Digest of Short Ballot Charters: A Documentary History of the Commission Form of Municipal Government*. New York: Short Ballot Organization, 1911.
Beman, Lamar T., comp. *Selected Articles on Current Problems in Municipal Government*. New York: H. W. Wilson Co., 1923.
Bradford, Ernest S. *Commission Government in American Cities*. New York: Macmillan Co., 1911.
Brigham, Johnson. *Des Moines: The Pioneer of Municipal Progress and Reform of the Middle West*. 2 vols. Chicago: S. J. Clarke Publishing Co., 1911.
Bruere, Henry. *The New City Government: A Discussion of Municipal Administration Based on a Survey of Ten Commission Governed Cities*. New York: D. Appleton and Co., 1912.
Chang, Tso-Shuen. *History and Analysis of the Commission and City Manager Plans*. University of Iowa Monograph, Studies in the Social Sciences, vol. 6. Iowa City, 1918.
Childs, Richard Spencer. *Short-Ballot Principles*. Boston: Houghton Mifflin Co., 1911.
Croly, Herbert. *Progressive Democracy*. New York: Macmillan Co., 1914.
DeWitt, Benjamin P. *The Progressive Movement*. New York: Macmillan Co., 1915.
Hamilton, John Judson. *The Dethronement of the City Boss*. New York: Funk & Wagnalls Co., 1910.
Lindsley, Philip. *A History of Greater Dallas and Vicinity*. 2 vols. Chicago: Lewis Publishing Co., 1909.
MacGregor, Ford Herbert. *City Government by Commission*. University of Wisconsin Bulletin #423, University Extension Series, vol. 1, no. 4. Madison, 1911.
Munro, William Bennett. *The Government of American Cities*. New York: Macmillan Co., 1912, 1916, 1920, 1926, 1929.
———, ed. *The Initiative, Referendum, and Recall*. New York: D. Appleton & Co., 1912.
Robbins, Edwin Clyde, comp. *Selected Articles on the Commission Plan of Municipal Government*. Minneapolis: H. W. Wilson Co., 1912.
Ryan, Oswald. *Municipal Freedom: A Study of the Commission Government*. Garden City: Doubleday, Page, & Co., 1915.

Ryan, P. H. *Foxy Government; or, Fallacies of the Des Moines Plan*. [Des Moines]: By the author, 1912.

Toumlin, Harry Aubrey, Jr. *The City Manager: A New Profession*. New York: D. Appleton and Co., 1917.

Woodruff, Clinton Rogers, ed. *City Government by Commission*. New York: D. Appleton & Co., 1911, 1920.

After 1920

Adrian, Charles R. *Governing Urban America*. New York: McGraw-Hill Book Co., 1955.

Aydelotte, William O., et al., eds. *The Dimensions of Quantitative Research in History*. Princeton: Princeton University Press, 1972.

Briggs, Asa. *Victorian Cities*. New York: Harper and Row, Harper Colophon Books, 1963, 1970.

Buenker, John D. *Urban Liberalism and Progressive Reform*. New York: Charles Scribner's Sons, 1973.

Childs, Richard Spencer. *Civic Victories: The Story of an Unfinished Revolution*. New York: Harper & Bros. Publishers, 1952.

———. *The First 50 Years of the Council-Manager Plan of Municipal Government*. New York: National Municipal League, 1965.

Crooks, James B. *Politics and Progress: The Rise of Urban Progressivism in Baltimore, 1895–1911*. Baton Rouge: Louisiana State University Press, 1968.

Dahlberg, Jane S. *The New York Bureau of Municipal Research*. New York: New York University Press, 1966.

East, John Porter. *Council-Manager Government: The Political Thought of Its Founder, Richard S. Childs*. Chapel Hill: University of North Carolina Press, 1965.

Gould, Lewis L. *Progressives and Prohibitionists: Texas Democrats in the Wilson Era*. Austin: University of Texas Press, 1973.

———, ed. *The Progressive Era*. Syracuse: Syracuse University Press, 1974.

Graham, Sam B. *Galveston Community Book: A Historical and Biographical Record of Galveston and Galveston County*. Galveston: Arthur H. Cawston, 1945.

Griffin, S. C. *History of Galveston, Texas: Narrative and Biographical*. Galveston: Arthur H. Cawston, 1931.

Griffith, Ernest S. *A History of American City Government: The Conspicuous Failure, 1870–1900*. New York: Praeger Publishers, 1974.

———. *A History of American City Government: The Progressive Years and Their Aftermath, 1900–1920*. New York: Praeger Publishers, 1973.

Harris, Arthur. *City Manager Government in Berkeley (California)*. Chicago: Public Administration Service, 1940.

Holli, Melvin G. *Reform in Detroit: Hazen S. Pingree and Urban Politics*. New York: Oxford University Press, 1969.

Johnson, Charles A. *Denver's Mayor Speer*. Denver: Bighorn Books, Green Mountain Press, 1969.

Kempner, Isaac Herbert. *Recalled Recollections*. Galveston: Privately published, 1961.

Kerney, James. *The Political Education of Woodrow Wilson*. New York: Century Co., 1926.

Link, Arthur S. *Wilson: The Road to the White House*. Princeton: Princeton University Press, 1947.

Lyon, Peter. *Success Story: The Life and Times of S. S. McClure*. New York: Charles Scribner's Sons, 1963.

McComb, David G. *Houston: The Bayou City*. Austin: University of Texas Press, 1969.

MacCorkle, Stuart A. *Austin's Three Forms of Government*. San Antonio: Naylor Co., 1973.

McKean, Dayton D. *The Boss: The Hague Machine in Action*. Boston: Houghton Mifflin Co., 1940.

Mason, Herbert Malloy, Jr. *Death from the Sea: Our Greatest Natural Disaster, the Galveston Hurricane of 1900*. New York: Dial Press, 1972.

Miller, A. George. *City Manager Government in Long Beach (California)*. Chicago: Public Administration Service, 1940.

Miller, William D. *Mr. Crump of Memphis*. Baton Rouge: Louisiana State University Press, 1964.

Morris, Margaret F., and Elliott West, eds. *Essays on Urban America*. Austin: University of Texas Press, 1975.

Municipal Year Book, 1934. Chicago: International City Managers' Association. 1934.

Municipal Year Book, 1976. Washington, D.C.: International City Management Association, 1976.

O'Neill, William L. *The Progressive Years: America Comes of Age*. New York: Dodd, Mead, and Co., 1974.

Overbeck, Ruth Ann. *Alexander Penn Wooldridge*. Austin: Von Boeckmann–Jones, 1963.

Reynolds, George M. *Machine Politics in New Orleans, 1897–1926*. New York: Columbia University Press, 1936.

Riorden, William L. *Plunkitt of Tammany Hall*. New York: E. P. Dutton & Co., 1963 [originally published 1905].

Sibley, Marilyn McAdams. *The Port of Houston: A History*. Austin: University of Texas Press, 1968.

Stave, Bruce M., ed. *Socialism and the Cities*. Port Washington, N.Y.: Kennikat Press, 1975.

Stewart, Frank Mann. *A Half-Century of Municipal Reform: The History of the National Municipal League*. Berkeley: University of California Press, 1950.

Stillman, Richard J., II. *The Rise of the City Manager: A Public Professional in Local Government*. Albuquerque: University of New Mexico Press, 1974.

Stone, Harold A.; Don K. Price; and Kathryn H. Stone. *City Manager Government in Austin (Texas)*. Chicago: Public Administration Service, 1939.

——. *City Manager Government in Dallas*. Chicago: Public Administration Service, 1939.

——. *City Manager Government in the United States*. Chicago: Public Administration Service, 1940.

Weems, John Edward. *A Weekend in September*. New York: Henry Holt and Co., 1957.

Weinstein, James. *The Corporate Ideal in the Liberal State, 1900–1918*. Boston: Beacon Press, 1968.

Willoughby, Alfred. *The Involved Citizen: A Short History of the National Municipal League*. New York: National Municipal League, 1969.

Wilson, Harold S. *McClure's Magazine and the Muckrakers*. Princeton: Princeton University Press, 1970.

Wright, William, ed. *New Jersey since 1860: New Findings and Interpretations*. Trenton: New Jersey Historical Commission, 1972.

ARTICLES

Before 1920

Allen, S. B.; F. E. Chadwick; and William B. Munro. "City Government by Commission: A Symposium on the Galveston, Newport, and Des Moines Plans." *Chautauquan* 51 (June 1908): 108–141.

"The American City, the Storm Center in the Battle for Good Government." *Arena* 38 (October 1907): 429–436.

Bradford, Ernest S. "Financial Results under the Commission Form of City Government." *National Municipal Review* 1 (July 1912): 372–377.

———. "History and the Underlying Principles of Commission Government." *Annals of the American Academy of Political and Social Science* 38 (November 1911): 3–11.

———. "Twelve Years of Commission Government." *Municipal Engineering* 45 (December 1913): 502–510.

———, and H. S. Gilbertson. "Commission Form Versus City-Manager Plan." *American City* 10 (January 1914): 37–40.

Carpenter, Dunbar F. "Some Defects of Commission Government." *Annals of the American Academy of Political and Social Science* 38 (November 1911): 192–200.

Cheesborough, E. R. "Galveston's Commission Plan of City Government." *Annals of the American Academy of Political and Social Science* 38 (November 1911): 221–230.

"Chicago and Galveston." *McClure's Magazine* 28 (April 1907): 685–686.

Childs, Richard S. "How the Commission-Manager Plan Is Getting Along." *National Municipal Review* 4 (July 1915): 371–382.

———. "The Lockport Proposal: A City That Wants to Improve the 'Commission Plan.'" *American City* 4 (June 1911): 285–287.

———. "The Short Ballot and the Commission Plan." *The Annals of the American Academy of Political and Social Science* 38 (November 1911): 146–152.

"City Government by Commission: A Report." *National Municipal Review* 1 (January 1912): 40–48.

"The Coming of the City Manager Plan." *National Municipal Review* 3 (January 1914): 44–48.

Cooper, Walter G. "Objections to Commission Government." *Annals of the American Academy of Political and Social Science* 38 (November 1911): 183–191.

Crosby, John. "Municipal Government Administered by a General Manager—The Staunton Plan." *Annals of the American Academy of Political and Social Science* 38 (November 1911): 207–213.

"Does the Commission Form Increase City Efficiency?" *American City* 7 (November 1912): 407.

"Driving Politics out of Dayton." *Literary Digest*, January 24, 1914, pp. 147–148.

Eliot, Charles W. "City Government by Fewer Men: The Superiority of a Small Commission over the Antiquated System of Mayor and Councilmen." *The World's Work* 14 (October 1907): 9419–9426.

Fassett, Charles M. "The Weakness of Commission Government." *National Municipal Review* 9 (October 1920): 642–647.

Gardner, Charles O. "The Initiative and Referendum in Commission Cities." *Annals of the American Academy of Political and Social Science* 38 (November 1911): 153–162.

Gemunder, Martin A. "Commission Government: Its Strength and Its Weakness." *National Municipal Review* 1 (April 1912): 170–181.

Gilbertson, H. S. "Some Serious Weaknesses of the Commission Plan." *American City* 9 (September 1913): 236–237.

Hamilton, John J. "What Government by Commission Has Accomplished in Des Moines." *Annals of the American Academy of Political and Social Science* 38 (November 1911): 238–246.

Haskell, H. J. "The Texas Idea: City Government by a Board of Directors." *Outlook,* April 13, 1907, pp. 839–843.

Hornaday, J. R. "Amazing Growth of a New Idea." *Uncle Remus's Home Magazine* 28 (March 1911): 9–11, 40.

McClure, S. S. "The Tammanyizing of a Civilization." *McClure's Magazine* 34 (November 1909): 117–128.

McFarland, J. Horace. "The Relation of the Commission Form of Government to Public Improvements." *American City* 5 (July 1911): 36–39.

Munro, William Bennett. "Ten Years of Commission Government." *National Municipal Review* 1 (October 1912): 562–568.

Putnam, Frank. "Galveston, an Epitome of American Plunk." *New England Magazine* 42 (June 1907): 387–403.

"The Relation of Charter Forms to Municipal Improvements: Are Commission-Governed Cities Making More Real Progress Than Those under Other Forms of Charter?" *American City* 6 (April 1912): 647–650.

Ryan, Oswald. "Commission Plan of City Government." *American Political Science Review* 5 (February 1911): 38–56.

———. "The Real Problem of Commission Government." *Popular Science Monthly,* September 1912, pp. 275–283.

Seberger, P. J. "Municipal Improvements and Lower Taxes under the Commission Form." *American City* 12 (February 1915): 106–110.

Shambaugh, Benjamin F. "Commission Government in Iowa: The Des Moines Plan." *Annals of the American Academy of Political and Social Science* 38 (November 1911): 28–48.

"A Summary of State General Laws and Constitutional Provisions Concerning Municipal Organization." *Equity* 18 (October 1916): 181–309.

Turner, George Kibbe. "Galveston: A Business Corporation." *McClure's Magazine* 27 (October 1906): 610–620.

———. "The New American City Government: The Des Moines Plan—A Triumph of Democracy. Its Spread across the United. States." *McClure's Magazine* 35 (May 1910): 97–108.

Waite, Henry M. "The Commission-Manager Plan." *National Municipal Review* 3 (January 1915): 40–49.

Woodruff, Clinton Rogers. "Simplicity, Publicity, and Efficiency in Municipal Affairs." *National Municipal Review* 2 (January 1913): 1–10.

After 1920

Bernard, Richard M., and Bradley R. Rice. "Political Environment and the Adoption of Progressive Municipal Reform." *Journal of Urban History* 1 (February 1975): 149–174.

Byers, H. W. "Des Moines after 15 Years' Commission Plan Government." *National Municipal Review* 12 (July 1923): 386–389.

Childs, Richard S. "The City Manager Plan Will Endure." *American City* 55 (May 1940): 35–36.

———. "Woodrow Wilson Legacy." *National Municipal Review* 46 (January 1957): 14–19.

"Galveston Repents at Last." *National Civic Review* 49 (May 1960): 228–229.
Hays, Samuel P. "The Politics of Reform in Municipal Government in the Progressive Era." *Pacific Northwest Quarterly* 55 (October 1964): 157–169.
Kempner, I. H. "The Drama of the Commission Plan in Galveston." *National Municipal Review* 26 (August 1937): 409–412.
Lubove, Roy. "The Twentieth-Century City: The Progressive as Municipal Reformer." *Mid-America* 41 (October 1959): 195–209.
Pease, Otis A. "Urban Reformers in the Progressive Era: A Reassessment." *Pacific Northwest Quarterly* 62 (April 1971): 49–58.
Price, D. K. "The Promotion of the City Manager Plan." *Public Opinion Quarterly* 5 (Winter 1941): 563–578.
Rice, Bradley R. "The Galveston Plan of City Government by Commission: The Birth of a Progressive Idea." *Southwestern Historical Quarterly* 73 (April 1975): 365–408.
Ringle, William M. "The Businessman Who Brought the Pro to City Hall [R. S. Childs]." *Nation's Business* 59 (December 1971): 30–32.
Scott, Thomas M. "The Diffusion of Urban Governmental Forms as a Case of Social Learning." *Journal of Politics* 30 (November 1968): 1091–1108.
Walker, Jack L. "The Diffusion of Innovations among the American States." *American Political Science Review* 63 (September 1969): 880–899.
Weinstein, James. "Organized Business and the City Commission and Manager Movements." *Journal of Southern History* 28 (May 1962): 166–182.

MISCELLANEOUS PUBLICATIONS

Cheesborough, Edmund R. *Galveston's Commission Form of City Government: Its History, Details, and Practical Workings*. Galveston, 1910.
Childs, Richard S. *The Short Ballot: A New Plan of Reform*. New York: By the author, [1908].
———. *The Story of the Short Ballot Cities: An Explanation of the Success of the Commission Form of Municipal Government*. New York: Short Ballot Organization, 1914.
Denver Chamber of Commerce. *Reports of the Special Committee on Commission Form of Government*. September 30, 1911.
National Municipal League. *Commission Plan and Commission-Manager Plan of Municipal Government: An Analytical Study by a Committee of the National Municipal League*. Philadelphia, 1914.
Short Ballot Organization. *Certain Weaknesses in the Commission Plan of Municipal Government: Why the Commission-Manager Plan is Better*. New York, various editions.
U.S. Bureau of the Census. *Comparative Financial Statistics of Cities under Council and Commission Governments, 1913 and 1915*. Washington, D.C.: Government Printing Office, 1916.

Duluth, Minnesota, 86

Earle, I. M., 38
efficiency: as goal of commission gov-
    ernment movement, 59–70, 90,
    95–96, 103
Eliot, Charles W., 31, 52, 58, 60, 80
El Paso, Texas, 27, 29
El Paso Herald, 26
Elyria, Ohio, 105
Emporia, Kansas, 76, 87
Erie, Pennsylvania, 57
Evans, I. H., 27
Ex Parte Lewis, 15

Fassett, Charles M., 96–97
Filene, Peter, xv
Fly, A. W., 4–5
Fort Wayne, Indiana, 61
Fort Worth, Texas: commission plan
    adopted in, 25–26; direct democracy
    in, 30, 72–73; results of commission
    plan in, 30–31, 64; mentioned, 10, 43,
    87, 109
Fort Worth Record, 25
Foulke, William Dudley, 105
franchises. *See* public service corpora-
    tions

Galveston, Texas: abandonment of
    commission plan by, 109; commission
    government begins in, 13–17; hur-
    ricane of 1900 in, 3, 8–9; invention of
    commission plan in, 7–13, 32; politics
    in, during the 1890s, 4–8; results of
    commission plan in, 17–18, 30–31,
    64–65, 68, 91; rivalry of, with Hous-
    ton, 19–20; role of commissioners in,
    29, 63; use of commission plan to
    boost city by, 66; mentioned, 35, 42,
    47, 52, 72, 80, 84, 97, 107, 108
Galveston City Club, 13–14, 16, 46
Galveston Daily News, 7, 12, 25
Galveston Deep Water Committee: de-
    scription of, 6–8; Galveston charter
    drafted by, 9–11; members of, 128n;
    mentioned, 15, 35, 61, 65
Galveston-Des Moines Plan: as name
    for commission plan, xiii
Galveston Journal, 12, 16
Galveston Plan: as name for commis-

sion plan, xiii, 38–39, 51, 73
Galveston Tribune, 3, 6, 10–11
Garner, John Nance, 12–13
Gaston, J. Z., 20–22, 24
Gilbertson, H. S., 91, 93, 101, 102
Gloucester, Massachusetts, 69, 96
Goodnow, Frank J., 80, 105
Grand Junction, Colorado, 76
Great Britain, 58
Greenville, Texas, 26, 30
Gresham, Walter Q., 9, 17
Griffith, Ernest S., xiv
Gunton's Magazine, 17

Hadley, Arthur T., 80
Hague, Frank, 98
Hamery, John L., 50, 72
Hamilton, John J.: in Des Moines poli-
    tics, 36–37, 41, 44, 49; mentioned, 67,
    77
Hanna, James R., 91
Harper's Weekly, 17
Harrisburg, Pennsylvania, 57
Hart, Albert Bushnell, 31
Hartford, Connecticut, 70, 86
Hatton, A. R., 105
Haverhill, Massachusetts, 52, 69, 78, 86,
    87, 91
Hays, Samuel P., xvi–xvii
Head, James M., 42
Herriott, F. I., 40–42, 46, 90, 100
Hoboken, New Jersey, 85
home rule, xii
Houston, Texas: abandonment of com-
    mission plan by, 109; adoption of
    commission plan by, 19–24; results of
    commission plan in, 24–25, 30–32, 86,
    96; rivalry of, with Galveston, 8,
    19–20; role of commissioners in, 29;
    mentioned, 46, 91
Houston Chronicle, 20, 22–24
Houston Post, 19, 21, 23, 32
Howe, Frederic C., 80
Hull, J. A. T., 40–41

Illinois: legislature of, studies commis-
    sion plan, 31, 53, 56
Independent, 17–18
Indiana, 57
Indianapolis, Indiana, 31, 70
Indianapolis plan, 37